Resurgent Islam and the Politics of Identity

Resurgent Islam and the Politics of Identity

By

Ali A. Mazrui

Edited by Ramzi Badran and Thomas Uthup

CAMBRIDGE
SCHOLARS

PUBLISHING

Resurgent Islam and the Politics of Identity, by Ali A. Mazrui
Edited by Ramzi Badran and Thomas Uthup

This book first published 2014

Cambridge Scholars Publishing

12 Back Chapman Street, Newcastle upon Tyne, NE6 2XX, UK

British Library Cataloguing in Publication Data
A catalogue record for this book is available from the British Library

ISBN (10): 1-4438-6326-2, ISBN (13): 978-1-4438-6326-1

CONTENTS

Contents

PREFACE AND ACKNOWLEDGEMENTS

This book project was initiated in 2011 as a new addition to the Mazruiana Islamica series. We began by selecting Mazrui's articles and lectures that are most relevant to the theme of the book. Mwalimu Mazrui is one of the most prolific writers of our time. Narrowing down the selection of articles from his many writings on this topic was a demanding task. The articles we selected span three decades of Mazrui's scholarship about Islam and the politics of identity. Our goal is to introduce the reader to a broad spectrum of Mazrui's contributions to the study of the relationship between Islam and modern politics of identity. The articles of this volume were integrated, updated, and revised in consultation with Mwalimu Mazrui.

Working on this project over the years, we have incurred many debts of gratitude to more people than we can mention here. We are very grateful to the invaluable advice and support we received from Dr. Seifudein Adem and A. Selase Adzima throughout this project.

This project would not have been possible without the wonderful support of Sarah A. Bull and Jennifer Winans. Sarah proofread drafts of the chapters in this volume and provided many useful inputs on the clarity and style of the manuscript, while Jennifer prepared the index and finalized the manuscript in readiness for publication. We are deeply grateful for their contributions.

We are also indebted to Pauline Mazrui and other members of the Mazrui family for facilitating our communication with Mwalimu Mazrui during his illness.

Our greatest thanks go to our families and friends for their love, encouragement, and unwavering support.

—Editors

INTRODUCTION

As a distinguished Africanist, Professor Ali A. Mazrui has attracted well-deserved attention for his wide-ranging intellectual contributions to African studies. In the 1980s, Mazrui's TV series, *The Africans*, elevated his stature as an academic luminary and public intellectual.[1] Yet, what has often received less attention is his work on Islam. While dealing with Islam has been an integral part to his Triple Heritage argument, he has not confined his explorations to the African continent, but indeed the global footprint across history of Muslims and Islam. But one could argue that in Mazrui's post-Michigan phase at Binghamton University, he has paid more attention to Islam. Indeed, in this phase he has been honored by several Muslim organizations and institutions for his work on Islam. In 2012 and 2013, he was designated as one of the "500 Most Influential Muslims" by the Royal Islamic Strategic Studies Centre in Amman, Jordan.[2] The rising prominence of religion generally—and Islam specifically—in international politics since the Iranian Revolution of 1979 has made Mazrui's writings on these subjects very pertinent to our contemporary age.

Religion is an important element of the culture of most people. We may not go as far as former Pope Benedict's characterization: "religion is an essential element of culture, is indeed its determinative center,"[3] but it would be quite fair to say that any treatment of cultural factors in international relations must engage with religion. Mazrui's seminal work on culture in politics, *Cultural Forces in World Politics,*[4] as well as the Institute of Global Cultural Studies (IGCS) founded by Mazrui in 1991, does not deviate from this conceptualization of the important role of religion in the study of culture. Mazrui and others at IGCS pay a great deal of importance to religion in their academic, public, and professional roles.[5] In *Cultural Forces in World Politics*, Mazrui offers a functional definition of culture, categorizing the functions as follows:

1) As lenses of perception and cognition;
2) As motives for human behavior;
3) To provide criteria for evaluation;
4) As a basis of identity;
5) As a mode of communication;

6) As a basis of stratification; and
7) In the system of production and consumption.[6]

In this functional approach to culture, we can easily see the integral role that religion plays in all of these functions, although its relative importance might vary across regions, religions, and time. In linking culture to identity, it is indeed true that we occupy simultaneous and multiple identities. As Nobel Laureate Amartya Sen has pointed out, a person can be:

> An American citizen, of Caribbean origin, with African ancestry, a Christian, a liberal, a woman, a vegetarian, a long-distance runner, a historian, a schoolteacher, a novelist, a feminist, a heterosexual, a believer in gay and lesbian rights, a theater lover, an environmental activist, a tennis fan, a jazz musician, and someone who is deeply committed to the view that there are intelligent beings in outer space with whom it is extremely urgent to talk (preferably in English).[7]

Nevertheless, we can safely say that for the vast majority of the Muslims in the world today, religion is of deep importance in many aspects.[8] The fourth function of culture (as a basis of identity) as well as what I see as the related sixth function (as a basis of stratification) are, for Muslims, powerfully influenced by their interpretation of Islam. One way of distinguishing between the two is to think of Islam as a basis of identity differentiating Muslims from non-Muslims—both in terms of theological Islam and historical Islam—and Islam as a basis of stratification affecting how Muslims view each other, mostly on the basis of historical Islam. The collection of essays in this book examines both these functions of Islam in affecting the identity of Muslims.

In "Islam between Secular Modernism and Civil Society," Mazrui examines two basic distinctions critical to understanding the ways in which identity and Islam are inextricably bound. The first of these distinctions is the distinction between theological Islam (the rules and restrictions enunciated in doctrine) and historical Islam, the way in which Muslims have lived. A second distinction, crucial in modern society, is the separation between religious institutions (mosque/church) and the state as opposed to the separation of religion and state. These distinctions have played out in the economic arena, affected the status of women, and ecumenical or interfaith tolerance of the 'other.' Through contemporary and historical examples, Mazrui argues that Islam and modernity are perhaps not as incompatible as many would think.[9]

Mazrui further argues in "Liberal Islam versus Moderate Islam," that liberal Islam should not be equated with moderate Islam. The latter could be seen as being more pro-Western, while the former can include those who are outraged at the state of Muslims and get radicalized.[10] Like other seasoned scholars of the Muslim World, Mazrui cites four principal reasons to explain the radicalization of the Muslim World. The first of these is the US imperial policy towards the Muslim World, manifested most obviously by the occupation of Iraq and periodic threats to states like Syria. A second reason, often seen as related to the first, is Israeli oppression of the Palestinians without any restrictions from the US, for the most part. A third reason is the 'multiple humiliations' of Muslims in a host of different countries, exacerbated in the post September 11th era by Western media-fed perceptions of Muslims as terrorists, and the weakening of Western condemnation of human violations of Muslims. These humiliations range from direct occupation by external powers to brutal as well as discriminatory treatment as minorities. Domestic factors such as authoritarianism, economic stagnation, corruption, and lack of freedoms are a fourth factor boosting radicalism among a few Muslims. To combat radicalism, Mazrui rightly cautions that modernization may not be a panacea, especially if modernization is seen as Westernization. Indeed, for many Muslims, that kind of modernization may even be seen as toxic.[11] But there are possibilities for liberalism, as revealed in many Muslims' approval of democracy, election of women to leadership positions, and—even if the news may suggest otherwise—the welcoming of interfaith dialogue by Muslim religious leaders. In the view of Mazrui, part of such a liberal approach would include welcoming *Ijtihad* as well as accepting the possibility of human history and its attendant advances in scientific knowledge as divine revelation. This would allow for a liberal Islam that could be a counter to radicalism. The challenge for liberal Muslims is to separate liberalism from Westernization and to look to their own traditions and writings to support democracy, women's rights, and interfaith cooperation as well as to counter the perversion of Islam by radicals.

There is a great deal of concern, both within Africa and in the West, about the presence and growth of Islamic radicalism. Apart from being hostile to other Muslims, radical Muslims may also be more prone to hostility towards Christians—the other major religious group in Africa. In "Christianity and Islam in Africa's Political Experience," Mazrui categorizes the relations between the two Abrahamic religions in Africa in three ways: as being conflictual where hostilities can often lead to violence; competitive when they are battling for increased market share of souls; and cooperative when they live together in mutual tolerance, if not in respect and harmony.[12] The type of relations may be determined by doctrinal, sociological, or historical experiences. Mazrui also deploys his Triple Heritage trope as an ameliorating or exacerbating factor in the interfaith relations of the two religions. Mazrui's comparative analysis of British versus French colonial policy towards Islam reveals the enduring impact of these policies on current interfaith relations, both positively and negatively.[13] He also advances two important generalizations of contemporary political Islam. The first is that Islam in military uniform in postcolonial Africa is more repressive than average, and the second is that Islam in civilian robes in Africa is more tolerant than average. In the end, he concludes that the rivalry between Islam and Christianity in Africa is increased when it coincides with other divisions, but decreased when there are other cross-cutting cleavages, such as ethnicity. In a contrarian fashion, Mazrui also makes the case that leveling the field of missionary work between Islam and Christianity—thanks to the petro-wealth of the former—has led to peaceful competition, rather than conflict. Conflict has also been reduced because many Christian non-governmental organizations (NGOs working in Africa are more interested in saving lives rather than souls. When Muslims are saved by Christian NGOs, whether in the form of mosquito nets to prevent malaria or in the form of a hospital to repair fistulas, conflict and hatred towards the 'other' is more difficult.

When it comes to the spread of Islam in Africa, missionary work has been just one of the factors that have helped to gain souls for Islam. Comparing "Islam between the Muslim Diaspora in Africa and the African Diaspora in the West," Mazrui observes that conquest, trade, migration, and revivalist *jihads* have also contributed to the significant numbers of Muslims in Africa today. In contrast, in Europe, Islam has been mainly spread by the migration of Muslims—mainly from North Africa, Turkey, and South Asia—while both migrants and indigenous (African American) are significant elements in US Islam.[14] Post-independence, Islam in Africa has been marked by both revivalism and expansion. Both these processes raise the possibilities of conflict. However, Mazrui argues that the tolerance of African indigenous religions has mitigated the competitiveness of the two religions—Christianity and Islam—that are battling for Africa's souls. As in other areas of the world, Mazrui points out that religious divisions lead to conflict particularly when those divisions reinforce other divisions. Further, conflicts also arise when a significant number of Muslims are marginalized and/or have their rights stripped. In the aftermath of the war on terror, African governments (such as Kenya) have felt relatively free to undertake measures that impinge on the rights of their Muslims. While earlier struggles between the Christian colonizers and their African subjects—whether Christian, Muslim, or indigenous—remained on African soil, the new battles between radicalized Muslims (including Africans) and the West are now being taken to the West on "planes, trains, and buses," in Mazrui's words. Globalization has facilitated and accelerated the reduction of the sense of safety felt in the past by the West.

In the first few decades of the United Nations, the world's premier global body of nation-states, the West enjoyed dominance. However, decolonization and a wave of accession to member status by new African and Asian states eroded their power, at least to some extent. Among the new member-states, Muslim member states organized collectively as the Organization of Islamic Cooperation (OIC), and emerged as the largest intergovernmental organization after the UN.[15] Mazrui's "The United Nations and the Muslim World: Allies or Adversaries" examines the relationship between the global body of states and the larger *Ummah* of Muslims around the world, whether in states represented in the OIC or not. In the adversarial column, Mazrui firstly argues that the UN has repeatedly been able to go against Muslim interests—even in recent times—thanks to the dominance of the West and the disunity of the Muslim World. In his usual unique comparison, Mazrui likens the ancient division of the world by Islamic law—*Dar al-Islam* (the Abode of Islam); *Dar al-Harb* (the Abode of War); and *Dar al-'Ahd* or *Dar al-Sulh* (the Abode of Peaceful Co-Existence or Contractual Peace)—to the divisions of the Cold War: the West, the Communist World, and the Third World. However, the conflict between the West and Communist World was not fought in the West or the Communist World, but in areas of the Third World, such as Korea, Vietnam, and in many parts of the Muslim and African World. The people of Somalia, Ethiopia, Egypt, Iraq, and Afghanistan have been among the victims of the Cold War between the West and the Communist World. Second, a Western/secular/Christian mindset prevails in the top leadership of the major UN agencies, from the Secretary General of the UN to the UNESCO Director-General. However, Mazrui does point out that the Muslim World and the UN can be allied in humanitarian and peacekeeping situations when the West is divided and the Muslim world is united and when there are pushes for decolonization and prosecution of war criminals. The jury is still out on whether the UN and the Islamic World can ally on the interests and rights of women, but in the end, as Mazrui mentions, both Islam and the United Nations have the objective of creating a peaceful world.

Peace and democracy are inextricably linked. Conditions of violence, war, terror, and brutality impinge on democracies, both in the Muslim

World and in the West. In his essay "Between the Pre-democratic *Ummah* and Post-democratic United States," Mazrui describes the current situation of Muslim states' evolution toward democracy and US democracy. Utilizing four principles of democracy—accountable rulers, participatory electorate, open socio-economic conditions, and basic social justice—Mazrui sees many Muslim societies as being 'pre-democratic' or undemocratic. Impediments to Muslim democracy include royalism (particularly in the Arab World), militarized rulers, weak states, and 'experimental' or infant democracies. On the other hand, Mazrui provocatively poses the question of whether the US is becoming post-democratic, in a negative sense. He points to the retreats on freedom (particularly in the wake of the war on terror), equity, and access. Recent US Supreme Court rulings have lopsidedly favored rich individuals and corporations. Inequality and discrimination has marginalized the participation of the poor and minorities in many Western democracies, leading to democratic decay. If the West is in a post-democratic phase, Muslim countries—at least a few—are in a pre-democratic phase. But even more Muslims countries face significant challenges in their evolution into democracy, particularly those that have dual societies, or have historically been in states of anarchy or tyranny.[16]

Among Muslim countries that have made some progress towards democracy, Turkey stands out as a particularly hopeful example, notwithstanding some concerns in the last couple of years.[17] In "Is Istanbul a Secular Jerusalem? Lessons from Atatürk and Tahrir Square," Mazrui makes yet another insightful comparison between Istanbul as a convergence of civilizations while Jerusalem may be seen as a convergence of religions. In its physical location, Istanbul connects Asia and Europe. In its role as a center for the convergence of civilizations, Istanbul regularly hosts meetings bringing the world together, such as the UN Alliance of Civilizations Global Forum in 2009, and the IV UN Conference on the Least Developed Countries in 2011. Istanbul also shows the possibility of melding European civilization—minus European Christianity—with Islamic religion. As the country in which Istanbul is located, Turkey has symbolized also the applicability of the Qur'an to modernity, both historically and in the contemporary era. Its historic acceptance of minorities and acceptance of a female head of government make it a paragon for other Muslim countries. Mazrui's reading of Turkish history emphasizes the simultaneous processes of Westernization, secularization, and democratization through the leadership (at times brutal) of Kemal Ataturk and his heirs, mostly in the military. Mazrui sees this as "democratization from above." The Islamist-based popular party of Prime

Minister Recep Tayyip Erdoğan has taken several steps towards liberalization. The recent pushbacks the Erdoğan government received over its attempts to repress protests, even if only from a small minority, is indicative of a society that guards its rights as a democracy zealously. It is still possible to say that the many labels of identity for Turks include that of being Muslim and a democrat. On the other hand, the so-called Arab Spring uprisings, most notably Tahrir Square uprisings in Egypt's Cairo in February 2011 and the earlier uprising in Tunisia a month earlier are seen by Mazrui as "democracy from below." As he rightly points out, while these were effective in ending dictatorial regimes of decades, they have been less successful in shaping new democratic regimes that can stand the test of time. Indeed, Egypt may even have regressed while Tunisia's fate is still up in the air.

Egypt was one of the most prominent countries—certainly from Africa—at what Mazrui argues has been the "most important conference of Afro-Asian solidarity in the twentieth century"—the 1955 Bandung Conference in Indonesia. In Mazrui's chapter on "From Bandung to Benghazi: Muslim Nationalists in Comparative Perspective," he traces the evolution of united Afro-Asian solidarity in the nationalist struggle to a divided Afro-Asian bloc of today. The camaraderie of revolutionary socialist guerilla fighters has given way to competition over the significant possibilities of trade and aid (even if the latter is declining in real terms). As Mazrui describes, the Bandung Conference was a precursor to the high points of Afro-Asian solidarity from the 1960s to the 1980s, with unity on anti-colonialism and North-South relations.[18] The Bandung Conference also took place in the midst of momentous changes in the world with repercussions that last to this day. These changes include: the end of the Korean War, the defeat of the French colonizers by the Vietnamese and the beginning of the Algerian-French Conflict, and the Supreme Court Case of Brown v. Board of Education. These events also presaged the overthrow of the oldest colonial empire (Portugal) in the 1970s, the defeat of the Americans in Vietnam and the retreat of the Russians in Afghanistan.

In the battles between the Afro-Asian bloc and Europe (including Russia) and the United States, blood was mostly shed in the African and Asian theater. Of course, this changed in the 21st century when Saudis, Egyptians, Moroccans, and Pakistanis took their grievances against the West to the metropoles of New York City, Washington, DC, Madrid, and London. But it is not just violence from Asia and Africa that has penetrated the West. Gandhi's ideas of nonviolence and peaceful tactics of resistance such as hunger strikes influenced African Americans, the Irish struggle against Britain, and anti-nuclear activists. Less influential has been what Mazrui has termed "Africa's short memory of hate," with perhaps the European Union as one of the few examples of victors and vanquished overcoming differences. In the global arena, Africans and Asians collaborated in their struggles against imperialism and neocolonialism, notably in the UN and as part of the Non-Aligned Movement. In these matters, they were often joined by Latin America. However, the end of the Cold War saw new challenges to this solidarity.[19] A Muslim World that had largely seen itself as Brown and Black (with perhaps the exception of Turkey) now had the phenomena of European Muslim states. Oddly enough, the West, through the mechanism of NATO, ended up defending Muslim lives in places like Kosovo and Bosnia. NATO's intervention in Libya to overthrow Muammar Gaddafi reflected another confusing aspect to the previous solidarity of Afro-Asian unity against intervention. The African Union was leery of the intervention, while the Arab League, in the words of Mazrui, "virtually encouraged NATO to attack Libya as a way of helping the rebels." Gaddafi was overthrown, and Libya is how gingerly taking steps towards a functioning liberal regime.

Libya's North African counterpart, Tunisia—the first successful case of the Arab Spring—appears to have emerged with a slightly more stable new government, at the time of writing. As Mazrui asks in his short essay on "The Arab Spring and Female Empowerment," was it a coincidence that Tunisia had also pioneered women's liberation in the Arab World early in the 20th century? Tunisia was also in the forefront of emancipating its women immediately after independence. Both in Tunisia and in Egypt, women were active participants in the struggles, although often subject to sexual harassment and molestation in the latter country.[20] Of course, Egypt has had strong female leaders—in the pre-Islamic era. Yemen, yet another Arab country with a strong precedent of a female leader in the form of Sheba (at least according to some versions) also contributed a strong female in its own struggles against dictatorship. Tawakkol Karman, a Yemeni journalist, won the 2011 Nobel Prize for her efforts and made the Arab World proud as its first woman and the youngest Nobel Peace Laureate. Now, Mazrui has maintained that the term "Arab Spring" is a misnomer, partly because he sees precedents in 1964 and 1985 Sudan of civilian nonviolent demonstrations against military rule. When it comes to female participation in these uprisings, Sudan did see an increase from 1964 to 1985, partly as a function of more educated women. Perhaps because of this linkage between education and participation,

Mazrui is more optimistic about a female leader emerging in Tunisia or Egypt.

In "Political Islam: Piety, Patriarchy and Petroleum in African and Comparative Experience," Mazrui puts on his political economy lenses to examine the relationship between resources, democracy, and religion. As usual, his proposition is simple but profound: the discovery of resources after the maturity of democracy helps to stabilize democracy, but if resources are discovered before democracy is established, it may delay the democratizing process. To make his case, Mazrui draws on cases from Europe and Africa, such as Norway, Scotland, Libya, Congo, Nigeria, and South Africa. In his discussion on the relationship between resources and regime-type in the case of Muslim countries, Mazrui distinguishes between plutocracy (the power of wealth), democracy (the power of votes), and militocracy (the power of the military). He further distinguishes between coup-prone countries and coup-proof countries, but does point out that these are not static categories. He then moves to a discussion on the predominant identity affiliations of the late Muammar Gaddafi, President of Libya. Gaddafi saw himself as an international revolutionary and, especially in the last decades of his life, had increasingly seen himself as more African than Arab or Muslim.[21] Libya is just one of the several Muslim countries with oil resources. Nigeria is an African country where the oil resources are not to be found in its Muslim areas, and this helped to trigger Shari'acracy in those Muslim areas as a challenge to the concentration of political and economic power in non-Muslim areas. Oil resources appear to be negatively correlated with the empowerment of women—with perhaps the exception of Libya's Gaddafi—in Africa and the Muslim World. However, it is possible that this could change as the Information Revolution becomes more widespread, and the digital divide narrows in the Muslim World.

We began this introduction by looking at the significance of culture in Mazrui's writings, and in particular by looking at the identity functions of religion and Islam. In his last essay for this volume, on "From the Old Politics of Race to the New Politics of Culture," Mazrui raises the issue of whether race has become less significant as a dividing line than culture. It is certainly true—with the election of a black US President, the end of apartheid in South Africa, and an increasingly multiracial Europe—that one could make the case that overt racism is declining. On the other hand, increasing prejudice based on conflicting values, largely based on religion, and in particular in opposition to those who claim a Muslim identity (as in places from Myanmar to the Central African Republic) or those whose Muslim identity is questioned by other Muslims (Pakistan and Iraq being such examples) are increasingly becoming common. The conflict between political Islam and American anti-terrorism efforts has also become a central cultural dividing line, with Africa as a central theater of operations. Further, "from the politics of color-identity to the politics of the identity of shared cultural experience," we are witnessing a new global apartheid which is not based on race as much as culture and knowledge. In this new apartheid system, Muslims are more often victims than victimizers. In some senses, as Mazrui demonstrates through his analysis of two of Shakespeare's most famous plays—*Othello* and *The Merchant of Venice*—we may be reverting back to an earlier age, when Islamophobia and anti-Semitism were more acceptable and prevalent than 'Negrophobia.'

The last entry in this volume, "The Afrabian Awakening in Comparative Perspective" is an interview of Ali Mazrui conducted in July 2011 by Nirvana Tanoukhi.[22] This interview explores the implications of the Arab Spring (or what may be more accurately termed the 'Afrabian Awakening') for Africa, the Muslim World, and the large universe of developing and developed countries. Mazrui clearly sees the tentative nature of these uprisings, but sees hope in the goals of liberty (rather than liberation) among the protestors. He is regretful about the implications of the end of Gaddafi for African solidarity and the violence of the conflict. Mazrui also discusses Muslim-Christian relations in Africa, including the post-revolution Coptic-Muslim relations in Egypt, and offers an optimistic take on the future of Tunisia and Egypt. He also offers the Atatürk Revolution, the Iranian Revolution, the Arab Revolution, and perhaps the partition of British India as being among the more important events affecting the Muslim World in his lifetime. He concludes the interview by calling on North Africa to see itself as part of Africa and increase its commitment to the African continent.

The volume presents the reader with a solid foundation for understanding processes of identity formation within Muslim communities. It further addresses vital and timely questions about the relationship between Islam, political culture, modernity, and political institutions in the developed and the developing worlds. The volume offers an original interpretation of Islamic political culture. It illuminates the complexities of social and political dilemmas facing Muslim societies around the world today. It also presents thought-provoking analyses of the paradoxes in contemporary identity politics. Mazrui makes important contributions to key debates on modern Islamic political ideology.

—*Thomas Uthup*

Notes

[1] The companion volume to the series is Ali A. Mazrui, *The Africans: A Triple Heritage* (Boston: Little, Brown, 1986).

[2] See Royal Islamic Strategic Studies Centre, *The Muslim 500: The World's 500 Most Influential Muslims 2013/14* (Amman, Jordan: The Royal Islamic Strategic Studies Centre), p. 108.

[3] Cited in R. Jared Staudt, "Religion and Culture" and "Faith and the Renewal of Society" in Christopher Dawson and Pope Benedict XVI, *Logos: A Journal of Catholic Thought and Culture* (Winter 2013), Vol. 16, No. 1, p. 37.

[4] Ali A. Mazrui, *Cultural Forces in World Politics* (Oxford, Nairobi and Portsmouth, NH: James Currey, EAEP and Heinemann, 1990, 2005 reprint).

[5] Co-Editor Thomas Uthup, who has been associated with the Institute of Global Cultural Studies in informal and formal capacities since its inception in 1991, wrote a dissertation on religious values and public policy and has continued to do research and work (including at the United Nations) on the interaction of religion and international relations. Co-Editor Ramzi Badran, who has been involved with the IGCS since 2006 has written several articles on political Islam and religion and peace.

[6] Mazrui, *Cultural Forces in World Politics,* pp. 7–8.

[7] Amartya Sen, *Identity and Violence* (New York: W. W. Norton, 2006), pp. xii–xiii.

[8] Pew Research Center, *The World's Muslims: Unity and Diversity* (Washington, DC: Pew Research Center's Forum on Religion & Public Life, August 9, 2012), p. 8. has varying figures by region on how important religion is to the world's Muslims.

[9] An excellent guide to the challenges of Islam and modernity may be found in Muhammad Khalid Masud, Armando Salvatore and Martin van Bruinessen, (eds.), *Islam and Modernity: Key Issues and Debates* (Edinburgh: Edinburgh University Press, 2009).

[10] Relatedly, consult Mahmood Mamdani, "Good Muslim, Bad Muslim: A Political Perspective on Culture and Terrorism," *American Anthropologist* (September 2002), Vol. 104, Issue 3, pp. 766–775.

[11] This is expressed in the idea of 'Westoxification' as expressed by Iranian writers such as Jalal Al Ahmad and Ali Shariati, who included the ulama as 'Westoxificated.' For more, see Homa Omid, "Theocracy of Democracy: The Critics of 'Westoxification' and the Politics of Fundamentalism in Iran," *Third World Quarterly* (December 1992), Vol. 13, Issue 4, pp. 675–690, and Shirin S. Deylami, "In the Face of the Machine: Westoxification, Cultural Globalization, and the Making of an Alternative Global Modernity," *Polity* (April 2011), Vol. 43, Issue 2, pp. 242–263.

[12] Here I prefer not to use Mazrui's term of "ecumenical" for two reasons: 1) The term "ecumenical" usually relates to unity among the world's Christian churches; and 2) "cooperative" fits better with the other two categories.

[13] Relatedly, consult Pade Badru, "Basic Doctrines of Islam and Colonialism in Africa," in Pade Badru and Brigid M. Sackey, (eds.), *Islam in Africa South of the*

Sahara: *Essays in Gender Relations and Political Reform* (Plymouth, UK: Scarecrow Press, 2013), pp. 27–46.

[14] According to the Pew Research Center, only one in five Muslim-Americans (about 22 percent) belong to a third or fourth or later generation of Americans; 26 percent of Muslim Americans are from the MENA region; 16 percent from South Asia; and 7 percent from Sub-Saharan Africa. See Pew, *Muslim-Americans: No Signs of Growth in Alienation or Support for Extremism* (August 2011), pp. 13–14. An earlier survey of US Muslims categorized them by race and found 30 percent to be Black, 33 percent South Asian, and 25 percent Arab (the survey did not include followers of the Nation of Islam); see *The Baltimore Sun* (April 27, 2001), p. 4. Other estimates put the African American Muslim population at a higher percentage (as high as 42 percent); for example, see Karen Leonard, "South Asian Leadership of American Muslims," in Yvonne Haddad, (ed.) *Muslims in the West: From Sojourners to Citizens* (Oxford and New York: Oxford University Press, 2002), p. 233.

[15] On the OIC, see Gokhan Bacik, "The Genesis, History, and Functioning of the Organization of Islamic Cooperation (OIC): A Formal-Institutional Analysis," *Journal of Muslim Minority Affairs* (Dec. 2011), Vol. 31, Issue 4, pp. 594–614.

[16] Relatedly, for two recent discussions on this topic, consult the following: Adeed Dawisha, *The Second Arab Awakening: Revolution, Democracy and the Islamist Challenge from Tunis to Damascus* (New York: W. W. Norton and Co., 2013) and Lily Zubaidah Rahim, *Muslim Secular Democracy: Voices from Within* (New York: Palgrave Macmillan, 2013).

[17] After a period where Turkey was seen as a model for the melding of Islam and democracy, in 2013 and 2014 Turkey saw protests that were savagely repressed, corruption scandals, emasculations of the judiciary, and attempts to ban major social media networks like Twitter and Youtube. See Alexander Christie-Miller, "Erdoğan's Missed Opportunity to Mix Islam and Democracy in Turkey," *Christian Science Monitor* (April 9, 2014).

[18] The famous African American writer, Richard Wright, wrote a report on the conference called *The Color Curtain: A Report on the Bandung Conference* (Banner, MS and Cleveland, OH: Banner Books and World Pub. Co., 1995, 1956).

[19] The rise and decline of the Non-Aligned Movement is briefly described in Martin Evans, "Whatever Happened to the Non-aligned Movement?" *History Today* (December 2007), Vol. 57, Issue 12, pp. 49–50 and its last summit in Tehran in 2012, less than a fourth of its membership's heads of state and government attended; see Behrooz Behbudi, "Iran and the Incubus of the Non-Aligned summit," *Middle East*, Issue 436 (Oct. 2012), pp. 30–31.

[20] On these, see the report by Kristen Chick "Egyptians Work to Reclaim a Tahrir Tainted by Sexual Assault," *Christian Science Monitor* (February 1, 2013) and Nawal El Saadawi, "The View From Cairo," *Middle East*, Issue 438 (Dec. 2012), p. 5.

[21] Relatedly, consult Yehudit Ronen, *Qaddafi's Libya in World Politics* (Boulder, CO: Lynne Rienner, 2008); and more specifically on Africa, see Herman J. Cohen, "Qadaffi and Sub-Saharan Africa," *Journal of International Peace Operations*

(Nov/Dec 2011), Vol. 7, Issue 3, pp. 37–38 and Onyekachi Wambu, "The End of the Affair," *New African*, Issue 510 (Oct. 2011), p. 98.

[22] This was published as "Arab Spring and the Future of Leadership in North Africa" *Transition*, Vol. 106, No. 1 (2011), pp. 148–162.

CHAPTER ONE

ISLAM BETWEEN SECULAR MODERNISM
AND CIVIL SOCIETY

There are two ways of trying to understand what Islam is all about. One way amounts to interpreting Islam theologically by answering the question: what do the rules say? The other method of research is an effort to interpret Islam historically by answering the question: what have Muslims done in history? Theological Islam is a matter of doctrine. Historical Islam is a matter of experience.

Theological Islam is profoundly distrustful of secularism, viewing it as a space where God's laws are not supposed to apply. Such a concept is doctrinally alien. Historical Islam, on the other hand, has interpreted secularism not as a space where God's laws do not apply, but as a space where God's laws are permissive in varying degrees.

In Islamic Shari'a, there are five categories of actions: *Halal*, which is permitted; *Makruh,* which is disapproved of but not forbidden; *Sunnah,* which is recommended but not commanded; *Haram*, which is truly forbidden; and *Fardh* or *Wajib*, which is obligatory.

Secularism is not a domain of God in absentia, but the domain of God's indulgent permissiveness—the divine green light. Historical Islam has distinguished between separating church (or mosque) from the state, on one side, and separating religion from politics (on the other side). Separating church from state is doable—this is an institutional differentiation. Separating religion from politics is *not* doable—this is behavioral separation in the actions of individuals.

The Republic of India is a secular state—separating church from state. But political behavior in India is constantly affected, reinforced or disrupted by religious factors. India has separated the temple from the state, but has not really sought to separate religion from politics in the hearts of the masses.

England, on the other hand, has not separated church from state. The Queen is both Head of State and Governor of the Church of England. The Archbishop of Canterbury is chosen with the participation of the Prime

Minister. And major doctrinal changes in the Church of England need at least the tacit approval of the British Parliament. I am, of course, subject to correction.

But although the British have not separated church from state (antidisestablishmentarianism), they have remarkably succeeded in separating religion from politics in the domain of individual behavior.

During the life of the Prophet Muhammad and of the first four caliphs (Abu Bakr, Omar, Uthman and Ali) there was in Islam neither separation of church from state institutionally nor separation of religion from politics behaviorally. The political secularization of Islam historically began with the royalization of Islam—the establishment of kings and sultans from the dynasties of the Umayyads and Abbasids onwards. The *Umayyads* reigned from 661 to 750 CE; and the *Abbasids* from 750 to 1258 CE. It became clearer across the centuries that there was a *Caliph* presiding over the Muslim *Ummah*, on one side, and a *Sultan* presiding over affairs of the state, on the other. In the Christian Bible, the command is "Give unto Caesar what is Caesar's; and unto God what is God's." In historical Islam, the injunction became "Give unto the Caliph what is the Caliph's and unto the Sultan what is the Sultan's."

The royalization of Islam was *de facto,* a process of partial political secularization—separating the Caliphate from the Sultanate. Mustafa Kemal Atatürk put an end to the Caliphate on March 3, 1924.

Religious values in the society as a whole remained very strong. What made Islam at the time compatible with the spirit of modernity was Islam's own spirit of creative synthesis. Islam was prepared to learn philosophy from the Greeks, architecture from the Persians, mathematics from the Indians, jurisprudence from the Romans—and to synthesize what was borrowed with Islam's own core values. That was a modern spirit.

The Muslim World went modernist long before the West did—but then the Muslim World relapsed back into premodernization. The ancient modernist phase of Islam has left its mark on the subsequent modernization of the West. The marks of Islamic modernism on the English language today include words borrowed from Arabic—like algebra, zero, tariff, and admiral. To recapitulate, Islam was born premodern, but receptive to modernism. Then it went modernist in the heyday of its civilization. Then Islam relapsed into premodernism, where it has been stuck to the present day.

Islam will return to the spirit of modernism when it returns to the spirit of creative synthesis—learning from others, letting others learn from Islam, and maintaining Islam's own core of authenticity.

Islam and Civil Society

When I turn to civil society, once again, Islam should be interpreted either theologically (identifying its laws and rituals) or interpreted historically (identifying how Muslims have lived Islam across the ages).

Of course, the theology and the history of Islam repeatedly intersect. For example, Islam is pro-profit but anti-interest. This dual-doctrine had consequences for civil society. Doctrinal opposition to interest led to the shrinking of a money-lending class in the history of Islam. The potential rudiments of a banking system were thus aborted at birth.

On the other hand, the Islamic green light for profit-making influenced the *suuq* or market-place culture in the political economy of Islam. The caravan linking one civil society with another encouraged trade across the Sahara Desert and stimulated the dhow trade across the Red Sea to Africa and across the Indian Ocean to east and south-east Asia. Transcultural trade helped to propagate Islam across huge cultural distances.

Islam's paradox of pro-profit and anti-interest also resulted in the complex culture of *awqaf*—a variety of charitable bequests whose civil society beneficiaries ranged from schools and clinics to *de facto* chambers of commerce, from social clubs for young people to grave yards for the poor.

The mosque itself is, in some Muslim countries, a major institution of civil society. In major cities like Tehran and Cairo the mosque sometimes tries to care for the homeless, either with free food or with shelter during rainy or cold seasons.

In sacred months, like the fasting month of Ramadan or the pilgrimage month and Ashura month of Muharram, the mosque can become a preeminent refuge for the poor and the homeless.

Some of the *awqaf* in Egypt are for the education of girls and women to prepare them for clear roles in civil society. Theological Islam has seemed to discourage women from performing high governing roles over men. However, historical Islam—starting from the great political influence of the Prophet Muhammad's widow, Aisha—has repeatedly propelled women to offices of power and influence.

Between 2001 and 2004, the largest Muslim country in population, Indonesia, had a woman President, Megawati Sukarnoputri. In Bangladesh, both the Prime Minister's office and the role of the leader of the opposition have been alternating between two women—Khaleda Zia and Sheikh Hasina Wajed. In Pakistan, Benazir Bhutto headed two governments before. Senegal, an African country with a Muslim population of over 94 percent, has had two female Prime Ministers—Mame Madior Boye and Aminata

Toure. And Turkey—a Muslim country with a secular state—has had a woman Prime Minister, Tansu Çiller.

Five Muslim countries have had female Heads of State or Heads of Government long before the United States has had a woman President, Italy a woman Prime Minister, France a woman President, Germany a woman Chancellor, or Russia a woman Head of State.

The United States has tried to protect religious minorities in the civil society through a separation of church and state. And yet, after 200 years, the United States has only once strayed from the Protestant fraternity. John F. Kennedy was elected in 1960 by the slimmest of margins. In 2000, the United States was tested to see if it would elect a Presidential package with a Jew for Vice President. The system rejected Gore and Lieberman. The United States has never elected a Jew to the White House—and may never elect a Muslim for President for another century.

Islam has protected its religious minorities, not through separation of church from state, but through ecumenicalism and the tolerance of Ahl al-Kitab. During the Ottoman Empire, Christians attained high office. Suleiman I (1520–1566) had Christian ministers in his government, as did Selim III (1789–1807). Moghul Emperor Akbar (1556–1605) integrated Hindus into government. Saddam Hussein in Iraq had a Chaldean Christian—Tariq Aziz—as Deputy Prime Minister. Egypt nurtured Boutros Boutros-Ghali (a Coptic Christian) through its foreign ministry and helped him become the Secretary-General of the United Nations.

The Republic of Senegal in West Africa—over 90 percent Muslim—repeatedly elected Léopold Senghor, a Roman Catholic, as President. Muslim societies have used ecumenical tolerance as a protection of religious minorities in their civil societies.

A Conclusion

Senegal's degree of ecumenicalism in its first half-century of independence constituted a degree of secular modernism far ahead of the level reached by any contemporary Western society. Where in the entire Christian West is it even conceivable for a Muslim to be elected President or Prime Minister? Even in those Western countries like France where the Muslim population is much larger than the number of Christians in Senegal, a Muslim would have a hard time being elected Mayor of a small town, let alone President of the Republic.

In the political culture of Muslim Senegal, I see signs of the historical proposition that Islam went modernist long before the Western World did. Most of the Muslim World then relapsed into a premodernist culture of legalistic lethargy and social conservatism. But even today, elements of modernist Islam can be found in unexpected places—from poverty-stricken Bangladesh ready to follow women in hijab as Prime Ministers to postcolonial Senegalese Muslims ready to elect a Christian for executive President.

CHAPTER TWO

LIBERAL ISLAM VERSUS MODERATE ISLAM: ELUSIVE MODERATION AND THE SIEGE MENTALITY*

There is a tendency to equate liberal Islam with moderate Islam. Yet there are occasions when to be liberal demands a sense of outrage and rebellion.

The causes of the political radicalization of Islam are different from the roots of theological conservatism. For decades, the Royal House of Saudi Arabia has been theologically conservative but not politically radical. Indeed, the monarchy in Riyadh was for a long time a classic example of how a Muslim regime could be politically pro-Western without being culturally Westernized. Was the Saudi regime politically moderate without being doctrinally liberal?

Common interests have been critical in the close alliance between the Saudi royals and Western states—particularly the United States. The Saudis sought an alternative to Great Britain, and future military protection against real or imagined enemies. On the other hand, the United States was aware, by the end of the Second World War, of Saudi Arabia's bountiful fields of oil and sought to ensure access. This alliance of mutual interests was solidified by a meeting on February 14, 1945 between President Franklin Roosevelt of the United States and King Abdulaziz Bin Saud.[1]

Of course, since the events of September 11, 2001, the United States has begun to be more concerned about the radicalization of Islam in Saudi Arabia. It was difficult to ignore the fact that a majority (15 of 19) of the 9/11 hijackers were Saudis, and that Osama bin Laden was from a rich Saudi family.[2]

A summer 2005 debate in the *American Journal of Islamic Social Sciences* (AJISS) was rich in trying to diagnose the nature of the radicalization of Islam, but relatively thin in diagnosing the causes of that radicalization.[3] The best diagnosis of causes of radicalism in that collection came from Graham E. Fuller, a former employee of the American Central Intelligence Agency (CIA).

The Muslim World, feeling itself under siege, and with its sensitivities heightened by its witness of the struggle of Muslims right across the global *Ummah*, is not currently operating in an environment conducive to intellectual openness or to liberal and reformist thought. The Muslim World is simply hunkered down in defensive and survivalist mode. Indeed, the forces of terrorism in the Muslim World must be brought to heel. But it will not happen unless we see a change in hegemonistic US policies, US explicit embrace of Israeli right-wing policies in the occupied West Bank, and linkage with American fundamentalist Christian attitudes.[4]

I have never heard the problem better formulated. There are indeed global causes of Islamic radicalism and global reasons why 'Muslim terrorism' has gone international. One factor is the 'Latin-Americanization' of the Middle East by US policy-makers and strategists. Just as Latin America had been regarded by the United States as fair ground for imperial manipulation and periodic military interventions for nearly two centuries, much of the Muslim World, especially the Middle East, has more recently been treated with similar imperial arrogance. US imperialism in Latin America had been an Empire of control rather than occupation.[5] The same is largely true of American imperialism in the Middle East. However, the Bush Doctrine of preemption saw the United States' willingness to occupy Iraq and periodically threatened other states like Syria and Iran.[6]

The second major trigger of globalized Islamic radicalization consists of the State of Israel, its brutal occupation of the Palestinian territory, the annexation of Jerusalem and the United States' enormous material, diplomatic, and uncritical support of the Jewish state. One table in this regard, below, of US aid to the world and Israel is instructive.

Table 2-1: US Aid to the World and Israel

July 1, 1945–September 30, 1997 (in millions of dollars)[7]

Area/Country	Total Economic and Military Assistance
World	492, 958
Israel	68,697

Israeli behavior cannot even be censured by the United Nations Security Council without encountering the American veto. Because of the United States, Israel has been enjoying almost total immunity since at least the 1967 Middle East War.[8] The United States provides Israel with an umbrella of impunity.[9] The resulting international frustration has aroused widespread rage throughout the Muslim World. In addition, the Arab-

Israeli dispute has provided license for many countries in the region to restrict domestic rights and democratic practices.[10]

The third international trigger of Islamic radicalism and major cause of Muslim terrorism is the multiple humiliations of Muslims in so many different countries. Two Muslim countries are under direct foreign occupation (whether acknowledged or not)—Afghanistan and Palestine. Two Muslim populations are under some kind of international trusteeship—Bosnia and Kosovo. Several Muslim minorities elsewhere are struggling for self-determination against enormous military odds—including Kashmir, Chechnya, Southern Philippines, Southern Thailand and elsewhere.[11] No other civilization in the contemporary world is under a comparable sense of siege. This is quite apart from lower intensity rivalries between Muslims and non-Muslims in Nigeria, the Ivory Coast [Côte d'Ivoire] and Ethiopia. (I regard the conflicts in the Sudan as more Arab versus less Arabized, rather than Muslims against non-Muslims). Politically and militarily, the Muslim *Ummah* is more sinned against than sinning.

Almost all the contributions in the AJISS debate agreed that there are also domestic causes of Muslim radicalization, as well as global causes. Such domestic causes include authoritarian Arab monarchs and other undemocratic Muslim regimes, resentment of sociocultural changes, economic stagnation, and lack of alternative channels of political protest. But even those domestic radicalizing forces might not have risen to levels of terrorism if they had not been reinforced by a resentment of American support for most Muslim dictators for decades—especially oil-rich dictators, but along with oil-poor Pakistan and Egypt. Moreover, aid to countries like these is largely military aid, not trade deals or aid that can help in raising the economic circumstances of unemployed Muslims.[12]

Political Islam in many Muslim dictatorships seeks to offer an alternative to governments that are not only anti-freedom, but also incompetent and corrupt. In 2005, it was pointed out that the Muslim Brotherhood would be seen as an appealing alternative if Egypt held truly free and fair elections; the Muslim Brotherhood won the elections in Egypt in 2012, as expected.[13] However, the Muslim Brotherhood's blunders in power did lead to their ousting by the military a year later.

Pro-democracy forces in countries like Egypt, Pakistan, and Saudi Arabia were enough to politicize Islam, and even to radicalize it.[14] But the rise of the temperature to terrorism is almost always ignited by anti-Americanism or anti-Westernism, even at the domestic level. This spark of anti-Americanism or anti-Westernism is not lit by who or what the West thinks in religious terms, but "rather from the plausible perception that the things they [Muslims] most love and value—God, Islam, their brethren, and Muslim lands—are being attacked by America."[15] Anti-Westernism is not a rejection of democracy. Indeed, data from the *World Values Survey* conducted from 1995 to 1996 and from 2000 to 2002 showed that with the exception of Pakistan, people in many Muslim countries surveyed thought highly of democracy. In Albania, Egypt, Bangladesh, Azerbaijan, Indonesia, Morocco, and Turkey, 92 to 99 percent of the public supported democratic institutions—more than the 89 percent in the United States.[16] Indeed, in some circumstances such as the election of female heads of government, or the toleration of minorities in power—as pointed out elsewhere in this volume—Muslims may be more liberal than even Westerners or Americans.

I am not a moderate Muslim in the US sense. Yet, at least on three issues, I regard myself as a liberal Muslim. I am against the death penalty; I am in favor of gender equality; and I believe that *ijtihad* will become increasingly crucial as a solution to Islam's doctrinal problems. On the death penalty, I came out of the closet during the uproar over *Satanic Verses* in the 1980s. I deplored the book, denounced the author, and dissented from the death penalty not just for Rushdie but also for anybody else regardless of the offense.[17]

On gender equality, I have had qualified reservations about polygamy, but not outright rejection. I had grown up in a polygamous family, and knew its strengths as well as weaknesses. It is also instructive to note the context of the Qur'anic permission of this practice. First, at the time of the Qur'an, permission to take multiple wives allowed the care of widows and female orphans in a society plagued by continuous warfare. Many women and children were left destitute by the deaths of their husbands or fathers in warfare. Second, prior to the coming of Islam, men were not limited to four wives. Third, the Qur'an demands husbands treat all wives equally, and, if it is not possible, restricts them to one wife (4:3). Fourth, in a later verse (4:129), it warns that it will not be possible to treat wives equally, perhaps effectively prohibiting polygamy.[18]

On the other hand, I have supported Amina Wadud's effort to end male monopoly of religious leadership. I have supported that effort of hers long before she dramatically demonstrated it in a Friday prayer in New York City in March 2005.[19] She had attempted it in a mosque in Cape Town, South Africa, in the 1990s, but with only limited success. I cheered her even then.

Liberal Islam on the Defensive

But those of us who see ourselves as liberal Muslims are greatly hampered by the external forces of Zionism, the American imperium and the global humiliation of Muslims from Kashmir to Chechnya. Once again, Graham E. Fuller captures the fundamentals when he says the following:

> As long as conditions in the Muslim World remain radicalized—by terrorism, the sweeping US military response, dictatorship across the region, and a sense of Islam under siege—only radical groups will flourish. Moderation and liberalization can only flourish in a quieter and freer environment where radical voices find limited response.[20]

In this paragraph, Fuller almost equates liberalization with moderation. In the literature about developing countries, there was a time when modernization was equated with Westernization. To be 'modern' was to be as 'Western' as possible. In the literature about Islam, more recently, the concept of moderation has come close to being equated with Westernization.[21] To be 'moderate' is now translated as being as 'Western' as possible. Sometimes the concept 'liberal' is also hijacked by the West—as when conservatives use it as a dirty word in election commercials and other political rhetoric.

But most African social scientists and thinkers, for example, would reject the proposition that the modern African society is necessarily the Westernized African society nowadays. What about thinkers of the Muslim World? Do they accept the proposition that the moderate Muslim society is the Westernized *Ummah*? It may be difficult to characterize someone like the Grand *Mufti* of Egypt, Ali Gomaa. The *Mufti*, appointed by the Egyptian government, has denounced fundamentalism and clerics who are narrow-minded or ignorant. He has also skewered patriarchal society's expectations of women's roles and proposed that Shari'a can be seen as a means towards a just and peaceful world. Gomaa could not be seen as Westernized since his lifestyle is appropriate for his religion and status. However, Gomaa may find it difficult to avoid the pressures of anti-Americanism as a result of the aggressive American foreign policy in the Middle East.[22] This illustrates the difficulties of attempts at reforms by Muslim liberals, since the reforms are difficult to implement in a broad climate of Islamophobia in the Western World and deepening Americophobia in the Muslim World. Muslims begin to lose their moderation.

Muqtedar Khan, one of the participants in the AJISS debate, would surely agree that anti-Western sentiment in the Muslim World is not necessarily anti-Christian. Al-Qaeda's strategy of September 11, 2001, seemed to have targeted the economic symbol of American power—the World Trade Center which they successfully destroyed. Al-Qaeda also appeared to target the military symbol of American power—the Pentagon. Thirdly, the airplane which crashed in Pennsylvania seemed to have been intended for either Capitol Hill or the White House, symbols of American political power. What was missing on September 11, 2001 was any attempt by Al-Qaeda to target a Cathedral in either Washington or New York as a symbol of American religiosity.

Al-Qaeda succeeded in demolishing a symbol of American economic might in New York. Al-Qaeda triumphed in damaging a symbol of American military hegemony in Washington, DC. Because the passengers in a fourth plane succeeded in overcoming the Muslim warriors, Al-Qaeda failed in hitting a symbol of America political power. What Al-Qaeda never targeted at all was a symbol of American Christian faith.[23]

All the contributors in the AJISS debate found a place for *ijtihad* (reinterpretation)—a 'juristic tool' and potential mechanism of reform. John L. Esposito gave *ijtihad* a wide role,[24] whereas Abid Ullah Jan narrowed the scope for *ijtihad*.[25] My position may lie somewhere between these two colleagues, but my reasons may be somewhat different. *Ijtihad* may make Muslims more liberal but not necessarily more moderate.[26]

My central thesis in this regard is that God deliberately reveals Himself in installments, partly through religious messengers and partly through the march of science and expanding human experience. Indeed, one could even say that the Islam of Prophet Muhammad was quite respectful of knowledge and encouraged its pursuit. Muslims, after all, believe that God's first words to the Prophet Muhammad were about knowledge, and God's first command to the prophet was the imperative *Iqra* (Read).

> Yet man doth transgress all bounds
> In that he looketh upon himself
> Verily to the Lord is the final return[27]

God "taught by the pen." In contemporary terms, "the pen" could be extended to include teaching by the computer and the Internet as well as continuing revelations about the natural and physical worlds, from the outer reaches of space to the inner workings of genes. God taught human beings "that which they did not know." Within the last one hundred years alone, this has included harnessing the awesome atom for good and evil, landing a man on the moon, exploring galaxies far away, mapping the human genome, and connecting people tens of thousands of miles apart through the Internet.[28]

Early Islam as a civilization may have been distinct because of its readiness to synthesize what was best from other cultures. Those early

Qur'anic verses stressed that all real knowledge came from God regardless of which human being *(insan)* discovered it. Every successful scientific discovery helped to reveal more of God. But some of the experiences may be radicalizing rather than moderating.

Human History as Divine Revelation

The reason why Islam recognizes so many prophets *(anbiya')* and so many messengers or apostles *(rusul)* is because Allah reveals himself in such installments across time and across space. The Prophet Muhammad was the last prophet *(nabi)*, but was he the last messenger *(rasul)*? Let us accept that he was also the last *rasul* in the form of a human person. But could Time be a continuing cosmic *rasul* or at least *risalah*? Is history a continuing revelation of God? Is expanding science a non-carnate *rasul*?

If God reveals Himself incrementally, and if history is a continuing revelation of God, should we not re-examine the message of Muhammad in the light of new installments of Divine Revelation? The early Muslims of the first century of *Hijrah* would not have understood much about distant galaxies. So Allah talked to them in simple terms about our own moon (as if it was the only moon) and about the sun in the Milky Way (as if it was the only sun). Fourteen centuries ago, the Arabs were overwhelmed by the Almighty as the creator of our own galaxy. Today, we know that God created billions of galaxies. Should we not reinterpret the verses about the sun and the moon in the Qur'an in the light of our new understanding of astronomy and the cosmos? One should not forget that early Islam was in the forefront of pursuing, collecting, and systematizing knowledge about science. Historically, Islamic culture refined what now is called "Arabic numerals," invented Algebra, developed the zero and pushed forward the frontiers of science.[29]

If one needs to reinterpret Qur'anic verses about astronomy, why cannot he reinterpret Islamic verses about ancient punishments *(hudud)*? The expansion of human knowledge is not only about the stars. It is also about human beings themselves and their behavior. If we now know more about the causes of crime, we also know more about the limits of culpability and guilt. We know that poverty, bad parenting, a sense of injustice, racial discrimination, chemical imbalance in the human body, a bad neighborhood, and a bad social environment can all be contributing factors towards turning a human being towards crime.[30] At times *ijtihad* can lead to both liberalization and moderation.

From these conclusions, I proceed to the belief that some verses of the Qur'an were about events during the Prophet's own time and other verses were eternal in purpose. One can illustrate with the *Sura* in the Qur'an about Abu Lahab (father of the flame). I believe the Prophet's contemporaries knew that the verses were about the Prophet's uncle Abd al-Uzza bin Abdul Muttalib. In the Prophet's own time, it was understood that the verses were about a specific individual enemy of Islam.[31]

Should we reinterpret Abu Lahab in a more timeless fashion? Alternatively, should we be reinterpreting Qur'anic verses in ways which would make them historically specific?

The Sudanese theologian Mahmoud Mohammed Taha had argued about the two messages of Islam—the time-specific message and the eternal.[32] The Nimeiry Government executed the old man in 1985 in the name of Islamic *hudud*. Taha rejected the criticism offered by some that the Shari'a—since it is perfect—does not need to evolve and develop. Taha pointed out, in his introduction to the 4th edition of his *The Second Message of Islam*:

> ... the perfection of the Islamic Shari'a lies in the fact that it is a living body, growing and developing with the living, growing, and developing life, guiding its step towards God, stage by stage.[33]

Taha thought that it was 'irrational' to think that the Shari'a of the seventh century is suitable for application to the current era.[34]

Taha's *Second Message* led him to some startling conclusions. For instance, he said:

> The good society ... is based on three equalities: economic equality, today known as socialism, or the sharing of wealth; political equality or democracy, or sharing in political decisions which affect daily life; and social equality which, to some extent, results from socialism and democracy, and is characterized by a lack of social class and discrimination based on color, faith, race, or sex.[35]

Mahmoud Taha was more of a force for doctrinal liberalization than for political moderation.

If God has been teaching human beings in installments about crime and punishment, and if there were no police, prisons, forensic science, or knowledge about DNA fourteen centuries ago, the type of punishments needed had to be truly severe enough to be a deterrent. Hence, the *hudud* had to be introduced. Since then God has taught us more about crime, its causes, the methods of its investigation, the limits of guilt, and the much wider range of possible punishments.

Did not the Prophet Muhammad say, "My people will never agree on error?"[36] If so, one can take it for granted that Muslims of the future will be less and less convinced that the amputation of the hand is a suitable punishment for a thief under any circumstances. This is a prediction. I have not the slightest doubt that the Islam of our grandchildren will never accept penal amputation of the hands of thieves as legitimate any longer. On such issues, doctrinal liberalism converges with social moderation.

Abid Ullah Jan rightly saluted the *Sahaba* and the Prophet's disciples. We revere them as the first converts to Islam and as supporters of our Prophet. But one must not forget that the *Sahaba* were not themselves prophets; most of them were not even saints. As ordinary human beings, they were the usual mixture of vices and virtues. That is why three of Islam's first four Caliphs were assassinated. That is also why there was an Arab civil war within little more than a decade after the Prophet's death— with the Prophet's widow Aisha fighting the Prophet's cousin and son-in-law, Ali![37] *Sahaba* behavior was often neither liberal nor moderate. Have we been idealizing the *Sahaba* too much?

If the Prophet's disciples could be fallible, so could the founders of the *Madhahib*. Indeed, for fourteen centuries, the Qur'an and *ahadith* have been interpreted almost exclusively by men. Male-centrism has also been a historic feature of Judaism and Christianity. There is enough in the Qur'an which supports gender-equity, but none of the four Sunni schools was founded by a woman. Abu Hanifa founded the Hanafi school; Mallik Ibn Anas founded the Maliki school; Muhammad Ibn Idris al-Shafi'i founded the Shafi'i school; and 1 founded the Hanbali school.[38]

The Grand *Mufti* of Egypt, Ali Gomaa, has pointed out that there have been noted female teachers in Islam—including at least fifty female sheikhs who taught Al Jili, one of the preeminent thinkers of Islam. He went on to say: "And yet there are those who deny that women have equal spiritual status in Islam. This is a disgrace."[39] It might have made a difference if one *madhhab* was founded by a woman like Amina Wadud. But one must take into account that all over the world in the Middle Ages, women were usually condemned to inferior status. But today a woman theologian like Wadud could be a voice of liberalization rather than moderation.

The Qur'an does not prohibit slavery (any more than does the Bible or the Torah), but the Qur'an goes further than the sister religions in encouraging the freeing of slaves. Islam is not anti-slavery, but it is pro-emancipation. If early Muslims had used *ijtihad* enough, the abolitionist movement would have started in the Muslim World a thousand years before William Wilberforce, John Brown, or Abraham Lincoln.[40]

There are many other humane gems in the Qur'an waiting to be fully revealed through *ijtihad*. Some may enrich liberal thought without encouraging political moderation. But current Islamic thought is indeed "mired in literalism, narrowness of vision and intolerance," to quote Fuller.[41] The necessary climate for an Islamic renewal is hampered by the forces which have put Islam on the defensive. Both political moderation and doctrinal liberalization among the Muslim masses will remain difficult as long as the United States remains imperial and Islamophobic in foreign policy; Israel continues to brutalize and occupy the Palestinian population; and the rest of the world permits the humiliation of Muslims from Chechnya to Afghanistan, from Kashmir to Iraq. When Muslims are politically radicalized, they often tend to be resistant to doctrinal liberalization. The ultimate causes of radicalization are primarily non-Muslim in origin. But the Muslim World suffers the most from the excesses of both political radicalism and doctrinal conservatism.

Notes

* An earlier version was written as part of an exchange on the theme, "Debating Moderate Islam: The Theopolitics of US–Islamic World Relations," guest-edited by M. A. Muqtedar Khan, in the *American Journal of Islamic Social Sciences* (Summer 2005), Volume 22, Number 3, pp. 83–89. My own arguments were partly developed in an Internet family debate with nephew Muhammad Yusuf in Canada and cousin Rafii Abdalla Shikely in Kenya. I am grateful for their stimulation.

[1] For some descriptions of this meeting, see Robert Baer, *Sleeping with the Devil: How Washington Sold Our Soul for Saudi Crude* (New York: Crown Publishers, 2003) pp. 82–83, and Michael T. Klare, *Blood and Oil: The Dangers and Consequences of America's Growing Dependency on Imported Petroleum* (New York: Metropolitan Books, 2004), pp. 35–36.

[2] There has been a spate of books describing and speculating on the Saudi-terrorism connection. See, for instance, Laurent Murawiec, trans. George Holoch, *Princes of Darkness: The Saudi Assault on the West* (Lanham, MD: Rowman & Littlefield Publishers, Inc. and distributed by National Book Network, 2005); Bob Graham with Jeff Nussbaum, *Intelligence Matters: The CIA, the FBI, Saudi Arabia, and the Failure of America's War on Terror* (New York: Random Books, 2004); Baer, *Sleeping With the Devil*; and Bernard Lewis, *The Crisis of Islam: Holy War and Unholy Terror* (New York: Modern Library, 2003).

[3] "Debating Moderate Islam: The Theopolitics of US–Islamic World Relations," guest-edited by M. A. Muqtedar Khan, in the *American Journal of Islamic Social Sciences* (Summer 2005), Volume 22, Number 3.

[4] Graham E. Fuller, "Freedom and Security: Necessary Conditions for Moderation," *American Journal of Islamic Social Sciences* (Summer 2005), Volume 22, Number 3, pp. 25–26. A more detailed and somewhat similar analysis of why the actions of the United States inspire violent Islamic reactions may be found in the work of

another former CIA employee; see Anonymous (later revealed as Michael Scheuer) *Imperial Hubris: Why the West is Losing the War on Terror* (Washington, DC: Brassey's, Inc., 2004), pp. 11–14. To sum up, Scheur has said: Rather, America is now regarded as a nation that supports and protects Arab tyrants from Rabat to Riyadh, that has abandoned multiple generations of Palestinians to cradle-to-grave life in refugee camps, and that blindly supports Israel, arming and funding her anti-Muslim violence and preventing Muslims from arming sufficiently to defend themselves.

—Anonymous, *Imperial Hubris*, p. 16.

[5] Under the Monroe Doctrine, enunciated first in December 1823, the United States gave notice to the world that it would not brook attempts by outside powers ("Europeans") to extend its system or control to Latin America; see Edwin P. Hoyt, *America's Wars and Military Excursions* (New York: McGraw-Hill Book Co., 1987), p. 179.

[6] The Bush Doctrine, first previewed in a speech at West Point in June 2002 and elaborated on in the National Security Strategy Overview in September 2002, has three major points:

- The US would not hesitate to act preemptively against terrorists
- The US would maintain its global military preeminence
- The US would seek to promote its democratic values overseas

[7] Data for this table is drawn from United States Agency for International Development, *US Overseas Loans and Grants and Assistance from International Organizations July 1, 1945–September 30, 1997* (Washington, DC: Office of Budget, Bureau of Management, US AID, 2000), pp. 4, 12, and 52. For discussions on US aid to Israel, see Mohammed Rabie, *The Politics of Foreign Aid: US Foreign Assistance and Aid to Israel* (New York, Westport, CT, and London: Praeger, 1988), and for a comparative look, consult Duncan L. Clarke, "US Security Assistance to Egypt and Israel: Politically Untouchable?" *Middle East Journal*, Volume 51, Number 2 (Spring 1997), pp. 200–214.

[8] For a detailed account of the US–Israel ties and the resultant Muslim outrage, see Anonymous, *Imperial Hubris*, pp. 226–229.

[9] Former President Bush declared that the US will come to Israel's aid if it is attacked by Iran; see Glenn Kessler, "Bush Says US Would Defend Israel Militarily," *The Washington Post* (February 2, 2006), p. A18.

[10] Sheikh Mohammad Hussein Fadlallah (former spiritual leader of Hezbollah and one of the first Muslim clerics to condemn the 9/11 bombing) has said:
"We have emergency laws; we have control by the security agencies; we have stagnation of opposition parties; we have the appropriation of political rights—all this in the name of the Arab–Israeli conflict."
David Ignatius, "Real Arab Reform," *The Washington Post* (March 12, 2004), p. A23. A detailed account of the impact of US support for dictators in the Arab World may also be found in Anonymous, *Imperial Hubris*, pp. 12–13.

[11] Also see Anonymous, *Imperial Hubris*, p. 12.

[12] This is pointed out in the case of Pakistan, for example, by Helene Cooper, "For Pakistan, American Aid Is All Guns, No Butter," *The New York Times* (February 16, 2006), p. A32.

[13] See Associated Press, "Islamic Candidates Make Gains in Egypt," *The Washington Post* (November 17, 2005), p. A22. Authorities in places like Egypt often argue that full democratization would lead to victory for Islamists. However, as Saad Eddin Ibrahim, an Egyptian dissident and democracy activist has noted:
... isn't it Mubarak's repression of secular civil forces that has kept the field empty for the Islamists in Egypt, where there are now more than 100,000 mosques where they can freely preach their message—but only a handful of registered political parties and human rights groups?
Saad Eddin Ibrahim, "Questions for Mubarak," *The Washington Post* (February 11, 2005), p. A25.

[14] Reformers in the kingdom of Saudi Arabia have been emboldened to press for political reforms, but some of the bolder ones were jailed, days before Secretary of State Colin Powell's 2004 visit to Riyadh. See Reuters, "Saudi Arabia Detains Reformers," *The Washington Post* (March 17, 2004), p. A17 and Elizabeth Rubin, "A Saudi Response on Reform: Round Up the Usual Dissidents," *The New York Times* Week in Review Section, (March 21, 2004), p. 3.

[15] Anonymous, *Imperial Hubris*, p. 9.

[16] Ronald Inglehart and Pippa Norris, "The True Clash of Civilizations," *Foreign Policy* (March/April 2003) Issue 135, pp. 62–70.

[17] See Ali A. Mazrui, "*The Satanic Verses* or a Satanic Novel?: Moral Dilemmas of the Rushdie Affair," *Third World Quarterly*, Vol. 12, No. 1 (1990), pp. 116–39.

[18] For discussions on this issue, consult Mahmoud M. Ayoub, *Islam: Faith and History* (Oxford, UK: Oneworld Publications, 2004), p. 184 and Reza Aslan, *No God but God: The Origins, Evolution, and Future of Islam* (New York: Random House, 2005), p. 63.

[19] The prayer did have to be carried out in secrecy due to threats; see Mona Eltahawy, "A Prayer toward Equality," *The Washington Post* (March 18, 2005), p. A23.

[20] Fuller, "Freedom and Security: Necessary Conditions for Moderation," p. 26.

[21] To be Westernized may be suspect in many Muslim eyes; thus Jalal Al-e Ahmad coined the term "Westoxification,"—or in Farsi, *gharbzadegi*—to denote the absorption of Western culture in Muslim lands. Cited by Aslan, *No God but God,* p. 237.

[22] Gomaa's views are outlined in G. Willow Wilson's, "The Show-Me Sheikh," *The Atlantic Monthly* (July/August 2005), pp. 40–44.

[23] Similarly, in a December 2004 audio tape, Osama bin Laden said President Bush was wrong to "claim that we hate freedom." Bin Laden's response: "If so, then let him explain to us why we don't strike, for example, Sweden." Don Van Atta Jr., "Sizing Up the New Toned-Down Bin Laden," *The New York Times* (December 19, 2004), Week in Review Section, p. 1.

[24] Esposito's thoughts on *ijtihad* may be found in his "Moderate Muslims: A Mainstream of Modernists, Islamists, Conservatives, and Traditionalists," in *American Journal of Islamic Social Sciences*, Volume 22, Number 3 (Summer 2005), p. 15.

[25] Abid Ullah Jan's views on *ijtihad* are expressed in, "Moderate Islam: A Product of American Extremism," *American Journal of Islamic Social Sciences*, Volume 22, Number 3 (Summer 2005), pp. 33–34.

[26] Some further discussions on *ijtihad* may be found in H. H. A. Rahman, "The Origin and Development of *Ijtihad* to Solve Complex Modern Legal Problems," *Bulletin of the Henry Martyn Institute of Islamic Studies* 17 (January–June 1998), pp. 7–21, and also Frank E. Vogel, "The Closing of the Door of *Ijtihad* and the Application of the Law," *American Journal of Islamic Social Sciences* 10 (Fall 1993), pp. 396–401.

[27] Sura *Iqra* or *Alaq*/Sura 96, Verses 1–8.

[28] These issues are discussed more fully in Ali A. Mazrui and Alamin M. Mazrui's, "Islam and Civilization" (eds.) Majid Tehranian and David W. Chapell, *Dialogue of Civilizations: A New Peace Agenda* (New York: L. B. Tauris, 2002), pp. 139–160.

[29] For details on the Islamic contribution to scientific knowledge, consult C. M. Stanton, *Higher Learning in Islam: The Classical Period, AD 700 to 1300* (Savage, MD: Rowman and Littlefield, 1990), pp. 103–119.

[30] For an overview of the causes of crime, consult George B. Vold, Thomas J. Bernard, and Jeffrey B. Snipes, *Theoretical Criminology* (New York: Oxford University Press, 2002).

[31] The relevant Sura about Abu Lahab is Sura 111. See Faruq Sherif, *A Guide to the Contents of the Qur'an* (Reading, UK: Garnet Pub., 1995), p. 4.

[32] Mahmoud Mohamed Taha, *The Second Message of Islam*, translation and introduction by Abdullahi Ahmed An-Na'im (Syracuse, NY: Syracuse University Press, 1987).

[33] Taha, *The Second Message of Islam*, p. 39.

[34] Taha, *The Second Message of Islam*, p. 39.

[35] Taha, *The Second Message of Islam*, p. 153.

[36] This is a *hadith* attributed to the Prophet; see Fazlur Rahman, *Islam*, 2nd edition (Chicago: University of Chicago Press, 1979), p. 78.

[37] On the struggles in early Islam, see Frederick Mathewson Denny, *An Introduction to Islam*, 2nd edition (New York: Macmillan Pub. Co., 1994), p. 90.

[38] The growth and spread of these schools is discussed in Rahman, *Islam*, pp. 82–83.

[39] Wilson, "The Show-Me Sheikh," p. 40.

[40] A quick overview of Islam and slavery may be found in Paul E. Lovejoy, *Transformations in Slavery: A History of Slavery in Africa* (Cambridge and New York: Cambridge University Press, 2000), pp. 15–18, while comparative work on justifications and ideas on slavery may be found in Peter Garnsey, *Ideas of Slavery from Aristotle to Augustine* (Cambridge and New York: Cambridge University Press, 1996).

[41] Fuller, "Freedom and Security: Necessary Conditions for Moderation," p. 25.

CHAPTER THREE

CHRISTIANITY AND ISLAM IN AFRICA'S POLITICAL EXPERIENCE: PIETY, PASSION AND POWER

Introduction

Has the impact of religion in developing societies declined? Today, modernization theories and their postulates about the imminent demise of religion in developing regions are increasingly being discredited by empirical evidence of the surprising resilience of religion.[1] Beliefs in the Hereafter, and in God, apparently are influential in terms of political behavior here on Earth—whether on issues of sexual orientation, nationalism, or terrorism.[2]

Sometimes, these modes of behavior are paradoxical. Given the fact that Islam plays a major role in African affairs, this chapter will discuss some of the paradoxes of Islam's relationship with Christianity in Africa's experience. I analyze in this chapter the impact of colonialism on Christian–Muslim relations; the interplay between religion and civil–military relations; the influence of religious culture on levels of social violence; and the relevance of religious culture for the distribution of the AIDS epidemic in Africa.

Two points may be noted. First, I sometimes use the term "Islam" here metaphorically to mean followers of the religion rather than the pristine doctrines of the religion necessarily. Second, to facilitate the analysis, I may also draw on comparisons from non-Islamic and non-African states and societies. However, my focus will remain on the interplay between Islam and Christianity in the African experience.

Between Faith and Friction

Relations between Islam and Christianity can be conflictual as they currently seem to be in parts of the Nile Valley or Nigeria, or competitive as they seem to be in East Africa, or ecumenical as they have often been in countries like Tanzania. Christianity and Islam are in conflictual relations when hostilities are aroused, and the two great religions re-enact in Africa a shadow of the Crusades. Christianity and Islam are in competition when they are rivals in the free market of values and ideals, scrambling for converts without edging towards hostility. Christianity and Islam are in an ecumenical relationship when they appear to accept each other as divergent paths towards a convergent truth, different means towards a shared ultimate end. Minimally, the ecumenical spirit is a spirit of 'live and let live.' Maximally, the ecumenical spirit is a spirit of cooperation. Muslim-Christian dialogues tend to fall in between.[3]

Whether Christian–Muslim relations are conflictual, competitive, or ecumenical, they are themselves determined by three forces—the import of doctrine, the sociological balance in a given society, and the legacy of history in that particular society. Doctrinal, sociological, and historical forces help to shape relations between Christians and Muslims in a given part of the world.

In Africa, these two triads (conflict, competition, and cooperation on one side, and doctrine, sociology, and history on the other) operate within yet another triad—the triple heritage of twentieth century Africa: indigenous, Islamic, and Western civilizations.[4]

Africa in the twentieth century has been a confluence of these three civilizations. The Muslim parts of the populations of Nigeria, Egypt, and Ethiopia added together may well account for more than a quarter of the total of the population of the African continent as a whole. Nigeria has more Muslims than any Arab country, including Egypt.[5] In 1994, the Republic of South Africa celebrated not only its first multiracial democratic elections, but also the 300th anniversary of the arrival of Islam in the country—a minority religion which has proven more historically resilient than anyone would have expected.[6] The Republic of Malawi elected its first Muslim President also in 1994.

Africa's triple heritage of indigenous culture, Islam, and Western culture is sometimes a source of cultural enrichment, and at other times a cause of social and political tensions. Within the context of this triple heritage, Christianity and Islam have sometimes been in conflict, sometimes been in gracious competition, and have increasingly sought areas of ecumenical cooperation.

The impact of the West came initially through colonization, and this impact had a direct bearing on the fortunes of Christianity, Islam, and indigenous culture in Africa. The cornerstone of British colonial policy in Africa became Lord Lugard's doctrine of Indirect Rule—a strategy of ruling subject people primarily through their own "native authorities and institutions," such as the Maharajahs in India, the Emirs in northern Nigeria, and the Kabaka (King) in Buganda.[7]

In its application in Africa, Indirect Rule favored Islam in those areas which were already Islamized before the British came, but favored Christianity in areas where traditional African religion still prevailed. Thus, Indirect Rule favored Islam in northern Nigeria (which owed its Islam to precolonial times), but favored Christianity in Buganda and southern Sudan where the prevailing mores and beliefs were indigenous.

But in what ways did British Indirect Rule favor either Islam or Christianity? One extreme strategy was to keep Islam out of a particular area altogether. This was true of British policy for southern Sudan during the colonial period. Any Muslim missionary activity was kept out of the South.

In northern Nigeria, the British rulers discouraged Christian missionary work in the most Islamized parts of the North such as Sokoto and Zaria, but permitted Christianization in parts of the North which were not yet under the sway of Islam.

In most other parts of their African empire, the British helped Christianity by facilitating and subsidizing Christian mission schools and Christian mission clinics. Even British language policy in the colonies favored Christianity more than Islam. The British helped to promote a number of African languages and to create orthographies for them. Missionaries became allies in this enterprise. The Bible has been translated into many more African languages than the Qur'an.

Have the consequences of Indirect Rule after independence promoted conflict, competition, or cooperation between Christianity and Islam? Some would argue that the most dramatic postcolonial consequences have been conflictual. In Sudan, the colonial policies of ethno-religious apartheid separating north from south were a major cause of the first Sudanese Civil War (1955–1972) and a contributory factor to the Second Sudanese Civil War which started in 1983 and continued for decades.[8]

British policies of Indirect Rule in Nigeria might also have deepened the North-South divide in the country, and aggravated ethnic and sectarian tensions. British policies were more respectful of Islam and indigenous culture than the policies of any other European power in Africa, but, nevertheless, British concessions to indigenous institutions did carry a postcolonial cost within the artificial boundaries which colonialism had created.

The French colonial authorities, on the other hand, had put great emphasis on a policy of assimilation. At its most ambitious, French colonialism sought to turn Africans into Black French men and French women. And since for most of their history the French people had not been Muslim, the assimilation policy was implicitly a rejection of Islam—and a declaration of cultural war on indigenous traditions.

However, outside North Africa, French assimilationist policy hurt indigenous cultures more deeply than it hurt Islam. Paradoxically, assimilationist policies weakened indigenous resistance to Islamization— and therefore helped the spread of Islam in West Africa.

French assimilationist policy made Africans ashamed of their own native cultures—but that did not necessarily make them French. Islam therefore continued to thrive even in such long-established French colonies as Senegal, which the French regarded as their own cultural showpiece, and part of which they had colonized for well over a century.

Other Muslim countries in French West Africa included Western Sudan (now Mali), Niger, Guinea (Conakry), parts of the Côte d'Ivoire, and Mauritania in the Northwest. In all of them, Islam survived French assimilationist policy and was sometimes even inadvertently helped by it.

This configuration of doctrine, sociology, and history during the colonial period had consequences for the postcolonial era. Some of these consequences were dialectical, replete with contradictions and paradoxes. Especially significant are the consequences in postcolonial political experience. It is to this political experience that I must now turn, with all its paradoxes.

On Governance and Religious Culture

Our first postcolonial paradox is at once stimulating and disturbing; it is both fascinating and disquieting.

The paradox is as follows: Islam in military uniform in postcolonial Africa is more repressive than average; Islam in civilian robes in Africa is more tolerant than average. Militarized Islam in Africa is extra-dictatorial; civilian Islam in Africa is extra-tolerant.

What are the facts of the case? What are the causes? What are the consequences? Nigeria's experience of maximum open society has been under civilian Muslim administrations. Nigeria's experience of maximum repressive society has been under military Muslim administrations. Nigeria's Muslim civilian rulers have taken the country so far in openness and freedom that Nigeria was at times on the brink of anarchy. Nigeria's Muslim military rulers have taken the country so far in repression that the country has entered the gates of tyranny. Nigeria's non-Muslim rulers have been Christian.

Every time Nigeria has held free civilian elections, it has produced a Muslim Chief Executive or Muslim President—until Christian Olusegun Obasanjo was elected twice, and Christian Goodluck Jonathan was elected in the 2011. The greatest period of the open society in Nigeria was perhaps under Alhaji Shehu Shagari.[9] Under Shagari, political freedom was virtually unrestricted and economic freedom became license for plunder. The Shagari years of 1979 to 1983 were perhaps the greatest years of freedom of expression in Nigeria in the twentieth century. All shades of opinion could say absolutely anything—and the President of the Republic was subjected to the widest range of name-calling, from sheikh to satan, from *maallem* to monster.[10] Newspapers proliferated right and left, breathed or died in response to the market rather than to the musket. Newspapers were, more or less, instruments of party politics, and as such, were highly partisan. As Adigun Agbaje has pointed out: "... the newspaper press became an important part of the partisan struggles that wracked the Second Republic..."[11]

On the other hand, under Muslim military rulers, Nigeria experienced brutal repression. The most benign military rulers of Nigeria were Christians—especially the remarkably humane General Yakubu Gowon (Head of State 1966–1975) and General Olusegun Obasanjo (Head of State 1976–1979 and President from 1999–2007). Obasanjo was the only Nigerian leader to hand over power to a freely elected alternative government.

Somalia, before it got militarized, was one of the most democratic countries not only in Africa but almost anywhere in the world. A kind of pastoral democracy emerged after the unification of Italian Somaliland and British Somaliland and the establishment of independent Somalia in July 1960.[12]

This open society lasted for less than a decade. On October 21, 1969, a military regime was installed. For almost two decades, the country became a pawn in the Cold War between the Soviet Union and the United States in the Horn of Africa, switching sides between the former and the latter. The soldier Siad Barre remained in power as a military dictator, getting more and more repressive, until he was forced to leave the country in January 1991.[13]

Somalia after 1969, once again, demonstrated that Muslim political authority in Africa in uniform was often more repressive than average; whereas Somalia before 1969 illustrated the proposition that Muslim civilian authority in Africa was more tolerant than average.

Sudan has been a more complex case. South Sudan has been in turmoil on and off since 1955. The South is largely, but not completely, non-Muslim. The majority part of Sudan is the Islamized Northern Sudan. In the North, it has indeed been true that Muslim civilian authority has been exceptionally tolerant—except with regard to the civil war in the South,[14] and more recently in what may be a sort of ethnic intolerance mixed with anarchy in Darfur.[15]

Like several other African states, Sudan has had both military and civilian regimes.[16] Under civilian rule in Sudan, political detainees were virtually unknown; the one-party state was unthinkable; political trials were never staged; political assassinations were not carried out.

But Sudan's military governments started by also being relatively soft. Lt. General Ibrahim Abboud captured power in November 1958. It became the first military government in Africa to be dislodged by civilian demonstrations in October–November 1964. So soft was the regime that it let itself be pushed out by angry civilians.

Again the succeeding multi-party civilian rule in the Sudan was exceptionally tolerant. But this relative calm was ended in May 1969 when Col. Gaafar Muhammad Nimeiry, then left-wing, overthrew the civilians and established a so-called ten-man revolutionary council.

Nimeiry had himself elected President in 1971. He later dissolved the Revolutionary Council and established the Sudanese Socialist Union as the only legitimate political party.

Unlike the Ibrahim Abboud military regime of 1958–1964, Nimeiry's military rule was not so soft. From a religious point of view, its most merciless action was the execution of an old man, Mahmoud Mohammed Taha, on charges of heresy and apostasy. On the other hand, Nimeiry did negotiate and reach the Addis Ababa accords with South Sudan in 1972 and gave southern Sudan a decade of peace.

And Nimeiry's regime was also soft enough to allow itself to be chased out of office by popular demonstrations in the streets of Khartoum in 1985.

After a brief Transitional Military Council for one year under General Siwar al-Dahab from April 1985 to May 1986, Sudan once again returned to civil rule under Sadiq al-Mahdi as Prime Minister. It lived up to its reputation that Muslim civilian authority was above average in tolerance.

Unfortunately, this civilian phase did not last long either. On June 30, 1989 the government of Sadiq al-Mahdi was overthrown by General Omar Hassan Ahmad al-Bashir. His government was indeed to demonstrate that Muslim authority in military uniform was above average in repression. Bashir's regime is the toughest of all the military regimes Sudan has had.[17] It also happens to be the most self-consciously Islamic. Sudan now completes both parts of our dual-interpretation—that Islamic authority in civilian robes is extra-tolerant; and Islamic authority in military uniform is extra-repressive.

Uganda has had a Muslim ruler in military uniform, but has had no Muslim ruler in civilian robes. The one half of our proposition does hold—the Muslim ruler in military uniform in Uganda was more repressive than were the Christian soldiers who ruled Uganda. Idi Amin (1971–1979) did more damage to Uganda than did any other ruler of Uganda, military or civilian.[18]

Some have argued that Milton Obote's second administration was as bad if not worse than Idi Amin's rule. Possibly more people died under Obote's second administration (1980–1985). But one must remember that they died as much from a civil war as from tyranny. Most of Amin's slaughter, however, was due to tyranny or anarchy.[19] In any case, Obote himself was not a military ruler.[20]

In Malawi, there has been one ostensibly devout Christian ruler called Hastings Banda; a Muslim President called Bakili Muluzi, elected President of Malawi on May 17, 1994; and a Christian President called Bingu wa Mutharika (named Brightson Thom at birth, and then Webster Ryson Thom as a youth) who was elected in 2004[21]; and Christian Joyce Banda who ascended to office after the April 5, 2012 death of President Mutharika.

Banda was in power from 1964 to 1994, ruling for 30 years in an arbitrary fashion. He was one of Africa's worst postcolonial tyrants. Banda belonged to the Church of Scotland and was an elder in the church. Under Banda, Malawi plunged into desperate economic conditions and political staleness, since he ruled the country with an iron hand and prevented meaningful opposition.[22]

On balance, Bakili Muluzi was a much more democratic ruler of Malawi even if there was inevitable deterioration from the high standards when he took office.[23] Although Mutharika received high marks during his first term for Malawi's economic growth and political stability, his second term was marked by attempts to elevate his brother as successor, political unrest, and crackdowns on protestors. Malawi therefore authenticates the proposition that a Muslim ruler in civilian robes is above average in tolerance.

Tanzania may be heading for a system in which the President alternates between a Christian incumbent and a Muslim incumbent. The first Christian incumbent was of course Julius K. Nyerere who was chief executive from independence in 1961 until his resignation from the presidency in 1985. Nyerere was an exceptionally strong and creative chief executive. He was a Roman Catholic.[24]

Tanzania's second President was Ali Hassan Mwinyi who held office from 1985 to 1995. President Mwinyi was definitely less charismatic and less energetic and less influential than his predecessor, Julius Nyerere. But President Mwinyi was also more gentle and more tolerant than his great predecessor. President Mwinyi was a Muslim.

Mwinyi was followed by a Christian President again. Benjamin Mkapa of *Chama cha Mapenduzi* stepped into the Presidential State House in 1995, though with many cries of 'Foul' from the opposition. Benjamin Mkapa was followed by a Muslim President, Jakaya Kikwete.

Senegal poses even more intriguing questions about politics and religious affiliation. In the 1988 census, 94 percent of the population was identified as Muslim.[25] The population of Senegal has a higher proportion of Muslims than the population of Egypt.

And yet this overwhelmingly Muslim country, Senegal, had a Roman Catholic President in its postcolonial history not for five or ten years—but for twenty years. From 1960 to 1980, Roman Catholic Léopold Sédar Senghor ruled one of the more free governments on the African continent.[26] Senghor did bestride this narrow Muslim World like a colossus—not because everybody worshipped him, but because the Senegalese society was extra-ecumenical. Although a mostly Islamic society, Islam has emerged not as a competitor for state power, but as a locus for countervailing power in civil society that limits the reach of state action and, thus, acts as a check on state power. As Villalon has pointed out: "... the political importance of Islam in Senegal has been concentrated in the domain of state–society relations and not in the struggle for control of the state."[27]

Since Senegal was a relatively open society, Senghor was called many abusive names—lackey of the French, Negritudist hypocrite, political prostitute. But he was almost never denounced as *kaffir*, or infidel.

Consider how far ahead this situation was of any political–religious situation in the Western World. After two hundred years as a secular state, the United States strayed only once from the Protestant fraternity for the White House. We are not even sure John F. Kennedy was truly elected—we only know that he became President. There were some circumstances in Illinois which might have robbed Nixon of victory.[28] Kennedy's victory was exceptionally narrow.

No Jew has become President of the United States. There are now as many Muslims as Jews in the US, if not more.[29] Yet, a Muslim President of the United States is still a mind-boggling concept. Indeed, Senator John McCain, one of the contenders for the US Presidency in 2007, has said that Muslims are less suited to lead the United States because "this nation was founded primarily on Christian principles."[30] Yet there was Muslim Senegal with a Roman Catholic President for 20 years without upheavals in the streets or any attempted assassinations.

Now Senegal does at last have a Muslim President, and the first lady is also a Muslim. By almost all standards, the Muslims of Senegal have been remarkably ecumenical in the twentieth century. This has undoubtedly been a critical factor in the remarkable durability of Senegalese liberal democracy in a region of the world where there are too few of these regimes.[31]

Are there exceptions to this sweeping generalization that civilian Islam in Africa is more tolerant than average? Is there an exception to the generalization that military Muslim authority in Africa is more repressive than average?

There are indeed exceptions which hopefully prove the rule. Guinea (Conakry) produced a heroic Muslim leader, Ahmed Sékou Touré, who became one of the longest serving heads of state in Africa. He was President from 1958 until he died in a hospital in the United States in March 1984. Sékou Touré stood up against the French, and served for a while as Chairman of the Organization of the Islamic Conference. Nevertheless, he was one of the worst civilian dictators postcolonial Africa has had. A quarter of the population fled into exile. Despite several real or alleged attempts to overthrow Touré, he was unshakable from power until his death in 1984.[32] Mali, another overwhelmingly Muslim country, has also produced bad rulers both civilian and military. Mali is, therefore, another exception. It does not fit my thesis about the dual-tendency.

Arab civilian regimes of North Africa basically do conform to my generalization. Under civilian rulers, Tunisia and Morocco have been, at least until recently, more tolerant than average—both as compared with most other African countries and as compared with most other Arab countries. At least since 1992, I may conclude that the Algerian military regime has conformed to the other part of my generalization. A brief blossoming of political liberalization since 1989 was abruptly aborted in 1992, leading to a severe civil war. It has become more repressive than average. Several countries, particularly France, are concerned about the prospects of Algeria becoming another Iran.[33] Although Algeria, in the first decade of the twenty-first century, has continued to follow a path of 'national reconciliation,' the scars of the civil war still remain.

What about Egypt? How much of a military regime was Egypt's government? To what extent has it been civilianized by durability from 1952 to 1995? Egypt is more difficult to classify—but its previous regime conforms to the generalization that Muslim civilian or civilianized regimes in Africa are more tolerant than average.[34]

Observers are divided about Muammar Gaddafi's time as Head of State of Libya. Gaddafi captured power in 1969. Was his regime more repressive than average? Or was it a particularly generous military regime in material terms and a particularly egalitarian one in ideological terms? By the 1990s, the arbitrariness of the regime had probably tilted the balance on the side of repression. The expulsion of Palestinian and Sudanese workers in 1995 was symptomatic of a deepening repressiveness in the regime. Although Libya appeared to be largely rehabilitated in the eyes of the United States,[35] it was still a repressive regime.[36]

Culture and Violence

It is not clear why the twin-tendency of my thesis seems to hold up in Africa—that Islam in military uniform is extra repressive; that Islam in civilian robes is extra tolerant. But it may be related to another twin-tendency—that Muslim cities in Africa are routinely less violent than non-Muslim cities—but from time to time Muslim cities are nevertheless more prone to politicized riots or demonstrations. Islam does not inspire mugging in the streets, but it often inspires fiery protest.

Kano in Nigeria is much more of a Muslim city than Ibadan. On a day-to-day basis, Kano's streets are much safer than the streets of Ibadan from muggers and robbers. But Kano is competitive even with Lagos when it comes to politicized riots.

Mombasa is more of a Muslim city than Nairobi in Kenya. The streets of Mombasa are still, relatively speaking, safer than the streets of Nairobi. But Mombasa is beginning to be competitive with the capital city in politicized riots.

As for the really protected small Muslim enclave of Lamu in Northeast Kenya, it was for centuries almost entirely devoid of crime in the Western sense. There may be lots of secret vices, like adultery and extra mistresses, but no mugging or rape or murder. The prison was often almost empty most of the time before the 1980s.

Also, one may compare Cairo, the biggest city in the north part of the African continent, with Johannesburg, the biggest city in the South. Although Johannesburg is less than a sixth of the population of Cairo, it has more than three times the rate of reported violent crimes.

Tanzania's largest city, Dar es Salaam, is a semi-Islamized city culturally (and not just by its Arabic name). It has only a fraction of the crime rate of Kinshasa in Zaire.

Outside Africa, Tehran is about the size of New York City in population—about eight million people. And yet in 1993, I witnessed women and children in Tehran picnicking in public parks late at night. I witnessed a comparable phenomenon of fearlessness about the streets at night in three other Iranian cities.

The conclusion to be drawn from all this is that in terms of pacifying the streets from day-to-day violence like mugging and the harassment of drug-dealers and drunks, Islam is a force for peace in the relevant African cities. But in terms of politicized riots or demonstrations and potential civil disobedience, Islam can be a force of excitability. Whether or not these factors are related to our twin-tendency of Islam in uniform versus Islam in civilian robes is a matter yet to be explored.

Conclusion

What is the balance between conflict, competition, and cooperation between Islam and Christianity in the twenty-first century? In Africa, Christianity and Islam are divisive only if they reinforce pre-existing divisions of other kinds. Thus, in Nigeria almost all Hausa are Muslims; almost all Igbo are Christians; and Yoruba are split between the two religions. Thus Islam reinforces Hausa identity; Christianity reinforces Igbo identity and the Yoruba people are caught in between.

In Sudan, the degree of Islamization is not the only difference between the North and the South of the country. The two sub-regions differ in a whole range of other cultural and historical differentiations. But where Islam and Christianity do not reinforce prior divisions (as in Senegal) those two religions are not conflictual. It is in this way that sociology and history help to moderate the consequences of doctrine.

Leveling the field of missionary work between Islam and Christianity also helps to diffuse conflict and turn it into peaceful competition for the soul of Africa. The petro-wealth of the parts of the Muslim World has made available resources for *tabligh*, *da'wa* and propagation unheard of for hundreds of years.

Muslim missionary work is still less efficient, less organized, less imaginative, and less endowed than the Christian missionary work. But the gap has narrowed as a result of petro-*da'wa*, *alhamdu lillah*. The sacred playing field is being slowly leveled.

A third factor which helps in reducing conflict and even promoting cooperation is an important change in the nature of the Christian mission in Africa. Many Christian groups have decided to concentrate on saving lives rather than saving souls, focusing more on service now than salvation for the hereafter. Such Christian groups will go to help in devastated

Muslim areas like Somalia to save Somali lives rather than Somali souls. They would concentrate on easing pain rather than spreading the Gospel.

In Africa, such service-oriented activists have their Muslim counterparts. An association of Muslim doctors in South Africa spends a lot of medical hours and resources helping the poor in South Africa regardless of religious affiliation. They build clinics or serve them, and give of their time to the sick.

Between these two universalistic religions, the three tendencies are still often there:

— the risk of conflict
— the inherent competitive tendency
— the potential for ecumenical cooperation

In Africa, the worst days of religious conflict north of the Sahara may unfortunately not be over, but south of the Sahara those worst days are probably receding into history, with the exception of aberrations like the Central African Republic. The days of rivalry between Christianity and Islam in Africa are alive and well—but the competition is getting more gracious and more considerate. The days of ecumenical cooperation between Christianity and Islam in Africa are now unfolding—and Africa may be the best setting in the world for such a Christo-Islamic ecumenicalism in the twenty-first century.

In distribution, Christianity is an Afro-Western religion—since almost all Christian nations are either in the Western World or in Africa. Asia, the largest continent in the world, has been far less receptive to Christianity. There are hardly any Christian nations in Asia apart from the Philippines, and perhaps South Korea. In distribution Islam is an Afro-Asian religion— since most Muslim nations are either in Asia or in Africa. Apart from small Albania, and Bosnia, there are no Muslim countries in the Western World. Turkey is divided between Asia and Europe.

If Christianity is primarily Afro-Western, and Islam is primarily Afro-Asian, what the two religions have in common geographically is mainly the 'Afro' part. Africa is, therefore, the preeminent theater for ecumenical cooperation between these two great religions—moderated by the traditional doctrines, the sociology, and the history of the African peoples themselves.

Notes

[1] Consult, relatedly, Steve Bruce (ed.), *Religion and Modernization: Sociologists and Historians Debate the Secularization Thesis* (Oxford and New York: Clarendon Press and Oxford University Press, 1992); Rabbi Jonathan Sacks, *The Persistence of Faith: Religion, Morality & Society in a Secular Age* (London: Weidenfeld and Nicolson, 1991); and Edward Tiryakian, "From Modernization to Globalization," *Journal for the Scientific Study of Religion*, Volume 31 (September 1992), pp. 304–310.

[2] For example, on the religious connections to resurgent nationalism, see Mark Juergensmeyer, *The New Cold War? Religious Nationalism Confronts the Secular State* (Berkeley: University of California Press, 1993).

[3] A special issue of the journal *Islam & Christian–Muslim Relations* (April 2007), Volume 18, Issue 2, has several articles on the relationship between Islam and Christianity in Sub-Saharan Africa. Overviews of the relationships may be found in Rabiatu Ammah, "Christian–Muslim Relations in Contemporary Sub-Saharan Africa," *Islam & Christian-Muslim Relations*, Volume 18, Issue 2 (April 2007), pp. 139–153, and Matthew Hassan Kukah, "Christian–Muslim Relations in Sub-Saharan Africa: Problems and Prospects," *Islam & Christian–Muslim Relations*, Volume 18, Issue 2 (April 2007), pp. 155–164. There are also several case studies in this issue.

[4] This has of course been explored more fully in Ali A. Mazrui's television series, *The Africans: A Triple Heritage* (BBC/PBS and Nigeria's Television Authority, 1986).

[5] Because of religious and political issues over the implications of population numbers, estimates of the numbers of Muslims in Nigeria are disputed often. Moreover, population estimates are quite unreliable. However, based on the US State Department's *2006 Report on International Religious Freedom*, the Muslim population of Nigeria may be between 70–75 million, while that of Egypt may be estimated to be about 67 million. According to an earlier Associated Press report, "Muslim Mobs, Seeking Vengeance, Attack Christians in Nigeria," *New York Times* (May 13, 2004), "Many of Nigeria's 126 million people, [are] split almost evenly between Muslims and Christians..." One report estimates the percentage of Muslims in Nigeria at 75 percent; see <http://www.islamicweb.com/begin/population.htm>, accessed May 28, 2004. In 2006, Nigeria did conduct another census—without asking respondents' religion. See Michelle Faul, "Nigeria Tries to Take a Head Count," *The Washington Post* (March 25, 2006).

[6] Consult relatedly, Shamil Jeppie, "Commemorations and Identities: The 1994 Tercentenary of Islam in South Africa," in Tamara Sonn, *Islam and the Question of Minorities* (Atlanta, GA: Scholars Press, 1996), pp. 73–92.

[7] For specific cases and discussions of "indirect rule" in Nigeria, see Toyin Falola, (ed.), *Nigerian History, Politics and Affairs: The Collected Essays of Adiele Afigbo* (Trenton, NJ: Africa World Press, 2005), pp. 253–295; Olufemi Vaughan, *Nigerian Chiefs: Traditional Power in Modern Politics, 1890s–1990s* (Rochester, NY: University of Rochester Press, 2000), pp. 22–68; J. A. Atanda, *The New Oyo*

Empire: Indirect Rule and Change in Western Nigeria, 1894–1934 (London: Longman, 1973); and A. E. Afigbo, *The Warrant Chiefs: Indirect Rule in Southeastern Nigeria, 1891–1929* (New York: Humanities Press, 1972).

[8] For overviews of these Sudan conflicts, consult Douglas H. Johnson, *The Root Causes of Sudan's Civil Wars* (Oxford; Bloomington, IN and Kampala: James Currey; Indiana University Press; and Fountain Publishers, 2003); and Catherine Jendia, *The Sudanese Civil Conflict, 1969–1985* (New York: Peter Lang, 2002).

[9] Biographical portraits of Shagari may be found in David Williams, *President and Power in Nigeria: The Life of Shehu Shagari* (London and Totowa, NJ: F. Cass, 1990) and A. Okion Ojigbo, *Shehu Shagari: The Biography of Nigeria's First Executive President* (Lagos, Nigeria: Tokion Co., 1982).

[10]. For an example of unbridled attacks on Shagari, see Adigun Agbaje, "Freedom of the Press and Party Politics in Nigeria: Precepts, Retrospect and Prospects," *African Affairs* Volume 89 (April 1990), p. 211.

[11] Agbaje, "Freedom of the Press and Party Politics in Nigeria," p. 223.

[12] A useful guide to Somali history and politics since independence is I. M. Lewis, *A Modern History of Somalia: Nation and State in the Horn of Africa* (Revised, updated, and expanded edition) (Boulder, CO: Westview Press, 1988).

[13] Somalia's repression is well-detailed in Jama M. Ghalib, *The Cost of Dictatorship: The Somali Experience* (New York, NY: L. Barber, 1995); on the Cold War connections, see Gerry O'Sullivan, "Another Cold War Casualty," *The Humanist* (Volume 53) (January/February 1993), pp. 36–37.

[14] See Johnson, *The Root Causes of Sudan's Civil Wars* and Jendia, *The Sudanese Civil Conflict, 1969–1985* as also Dunstan M. Wai, *The African–Arab Conflict in the Sudan* (New York: Africana Pub. Co., 1981).

[15] Darfur has attracted worldwide attention because of the fears of another Rwanda, but it has also become a complex issue; consult, on the various dimensions of the Darfur conflict, Alex de Waal and Julie Flint, "In Darfur, From Genocide to Anarchy," *The Washington Post* (August 28, 2007); Mahmood Mamdani, "The Politics of Naming: Genocide, Civil War, Insurgency," *London Review of Books* Volume 29, Number 5 (March 8, 2007); Julie Flint, "The Arabs are Victims Too," *The Washington Post* (November 19, 2006); Sam Dealey, "Misreading the Truth in Sudan," *New York Times* (August 8, 2004); and Scott Anderson, "How Did Darfur Happen?" *New York Times Magazine* (October 17, 2004).

[16] Consult, for an overview of the various regimes in Sudan, Muddathir Abd Al-Rahim et al. (eds.), *Sudan Since Independence: Studies in the Political Development since 1956* (Aldershot, UK and Brookfield, VT: Gower, 1986).

[17] Part of this is, of course, the violation of human rights in Darfur; see Warren Hoge, "U.N. Mission Says Sudan Took Part in Rights Crimes," *New York Times* (March 13, 2007).

[18] On Uganda's experiences under Amin, a valuable tool for further reading is Martin Jamison, *Idi Amin and Uganda: An Annotated Bibliography* (Westport, CT: Greenwood Press, 1992).

[19] For a portrait of the hideous struggles of Ugandans under Amin, consult M. S. M. Semakula Kiwanuka, *Amin and the Tragedy of Uganda* (Munich: Weltforum Verlag, 1979).

[20] For a biography of this recurrent figure in Ugandan politics, consult Kenneth Ingham, *Obote: A Political Biography* (London and New York: Routledge, 1994).

[21] For a profile, see Grace Phiri, "Malawi: From Grass to Grace," *New African*, Issue 432 (August/September 2004), pp. 44–45.

[22] See T. David Williams, *Malawi, the Politics of Despair* (Ithaca, NY: Cornell University Press, 1978) and Andrew Meldrum, "Legacy of A Dictator," *Africa Report*, Volume 40 (March/April 1995), pp. 56–59.

[23] On the transition from Banda to Muluzi, see Mike Hall and Melinda Ham, "From Tyranny to Tolerance," *Africa Report*, Volume 39 (November/December 1994), pp. 56–57.

[24] For an early biography of Nyerere, consult William E. Smith, *Nyerere of Tanzania* (London: Gollancz, 1973); also see Andrew Meldrum, "Julius Nyerere: Former President of Tanzania," *Africa Report*, Volume 39 (September/October 1994), pp. 70–71.

[25] Arthur S. Banks, (ed.), *The Political Handbook of the World, 1994–1995* (Binghamton, NY: CSA Publications, 1995), p. 758.

[26] For a close look at the various influences on Senghor, see Janet G. Vaillant, *Black, French, and African: A Life of Léopold Sédar Senghor* (Cambridge, MA: Harvard University Press, 1990).

[27] Leonardo A. Villalon, *Islamic Society and State Power in Senegal: Disciples and Citizens in Fatick* (New York: Cambridge University Press, 1995), p. 262.

[28] One detailed account of the crucial but suspicious voting results in Chicago during the 1960 elections can be found in Edmund F. Kallina, *Courthouse Over White House: Chicago and the Presidential Elections of 1960* (Orlando, FL: University Presses of Florida; University of Central Florida Press, 1988), pp. 96–114.

[29] A figure of 5.944 million Jews in the United States is reported in Table 80 in the United States Bureau of the Census, *Statistical Abstract of the United States 1991*, 111th edition, (Washington, DC: Government Printing Office, 1991), p. 58; on the other hand, a *New York Times* (February 21, 1989) Section A, p. 1 report estimated the number of Muslims in the United States at 6 million.

[30] Stephen Laboton, "McCain Casts Muslims as Less Fit to Lead," *New York Times* (September 30, 2007).

[31] For a discussion of the factors in Senegal's exceptionally democratic record, see Robert Fatton, *The Making of A Liberal Democracy: Senegal's Passive Revolution, 1975–1985*, (Boulder, CO: L. Rienner Publishers, 1987).

[32] On Guinea under Touré, consult Ladipo Adamolekun, *Sekou Toure's Guinea: An Experiment in Nation-Building* (London and New York: Methuen, Harper & Row, and Barnes & Noble, 1976).

[33] See, for instance, Edward G. Shirley, "Is Iran's Present Algeria's Future?" *Foreign Affairs*, Volume 74 (May/June 1995), pp. 28–44.

[34] Rather than "disappearances" or execution—as in the case of Algeria—the Egyptian government's efforts to curb the Muslim Brotherhood, for instance, were

marked more by "detentions and legal changes," as reported by Ellen Knickmeyer, "Cairo Moving More Aggressively to Cripple Muslim Brotherhood," *The Washington Post* (October 1, 2007).

[35] See Colum Lynch, "U.S. Won't Block Libya's U.N. Bid," *The Washington Post* (September 30, 2007).

[36] "Still Bizarre, In A Bad Way," *The Economist*, Volume 383, Issue 8523 (April 7, 2007).

CHAPTER FOUR

ISLAM BETWEEN THE MUSLIM DIASPORA IN AFRICA AND THE AFRICAN DIASPORA IN THE WEST

For Africa, our use of 'diaspora' may often have to be metaphorical rather than literal. After all, a 'diaspora' is a dispersal of people rather than the spread of ideas. The Islamic presence in Africa is less of a demographic diaspora than the new Muslim populations in, say, Western Europe. Much of the Muslim presence in Western Europe is indeed the product of migration of Muslims rather than merely the transmission of Islamic principles and ideas, as is the case in Africa.[1]

The contemporary American experience constitutes an intermediate category. American Muslims from the Middle East, South Asia, and South East Asia do constitute a Muslim Diaspora in America. On the other hand, the African American Muslim population in the United States represents conversion to Islam rather than new immigrants from the Muslim World. The Black *Ummah* in America represents an indigenous *Ummah*.[2]

The concept of the diaspora started with the Jewish experience. It signified a combination of physical dispersal and spiritual resilience. The Jewish people were scattered abroad but remained focused on the rock of ancestry.[3]

What is the rock of ancestry for Islam from which we may identify an emerging diaspora elsewhere? One possible answer is the rock of Mecca and Medina and the Arabian Peninsula from which Islam emerged. More broadly, the ancestral home of Islam consists of the lands where the language of the Qur'an, Arabic, is now triumphant.

Agents of Islamic Expansion

Underlying the whole saga about diaspora-formation are the five modes by which Islam has spread in Africa. The most spectacular mode is expansion by conquest. Paradoxically, this affects mainly Arab Africa in the north of the continent—which was indeed Islamized initially by the sword. Sub-Saharan examples of Islamization by conquest are few and far between. Some conquests did take place—as in the case of the Almoravids' devastating incursions into West Africa from 1052 to 1076. Ibn Khaldun confirms that the conquerors did force Blacks to become Muslims.[4] But today's historians affirm that since Almoravids did not maintain a continuing presence, their short-term atrocities harmed the image of Islam rather than helping it. Such invasions were therefore not relevant for explaining the spread of Islam. People were subsequently converted in spite of the memory of the Almoravids.[5]

The second agency for the expansion of Islam was Muslim migration and settlement in non-Muslim areas. Arabs from Yemen and Oman, settling in East Africa, were among the cofounders of the Swahili civilization in what is today Tanzania and Kenya. The rapid Islamization and Arabization of North Africa was not only achieved through conquest, but also through migration and settlement.[6] Doctrinally, this mode of transmission of the Message goes back to the great *Hijrah* itself—the Prophet Muhammad's own migration mid-career from Mecca to Medina.[7]

As we indicated elsewhere, the migration may sometimes be of victims rather than victors. This is true of the exiles, slaves, and laborers imported into South Africa.[8] Islam arrived in chains in what later became the land of apartheid. These ex-slaves (now among the 'Coloreds' of South Africa) have kept the flame of Islam burning in South Africa for three hundred years.

The third agency for the spread of Islam was trade. By far the best illustration was once again the trans-Saharan trade. The camels which crossed the great desert carried varied commodities in each direction. Perhaps the greatest commodity of all was cultural diffusion—the spread of Islam from North Africa to Western Africa especially. Today, countries like Guinea, modern Mali, Senegal, and Niger are overwhelmingly Muslim in population.[9]

Arab and Swahili traders in Eastern, Central, and Southern Africa also played a part in carrying the torch of Islam to parts of what are today Uganda, Zaire, Malawi, and Mozambique. The commodities involved in the trade included ivory, copper, gold, manufactured goods from abroad and, tragically, also slaves.[10]

The fourth agency for the spread of Islam was actual purposeful missionary work, *d'awa*. In the earlier centuries this took the form of traveling imams, healers, and teachers. Muslim leaders acquired such a reputation that to the present-day a large portion of their patients in Africa include non-Muslims such as Christians, Hindus, and devotees of traditional religions. Their healing techniques have included the use of verses of the Qur'an, including the popular prescription of writing out the verse in washable ink on a slate, then washing it into a bowl, and having the patient "drink the sacred verse."[11] Grateful patients were sometimes converted to the faith.

In more recent times, Islamic missionary work has included material for use in *madrasas* and schools. Special books or pamphlets have been written in African languages to explain the religion not only to students but also to non-Muslims. Pamphlets in the Swahili language have poured forth from Zanzibar, the Kenyan Coast and the Coast of mainland Tanzania. And in the twentieth century the Qur'an was at last translated into Kiswahili—first by the controversial Ahmadiyya Movement, and later by Sunni scholars from Tanzania and Kenya. As the twentieth century was coming to a close there were three different Swahili editions of the Qur'an, though the third one was published only in part.

Some Muslims believed that translations of the Qur'an into other languages were a form of sinful imitation of the Holy Book.[12] The chief Muslim jurists of East Africa have given *fatwas* contradicting that doctrine. They have argued that if it was not sinful to translate the Qur'an orally in a sermon in a mosque, it was not sinful to translate it into writing.

Sunni and Shiite missionary work entered a new stage in the second half of the twentieth century with the arrival of petro-wealth in Saudi Arabia, Iran, Libya, and other parts of the oil-producing Muslim World. At last it was possible for the cause of Islam in Africa to command considerable financial resources. Schools could be built as well as mosques. Clinics were subsidized and scholarships to study abroad were offered.

On the whole, the petro-wealth was used not so much to attract new converts into the Muslim fold as to support the welfare and well-being of those who were already Muslims. But there were reparations favoring new conversions. Sunni Islam is still by far the main beneficiary of such conversions. Although itself Shiite, Iran has sometimes been ready to subsidize Sunni missionary work in Africa in the spirit of Muslim unity. As for the Ismaili Movement under the leadership of the Aga Khan (more Shiite than Sunni), it sometimes explicitly committed its missionaries to the propagation of Sunni Islam rather than to its own denomination.[13] The rationale was: Expanding the size of the Muslim *Ummah* in Africa is more important than creating more followers for His Highness the Aga Khan.

In examining the agencies for the spread of Islam in Africa, we have so far examined conquest, migration, trade, and missionary work. The fifth agency in Africa's historical experience has been periodic revivalist movements. These sometimes take the form of an internal morally purifying *jihad*, or are under the leadership of a *Mahdi*.

Among the most spectacular of these revivalist movements were those which unleashed the *jihad* led by Uthman dan Fodio in what is today Nigeria.[14] Until this upheaval, the Hausa states were at best an informal and loose confederation—sometimes allies, sometimes rivals. Katsina, Gobir, Zaria, and Kano vied with each other from about the fourteenth century. The North-South trade across the Sahara was at the core of much of their rivalry.

It was in the nineteenth century that the revivalist *jihads* led by Uthman dan Fodio, partly inspired by a glorified vision of the Abbasid Dynasty centuries earlier, burst onto the stage of West African history. Was it merely revivalism or was it conquest? In reality it was both. The long-term consequence was the relative unification of much of Hausaland under a single overarching sovereign. Uthman's son, Muhammad Bello, became the first Amir al-Mu'minin of Hausaland, Commander of the Faithful. Islam expanded as the Hausa got integrated.[15]

At least as spectacular was the movement in Eastern Sudan led by Muhammad Ahmad Ibn Abd Allah. This Muslim Reformation in Eastern Sudan started in 1881 in the wake of many years of Turco-Egyptian rule, compounded by British manipulations. Unlike the *jihad* of Uthman dan Fodio, that of Muhammad Ahmad was also a struggle for national independence. Religious revivalism intertwined with political nationalism.[16]

Muhammad Ahmad went further than Uthman dan Fodio. The Sudanese leader declared himself the *Mahdi*, appointed by God to reunite the Muslim *Ummah*. His vision extended well beyond his own ancestral Sudan. In a sense he wanted to fuse Pan-Islam with Pan-Africanism and Pan-Arabism. His dream was too big for his base, and too vulnerable to the new European imperialism. He was indeed defeated.[17] But Islam did make one more step forward in Sudanese history. And to the present day, the Mahdi's religious and political legacy lives on in the political configuration of Sudan. Indeed, the country's last elected Prime Minister of the 20th century was Sadiq al-Mahdi, his grandson.[18]

In Africa, since independence, two issues have been central to religious speculation—Islamic expansion and Islamic revivalism. Expansion is about the spread of religion and its scale of new conversions. Revivalism is about the rebirth of faith among those who are already converted. Expansion is a matter of geography and populations—in search of new worlds to conquer. Revivalism is a matter of history and nostalgia— in search of ancient worlds to re-enact. The spread of Islam in postcolonial

Africa is basically a peaceful process of persuasion and consent. The revival of Islam is often an angry process of rediscovered fundamentalism.[19]

Outside Arab Africa the central issue concerning Islam is not merely its revival—it is also the speed of its expansion. It is not often realized that there are almost as many Muslims in Nigeria as there are Muslims in any Arab country, including Egypt.[20] Muslims in Ethiopia are not a small minority—they are more than a third of the population.[21] Islam elsewhere in Africa has spread—however unevenly—all the way down to the Cape of Good Hope. Islam in South Africa is three hundred years old, having first arrived not directly from Arabia but from South East Asia with South-East Asian exiles, as we indicated.[22]

The largest countries in Africa in population are Nigeria, Egypt, Ethiopia, and Democratic Republic of Congo (Zaire). Between them these four countries account for close to 200 million Muslims. (The Islamic part of former Zaire is mainly in the East.) More than half the population of the continent is probably now Muslim.[23]

But Islam in Africa does not of course exist in isolation. The world of religious experience in Africa is rich in diversity. Let us look at Islam in this wider religious context.

Indigenous Ecumenicalism and Abrahamic Competitiveness

Of the three principal cultural legacies of Africa (indigenous, Islamic, and Christian) perhaps the most religiously tolerant is the indigenous tradition. It is even arguable that Africa did not have religious wars before Christianity and Islam arrived. Precisely because these two latter faiths were universalist in aspiration (seeking to convert the whole of humankind), they were inherently competitive. In Africa, Christianity and Islam have often been in competition for the soul of the continent. Rivalry has sometimes resulted in conflict.

Indigenous African religions, on the other hand, are basically communal rather than universalist. Like Hinduism and modern Judaism—and unlike Christianity and Islam—indigenous African traditions have not sought to convert the whole of humankind. By not being universalist in that sense, the African traditions have not been in competition with each other for the souls of other people. The Yoruba do not seek to convert the Ibo to Yoruba religion—or vice versa. Nor do either the Yoruba or the Ibo compete with each other for the souls of a third group like the Hausa. By not being proselytizing religions, indigenous African creeds have not fought with each other. Over the centuries, Africans have waged many kinds of wars with each other—but hardly ever religious ones before the universalist creeds arrived.

But what does this have to do with contemporary Africa? The indigenous toleration today has often mitigated the competitiveness of the imported Semitic religions (Christianity and Islam). Let us illustrate with Senegal which is over ninety percent Muslim.[24] The founder President of this predominantly Islamic society was Léopold Sédar Senghor. He presided over the fortunes of postcolonial Senegal for two decades—in basic political partnership with the Muslim leaders of the country, the Marabouts.[25]

His successor as President (partly sponsored by him) was Abdou Diouf, a Muslim ruler of a Muslim society at last. But the tradition of ecumenical tolerance continued in Senegal. The first lady of the country— Madame Elizabeth Diouf—was Roman Catholic. And several of the Ministers of the new President were Christian.

Senegalese religious tolerance has continued in other spheres since then. What in other Islamic countries elsewhere in the world might be regarded as provocative, in Senegal it has been tolerated. There have been occasions when a Christian festival like the First Communion—with a lot of feasting, merry-making, and singing—has been publicly held in Dakar right in the middle of the Islamic fast of Ramadan. And the Christian merry-makers have been left undisturbed.[26]

To summarize the argument so far, predominantly Muslim countries south of the Sahara have been above average in religious toleration. The capacity to accommodate other faiths may, to some extent, be part of the historical Islamic tradition in multi-religious empires. But far more religiously tolerant than either Islam or Christianity have been indigenous African traditions—especially since these do not aspire to universalism and are not inherently competitive. In Black Africa, this indigenous tolerance has often moderated the competitive propensities of Christianity and Islam.

Although the ecumenical spirit is more highly developed in Africa than almost anywhere else in the world, there are situations when it breaks down. Those conditions include the following: First, Islam and Christianity in Africa become divisive when they reinforce prior divisions. For example, in Nigeria almost all Hausa are Muslim; almost all Igbo are Christian; and the Yoruba are half Muslim, half Christian.[27]

Islam, therefore, reinforces Hausa identity; Christianity reinforces Igbo identity; and in Western Nigeria indigenous Yoruba culture moderates relations between Yoruba Muslims and Yoruba Christians. Because in most of Nigeria Christianity and Islam reinforce prior ethnic differences, the two Abrahamic religions become divisive themselves.

The same situation applies to Sudan. The political split between Sudan and South Sudan is culturally far deeper than simply the fact that the North is Muslim and the South is Christian-led. Here, again, Christianity and Islam reinforce prior cultural and ethnic differentiation between the 'tribes' of the North and the *kabilas* of the North. Such a situation carries the seeds of an ecumenical breakdown.[28]

Another situation which may lead to tensions between Christians and Muslims in Africa is when a country has a majority or a plurality of Muslims, but the Muslims are marginalized and the Christians assert supremacy.

One illustration of this is Côte d'Iviore (Ivory Coast) in which Muslims predominate, but political power has been disproportionately in Christian hands for most of the postcolonial period. The first postcolonial Head of State, Félix Houphouët-Boigny, was wise enough to give the Muslims a sense of political participation while the system maintained a Christian supremacy.

But after Félix Houphouët-Boigny's death in 1993, tensions began to mount between the Muslim majority (concentrated in the North) and the Christian minority (concentrated in the South). Eventually the political system collapsed into a low-intensity civil war from which it has yet to fully recover.[29]

A third cause of religious discord between Christians and Muslims in Africa is when a postcolonial regime deprives Muslims of religious rights which the European colonial regime had granted them for decades before independence. Such rights may include Islamic Courts of Law which the British colonial order permitted for its Muslim subjects, except in the field of criminal law. Muslims in places like Nigeria, Kenya, Zanzibar, and Tanganyika had their own Islamic courts for issues like marriage, divorce, inheritance, succession, and sometimes other civil areas of law.[30]

Some postcolonial Christian governments have threatened the existence of religion-specific courts of law on the dubious argument that since there are no Christian courts, there should be no Kadhis' courts.

Since September 11th and its aftermath, such debates about Islamic courts in Kenya have gathered momentum.[31] American Evangelical missionaries in Kenya have fuelled opposition to Kadhis' courts with the argument that any concession to the Shari'a (Islamic law) is a concession to Islamic fundamentalism. Kenyans debated a new constitution in anticipation of the constitutional referendum in November 2005. The Evangelical churches did not succeed in squeezing out Kadhis' courts from Kenya's judicial system, as they are recognized under Subordinate Courts in the new Constitution.

This brings us to the fourth major spark of discord between Muslims and Christians in Africa. This is the American-led war on terrorism worldwide. Pressures exerted by the United States on African governments to pass new anti-terrorism legislation sometimes result in Islamophobic tendencies in African countries.[32] Men who wear Islamic attire or grow Semitic-style beards run the risk of being subjected to regular surveillance. Sometimes African anti-terrorist legislation not only echoes the repressive potential of the US Patriot Act, but goes further than the US in anti-terrorist measures. Good relations between Muslims and Christians are put at risk.

The fifth potential trigger of religious discord in Africa is the anger generated by the new version of Pax Americana [the American Imperium], combined with the global Muslim rage over the Israeli occupation of Palestinians.[33] The new American imperium, as illustrated by the war on Iraq, and the United States' uncritical support of Israel, are probably the two greatest destabilizing forces in global politics since the end of the Cold War.[34]

What all these phenomena illustrate is, in part, the penetration of Africa by external forces, and Africa's internal response to those stimuli. If there is a Muslim Diaspora in Africa, it consists of both the migration of people and the transmission of ideas. Africa has been penetrated by Islam, by Christianity, by Arabs, by Europeans, by Americans, and others.

But, what about the counter-penetration of Muslim Africa into the Western World? Africa is not just a receptacle of the influences of others. It is also a counterforce on the destinies of other societies.

This draws our attention to the phenomenon of counter-penetration. Constructive counter-penetration of Africa into the West includes the role of Nigerian engineers in America, Ghanaian doctors in England, Senegalese teachers in France, a Kenyan-American representing Illinois on the US Senate, African nurses throughout the Western World—as well as African professors in the state of New York.[35]

But when African counter-penetration is combined with Islamic counter-penetration, we get results like the Nation of Islam as revised by Louis Farrakhan. Islamic values are fused with Black concerns as people of African descent seek to change America. Black Islam in the Western World is a dual diaspora of Islam and Africanity.

Towards Militarized Counter-Penetration

But counter-penetration of the West by Islam or the Third World is not always peaceful and civil. There is a new phenomenon of militarized counter-penetration. The concept of counter-penetration in the twenty-first century has opened up new possibilities. The Third World does not have to fight all its wars in the Southern Hemisphere.

The twentieth century opened with the Maji Maji War in Tanganyika against the Germans. The overwhelming majority of the casualties were, of course, Africans. Many of them were East African Muslims. What is more, African blood was spilled on African soil.[36] Also in those early years of the twentieth century, the Boers (now called Afrikaners) fought the British. These were White people fighting other White people—but strictly on African soil.[37]

Several decades later there was a struggle against apartheid. The economic and diplomatic war against apartheid was global. But the spilling of blood was overwhelmingly on African soil.

Next door in Zimbabwe, the Zimbabwe African National Union (ZANU) and the Zimbabwe African People's Union (ZAPU) fought against White minority rule.[38] Most of the White Rhodesians were of British descent, and many still had British passports. But ZANU and ZAPU did not export the anti-colonial struggle into the streets of Birmingham or the alleyways of Manchester.

In Angola, the People's Movement for the Liberation of Angola (MPLA) fought the Portuguese exclusively on Angolan soil. The anticolonial nationalists of the MPLA limited their military operations within the borders of the colony.[39] In military terms, Lisbon was never at risk from the liberation fighters within its own empire.

What the militants of the 21st century have demonstrated is that it is possible to punish Western imperial powers not just on the soil of the colonized people, but also on the planes, trains, and buses in Western capitals themselves. This is a whole new stage in the struggle against imperialism.

Colonial Kenya, on the other hand, had a very influential White settler community. Kenya's liberation required armed struggle. The Mau Mau Movement was indeed a liberation army which resorted to terrorist methods from time to time.[40] But Mau Mau never fought the British on British soil in the United Kingdom.

Zimbabwe's struggle against White minority rule even included the shooting down of a civilian airplane by Joshua Nkomo's liberation army in

1978. At least fifty people died (almost the same number as the fatalities of July 7, 2005 in the London mass transit bombing).

There were 26 survivors of the Rhodesia plane in 1978. But Joshua Nkomo's forces killed or attempted to kill a number of the survivors on the ground. This was clearly an act of terror, which Joshua Nkomo never denied.[41] But he was combating British people on African soil and not in Britain.

What the London bombs of July 7th and 21st, 2005 illustrated was a new Afro-Asian readiness to carry the anti-imperial struggle into the heartland of the new hegemonic forces. The vanguard of this new kind of imperialism consists of radicals from South Asia, the Middle East, and Eastern Africa, mainly of Muslim faith.

Two weeks after the London bomb blast of July 7th, new attempts were made on the London underground and on a London bus. Either by choice or because of incompetence, this second attack on London's transit system disrupted the city without killing anybody. While the main actors of July 7th in London seemed to be of South Asian descent (especially Pakistani origin), the main actors of the July 21st London attempt seemed to be Africans (from Eritrea, Somalia, Ethiopia and, conceivably Sudan).[42]

Was the relative failure of the second London attack due to the fact that African militants are less likely to kill themselves (suicide bombers) than South Asians or Middle Easterners are? Are there cultural taboos against suicide in African traditions which are stronger than anti-suicide taboos in South Asia or the Middle East? [43]

What is clear is that the phenomenon of heroic masochism is hundreds of years old in the Indian subcontinent. The Yogi tradition and readiness to sit on nails has for a long time been linked to Hindu asceticism. During the struggle against British rule in India, passive resistance became a version of heroic masochism—bearing British punishments in the cause of liberation. Mahatma Gandhi also repeatedly attempted to fast unto death as a way of forcing Britain's hand—a threat of suicide by self-starvation.[44]

As for the radical suicide bomber as a weapon of national liberation, it was started by the Tamils of South India and Sri Lanka (Ceylon) before Palestinians resorted to it. Rajiv Gandhi, a former Prime Minister of India, was assassinated by a woman suicide bomber in 1991. She approached him with a garland of flowers to adorn him and then released an explosive device which killed Rajiv, the woman, and a number of others. Additionally, the Tamil Tigers have been suicide bombers from before Palestinian self-destruction.[45]

Arabs are relative newcomers to the strategy of suicide bombing–long preceded by Asians. The Japanese kamikaze pilots during the Second

World War hurled their planes into American warships.[46] Relatedly, there have also been people in Asia who have burned themselves in protest (self-immolation) during the 1960s such as Buddhists protesting the American war in Vietnam and Tamil Hindus who protested the imposition of Hindi in India.

The most infamous Arab suicide bombers were the nineteen Arabs who hijacked four passenger planes on September 11, 2001 and hit the World Trade Center in New York, the Pentagon in Washington, DC, and a field in Pennsylvania. Nearly three thousand people were killed. Also Arab-led was the bombing in Madrid in 2004—though this did not involve suicides.

The most noteworthy south Asian suicide bombers against a Western power were indeed the blasts which hit London's transit system on July 7th, 2005. The other blasts, planned and feebly executed in London two weeks later, seem to have been an African project, undertaken by Muslims from the Horn of Africa.

This second plan might have stood a better chance of success if the militants had used the strategy of suicide bombing and were prepared to kill themselves in the process. Were African cultural taboos against suicide too strong for these young militants from the Horn?[47]

The new empire which is being attacked by these Muslim suicide bombers is the American empire, rather than the British Empire *per se*. The United Kingdom has allowed itself to become an extension of Pax Americana. Have British troops become a kind of 'mercenary army,' helping to fight American wars?[48]

Israel is also an extension of the American Empire—although paradoxically Israel has shown far more independence as an international actor than most British governments have.

This new American Imperium is an empire of control rather than of territorial annexation. The American flag does not fly on government buildings in Iraq or Afghanistan, but the United States is trying its best to maintain control in both countries. Indeed, there is some degree of American military presence in more than one hundred countries in the world, including about half the members of the African Union.[49]

International terrorism of the kind which hit the London and Madrid transit systems was fundamentally anti-American. So were the terrorist strikes in Nairobi and Dar es Salaam in August 1998. The attack on the Paradise Hotel in Mombasa in 2002 was more obviously anti-Israeli, which is widely regarded as a protégé of the United States.[50] Since the attack in Mombasa, Kenya was by a suicide bomber, it is most unlikely that the perpetrator was an indigenous African.

International terrorism is a form of global guerrilla war directed against new forms of transnational control and hegemony. What was unfair about the July 7th London blasts was the fact that they were directed against the British public rather than the British government. And the British public had been overwhelmingly against Britain's involvement in the American-led war in Iraq.[51]

If the London and Madrid bombers were anti-imperialists, they were venting their rage against the wrong targets. Public opinion in both Britain and Spain had opposed their own governments' involvement in the Iraqi War. But terrorism generally is always random in its casualties.

The ability of formerly colonized peoples to strike back militarily on Western soil directly may be an equalizing trend. But targeting friendly civilians in Western countries is not only unethical, it is counterproductive and self-defeating. The spirit of anti-imperialism at the global level needs to be guided by a higher moral standard than killing not only innocent civilians, but political allies as well.

Concluding Remarks

Between a Northern Hemisphere oppressed society and a Northern Hemisphere oppressor, there has been terrorist counter-penetration in the past. The Irish Republican Army (self-defined as defenders of the Irish people) has in the past bombed targets in England (perceived by the IRA as oppressors). Similarly, nationalists of Chechnya (self-defined as oppressed people) have from time to time bombed targets in Moscow (perceived as oppressors).

South-South terrorist counter-penetration includes activities by Kashmiri radicals (self-defined as oppressed people) against New Delhi (perceived as an oppressor of the Kashmiri Muslims).

North-South military penetration is also not new if the invading force comes from the North and proceeds to attack targets in Africa, Asia, or Latin America.

What is a new development in world politics is when even the poorest of the societies of the world (such as Somalia and Afghanistan) can find ways of punishing Western imperial powers within major Western cities themselves. The gain is in making all societies almost equally vulnerable (equal opportunity vulnerability). The loss lies in the indiscriminate nature of the weapon of terrorism—hitting the innocent as well as the guilty, killing political allies as well as imperial adversaries.

The blood of experience meanders on,
In the vast expanse of the valley of time,
The new is come and the old is gone,
And war abides a changing clime.

Notes

[1] Various discussions on Islam in Europe may be found in, for example, Gilles Kepel, *The War for Muslim Minds: Islam and the West* (Cambridge, MA: Belknap Press of Harvard University Press, 2004); Jack Goody, *Islam in Europe* (Cambridge, UK and Polity; Malden, MA: Blackwell, 2004); Robert J. Pauly, *Islam in Europe: Integration or Marginalization?* (Aldershot, Hants, England and Burlington,VT: Ashgate, 2004); and Tariq Ramadan, *Western Muslims and the Future of Islam* (Oxford and New York: Oxford University Press, 2004). Shorter portraits, including statistics, may be found in Ross Douthat, "A Muslim Europe," *The Atlantic Monthly*, Vol. 295, No. 1 (Jan/Feb 2005), 1, pp. 58–59, and Robert S. Leiken, "Europe's Angry Muslims," *Foreign Affairs*, Vol. 84, No. 4 (July/August 2005), pp. 120–135. For two comparative studies on Muslims in the US and Europe, consult, for example, Iftikhar H. Malik, *Islam and Modernity: Muslims in Europe and the United States* (London and Sterling, VA: Pluto Press, 2004) and Jocelyne Cesari, *When Islam and Democracy Meet: Muslims in Europe and in the United States* (New York, NY: Palgrave Macmillan, 2004).

[2] For some related discussions on Islam and Muslims in the United States, see, for example, Richard Wormser, *American Islam: Growing Up Muslim in America* (New York: Walker & Co., 2002); Asma Gull Hasan, *American Muslims: The New Generation* (New York: Continuum, 2002 Edition, 2nd ed.); Yvonne Yazbeck Haddad, (ed.), *Muslims in the West: From Sojourners to Citizens* (Oxford and New York: Oxford University Press, 2002); Yvonne Yazbeck Haddad and Jane I. Smith, *Muslim Minorities in the West: Visible and Invisible* (Walnut Creek, CA: AltaMira Press, 2002); Sam Afridi, *Muslims in America: Identity, Diversity and the Challenge of Understanding* (New York City, NY: Carnegie Corporation of New York, 2001); Yvonne Yazbeck Haddad and John L. Esposito, (eds.), *Muslims on the Americanization Path?* (Oxford and New York: Oxford University Press, 2000); and Jane I. Smith, *Islam in America* (New York: Columbia University Press, 1999).

Numbers of Muslims in the United States vary. According to one study conducted by Professor Ihsan Bagby of Shaw University in Raleigh, North Carolina (as part of a larger study of American congregations called "Faith Communities Today," coordinated by Hartford Seminary's Hartford Institute for Religious Research, there are approximately 6 million Muslims in the US with over 2 million of these being regularly participating adult attenders at the more than 1,209 mosques/masjids in the United States. (The full report is available at http://www.cair-net.org/mosquereport/, accessed April 19, 2004) .The television program *Frontline* points out that, "The estimated 5–7 million Muslims in the US include both immigrants and those born in America (three-quarters of whom are African-Americans)." "Portraits of Ordinary Muslims: United States," *Frontline*.

Aired on PBS Television on May 9, 2002. Retrieved on May 1, 2004 from (http://www.pbs.org/wgbh/pages/frontline/shows/muslims/portraits/us.html). According to one survey of US Muslims, 30 percent are Black, 33 percent South Asian, and 25 percent Arab (the survey did not include followers of the Nation of Islam); see *The Baltimore Sun* (April 27, 2001) p. 4. Other estimates put the African American Muslim population at a higher percentage (as high as 42%); for example, see Karen Leonard, "South Asian Leadership of American Muslims," in Haddad, (ed.) *Muslims in the West: From Sojourners to Citizens*, p. 233. Detailed analyses of the African American encounter with Islam may be found in, for example, Michael A. Gomez, *Black Crescent: The Experience and Legacy of African Muslims in the Americas* (Cambridge and New York, NY: Cambridge University Press, 2005); Richard Brent Turner, *Islam in the African-American Experience* (Bloomington, IN: Indiana University Press, 1997); and Aminah Beverly McCloud, *African American Islam* (New York: Routledge, 1995).

[3] For discussions on diaspora, see André Levy and Alex Weingrod, (eds.), *Homelands and Diasporas: Holy Lands and Other Places* (Stanford, CA: Stanford University Press, 2005); Erich S. Gruen, "Diaspora and Homeland," in Howard Wettstein, (ed.), *Diasporas and Exiles: Varieties of Jewish Identity* (Berkeley, CA: University of California Press, 2002), pp. 18–46; as also Gabriel Sheffer, "Is the Jewish Diaspora Unique?" in Eliezer Ben-Rafael, Yosef Gorny, and Yaacov Ro'I, (eds.), *Contemporary Jewries: Convergence and Divergence* (Leiden and Boston, MA: Brill, 2003), pp. 23–44.

[4] See Nehemia Levtzion, "Abd Allah b. Yasin and the Almoravids," in John R. Willis, (ed.), *Studies in West African Islamic History*, Vol. 1 (New York, Abingdon: Routledge, 1997), pp. 78–112.

[5] See Ronald A. Messier, "Rethinking the Almoravids, Rethinking Ibn Khaldun," in Julia Clancy-Smith, (ed.), *North Africa, Islam, and the Mediterranean World: From the Almoravids to the Algerian War* (London and Portland, OR: Frank Cass, 2001), p. 80.

[6] Relatedly, consult Ira M. Lapidus, *A History of Islamic Societies* (Cambridge and New York: Cambridge University Press, 2002), pp. 400–442.

[7] A brief description of this journey may be found in F. E. Peters, *Islam: A Guide for Christians and Jews* (Princeton, NJ: Princeton University Press, 2003), p. 67.

[8] Historically, three waves of Muslims are recorded as coming to South Africa; exiles from South East Asia, slaves from other areas of Africa, and indentured laborers from the Indian subcontinent. See Charlotte A. Quinn and Frederick Quinn, *Pride, Faith, and Fear: Islam in Sub-Saharan Africa* (New York: Oxford University Press, 2003), pp. 127–135 and Mervyn Hiskett, *The Course of Islam in Africa* (Edinburgh: Edinburgh University Press, 1994), p. 174. Shamil Jeppie has questioned the ascribing of "Malay" identity to the first wave of exiles; see Jeppie, "Commemorations and Identities: The 1994 Tercentenary of Ilsma in South Africa," in Tamara Sonn, *Islam and the Question of Minorities* (Atlanta, GA: Scholars Press, 1996), pp. 78–79.

[9] Relatedly, consult Lapidus, *A History of Islamic Societies* and Edward W. Bovill, *The Golden Trade of the Moors: West African Kingdoms in the Fourteenth Century* (Princeton, NJ: M. Weiner Publishers, 1995).

[10] See Paul E. Lovejoy, *Transformations in Slavery: A History of Slavery in Africa* (Cambridge and New York: Cambridge University Press, 2000), pp. 15–18 and also Joseph E. Inikori, *The Chaining of a Continent: Export Demand for Captives and the History of Africa South of the Sahara, 1450–1870* (Mona, Jamaica: Institute of Social and Economic Research, University of the West Indies, 1992).

[11] Fazlur Rahman, *Health and Medicine in the Islamic Tradition: Change and Identity* (Chicago, IL: ABC International Group, 1998), pp. 88–89.

[12] See Hussein Abdul-Raouf, *Qur'an Translation: Discourse, Texture and Exegesis* (Richmond, VA: Curzon, 2001), pp. 37–61, for an extended discussion on why the Qur'an cannot be translated.

[13] For an overview of this community, see Farhad Daftary, *A Short History of the Ismailis: Traditions of a Muslim Community* (Princeton, NJ: M. Weiner Publishers, 1998).

[14] A biography of this important figure in Nigerian Islam may be found in M. Hiskett, *The Sword of Truth: The Life and Times of the Shehu Usuman Dan Fodio* (New York: Oxford University Press, 1973).

[15] See David Robinson, *Muslim Societies in African History* (Cambridge and New York: Cambridge University Press, 2004), pp. 140–148.

[16] Robinson, *Muslim Societies in African History*, pp. 173–176.

[17] See Robert O. Collins, *The Southern Sudan, 1883–1898: A Struggle For Control* (New Haven, Yale University Press, 1962) and P. M. Holt, *The Mahdist State in the Sudan, 1883–1898* (Oxford: Clarendon Press, 1958).

[18] Consult Kamal Osman Salih, "The Sudan, 1985–9: The Fading Democracy," *The Journal of Modern African Studies*, Vol. 28, No. 2 (June 1990), p. 199.

[19] Consult Ali A. Mazrui, "African Islam and Competitive Religion: Between Revivalism and Expansion," *Third World Quarterly*, Vol. 10, No. 2 (1988), pp. 499–518.

[20] The estimation of the numbers of Muslims in Nigeria is somewhat controversial because of political issues over the census. According to an Associated Press report, "Muslim Mobs, Seeking Vengeance, Attack Christians in Nigeria," *New York Times* (May 13, 2004), "Many of Nigeria's 126 million people, [are] split almost evenly between Muslims and Christians..." However, another report estimates the percentage of Muslims in Nigeria at 75 percent; see http://www.islamicweb.com/begin/population.htm, accessed May 28, 2004. A more recent estimate in Pew Research Center, *The Future of the Global Muslim Population: Projections for 2010–2030* (Washington, DC: Forum on Religion & Public Life, January 2011), p. 160, puts the 2010 figure at 47.9 percent.

[21] Pew Research Center, *The Future of the Global Muslim Population*, p. 160, estimates the Muslim population in 2010 at about 33.8 percent of the population.

[22] Quinn and Quinn, *Pride, Faith, and Fear*, pp. 127–135, and Hiskett, *The Course of Islam in Africa*, p. 174.

[23] According to an estimate of the UAE Ministry of Islamic Affairs and Awaqf, 59 percent of Africa's population (in 1996) was Muslim; see http://www.fedfin.gov.ae/moia/english/e_growingreligion.htm, accessed May 28, 2004. The Pew estimates, cited above, for the continent are much more conservative.

[24] The population of Senegal in 2010 was 95.9 percent Muslim, according to Pew Research Center, *The Future of the Global Muslim Population*, p. 160.

[25] Relatedly, see Leonardo A. Villalón, *Islamic Society and State Power in Senegal: Disciples and Citizens in Fatick* (Cambridge and New York: Cambridge University Press, 1995).

[26] Consult Susan MacDonald, "Senegal: Islam on the March," *West Africa*, No. 3494 (London, Aug. 6, 1984), p. 1570.

[27] For discussions on these ethnic/religious divisions challenging Nigerian democracy, see, for example, Simeon O. Ilesanmi, *Religious Pluralism and the Nigerian State* (Athens, OH: Ohio University Center for International Studies, 1997) and Joseph A. Umoren, *Democracy and Ethnic Diversity in Nigeria* (Lanham, MD: University Press of America, 1996.

[28] Consult Ann M. Lesch, *The Sudan: Contested National Identities* (Bloomington, IN and Oxford, UK: Indiana University Press and J. Currey, 1998).

[29] See Norimitsu Onishi, "Dictator Gone: Ivory Coast Splits into Ethnic and Political Violence," *The New York Times* (Oct. 27, 2000).

[30] For an overview of Islamic Law in Africa under the colonial powers, see Allen Christelow, "Islamic Law in Africa," in Nehemia Levtzion & Randall L. Pouwels, (eds.), *The History of Islam in Africa* (Athens, OH; Oxford; and Cape Town: Ohio University Press, James Currey and David Philip, 2000), pp. 380–384.

[31] For more on the conflict between Kenyan Christians and Muslims, see Donal B. Cruise O'Brien, *Symbolic Confrontations: Muslims Imagining the State in Africa* (New York: Palgrave, 2003), pp. 92–117.

[32] The American concern over terrorism arising from Africa is expressed in Princeton N. Lyman and J. Stephen Morrison, "The Terrorist Threat in Africa," *Foreign Affairs*, Vol. 83, No. 1 (January–February 2004), pp. 75–86.

[33] Americans are not always willing to admit that the United States is an imperial power; see Dimitri K. Simes, "America's Imperial Dilemma," *Foreign Affairs*, Vol. 82, No. 6 (November–December 2003), p. 93.

[34] Critical discussions on the American empire may be found in, for instance, Chalmers Johnson, *Blowback: The Costs and Consequences of American Empire* (New York: Henry Holt, 2001, 1st Owl Books ed.) and Michael Parenti, *Against Empire* (San Francisco, CA: City Lights Books, 1995).

[35] For instance, according to a March 28, 2003, speech by United States Deputy Assistant Secretary of State, Pamela E. Bridgewater: "... there are now more than 250,000 scientists and physicians of African descent in the United States." See Pamela E. Bridgewater "The African Diaspora and its Influence on African Development," speech delivered at Kentucky State University, March 28, 2003. http://usembassy-australia.state.gov/hyper/2003/0403/epf410.htm), accessed Mar. 24, 2004.

On recent African immigrants to the United States, see Darlington I. I. Ndubuike, *The Struggles, Challenges and Triumphs of the African Immigrant in America* (Lewiston, NY: Edwin Mellen Press, 2002); John A. Arthur, *Invisible Sojourners: African Immigrant Diaspora in the United States* (Westport, CT: Praeger, 2000); Kofi A. Apraku, *African Emigres in the United States: A Missing Link in Africa's Social and Political Development* (New York, Westport, CT, and London: Praeger,

1991) and April Gordon, "The New Diaspora: African Immigration to the United States," *Journal of Third World Studies*, 15 (Spring 1998), pp. 79–103. Both general and specific discussions on African Diasporas may be found, for example, in the following: Joseph E. Harris, (ed.), *Global Dimensions of the African Diaspora*, 2nd ed. (Washington, DC: Howard University Press, 2003); Shihan de Silva Jayasuriya and Richard Pankhurst, (eds.), *The African Diaspora in the Indian Ocean* (Trenton, NJ: Africa World Press, 2003); Erna Brodber, *The Continent of Black Consciousness: On the History of the African Diaspora from Slavery to the Present Day* (London: New Beacon Books, 2003); John Hunwick and Eve T. Powell, *The African Diaspora in the Mediterranean Lands of Islam* (Princeton, NJ: Markus Wiener Publishers, 2002); Darlene Clark Hine and Jacqueline McLeod, (eds.), *Crossing Boundaries: Comparative History of Black People in Diaspora* (Bloomington, IN: Indiana University Press, 1999); E. L. Bute, *The Black Handbook: The People, History and Politics of Africa and the African Diaspora* (London and Washington: Cassell, 1997); Alusine Jalloh and Stephen E. Maizlish, (eds.), *The African Diaspora* (College Station, TX: Texas A&M University Press, 1996); Michael L. Coniff, *Africans in the Americas: A History of the Black Diaspora* (New York: St. Martin's Press, 1994); and Edward Scobie, *Global African Presence* (Brooklyn, NY: A & B Books, 1994).

[36] Consult John Iliffe, "The Organization of the Maji Maji Rebellion," and Patrick M. Redmond, "Maji Maji in Ungoni: A Reappraisal of Existing Historiography," in Gregory Maddox, (ed.), *Conquest and Resistance to Colonialism in Africa* (New York: Garland, 1993), pp. 217–252.

[37] For two views of the Boer War, see Denis Judd and Keith Judd, *The Boer War* (London: John Murray, 2002) and John Camaroff, (ed.), with Brian William and Andrew Reed, *Mafeking Diary: A Black Man's View of a White Man's War, by Sol T. Plaatje* (Cambridge, UK; Athens, OH: Meridor Press in association with J. Currey and Ohio University Press, 1990).

[38] On the Zimbabwe anti-colonial war, see David Martin and Phyllis Johnson, *The Struggle for Zimbabwe: The Chimurenga War* (London and Boston: Faber and Faber, 1981).

[39] See John Marcum, "Angola: Twenty-Five Years of War," *Current History*,Vol. 85 (May 1986), pp. 193–199 and Fola Soremekun, *Angola: The Road to Independence* (Ile-Ife, Nigeria: University of Ife Press, 1983).

[40] For descriptions and analyses of this armed struggle, consult Wunyabari Maloba, *Mau Mau and Kenya: An Analysis of a Peasant Revolt* (Bloomington, IN: Indiana University Press, 1993), pp. 102–109, and Marshall S. Clough, *Mau Mau Memoirs: History, Memory, and Politics* (Boulder, CO: L. Rienner, 1998), pp. 98–99. The British did not give up their colony in Kenya without a struggle and grievous violations of human rights; see, for some recent analyses, Caroline Elkins, *Imperial Reckoning: The Untold Story of Britain's Gulag in Kenya* (New York: Henry Holt, 2005) and David Anderson, *Histories of the Hanged: The Dirty War in Kenya and the End of Empire* (New York: W. W. Norton, 2005).

[41] See Richard Hull, "Rhodesia in Crisis," *Current History*, Vol. 76, No. 445 (March 1979), p. 107.

[42] For profiles of the two sets of bombers, see Craig Whitlock, "Trail from London to Leeds Yield Portrait of Three Bombers," *The Washington Post* (July 15, 2005); Kevin Sullivan, "Attempted Murder Charges Brought in London Attack," *The Washington Post* (August 9, 2005) and J. F. O. Mcallister, "The Terrorists Next Door," *Time* (August 8, 2005), pp. 30–31.

[43] Paul Bohannan, in *African Homicide and Suicide* (Princeton, NJ: Princeton University Press, 1960), p. 263, has pointed out that Africans do not see suicide as a "volitional act," but rather only "supernatural intervention can place a person in a suicidal state." Also, the act of suicide leads to the performance of several rituals to alleviate the pollution of the suicide site and ill-effects on the community. In one study, it has been pointed out that overall suicide rates in Sub-Saharan Africa is only 3.4 per 100,000 whereas in China it is 30.4 per 100,000; see E. Krug, A. Reza and J. A. Mercy, "Epidemiology of Violent Deaths in the World," Division of Violence Prevention, National Center for Injury Control and Prevention, Centers for Disease Control and Prevention at http://www.cdc.gov/ncipc/pub-res/epi_of_violence.htm (accessed October 15, 2005). On Hindu, Jewish, and Muslim attitudes to suicide see Norman L. Farberow, "Cultural History of Suicide," in Norman L. Farberow, (ed.), *Suicide in Different Cultures* (Baltimore, MD: University of Maryland Press, 1975), pp. 3–4.

[44] Gandhi's fasts were weapons not just against British imperialism but also against other South Asians' ill-treatment of castes and Muslims; see G. T. F. Jordens, *Gandhi's Religion: A Homespun Shawl* (Houndsmills, Basingstoke, Hampshire and New York: Macmillan Press and St. Martin's Press, 1998), pp. 199–221.

[45] Robert Pape places the Palestinians starting in 1994 and the Tamil Tigers of Sri Lanka beginning their campaign in 1990, although others have the Tigers starting even earlier in 1987. See Robert A. Pape, "The Strategic Logic of Suicide Terrorism," *American Political Science Review*, Vol. 97, No. 3 (August 2003), p. 348, and Mia Bloom, *Dying to Kill: The Allure of Suicide Terror* (New York: Columbia University Press, 2005), p. 60.

[46] For more on the kamikaze attackers, consult Bloom, *Dying to Kill*, pp. 13–16.

[47] Note that the background of these bombers also indicated lower educational levels and a life of petty crime prior to these bombings, leading to some speculation that their attacks may have failed due to incompetence; see Sullivan, "Attempted Murder Charges Brought in London Attack," *The Washington Post* (August 9, 2005); Mcallister, "The Terrorists Next Door," *Time* (August 8, 2005), pp. 30–31; and *The Economist* (July 30, 2005), p. 49.

[48] Indeed, according to a study:

Britain's position as a subordinate ally of the United States has been a "high-risk policy" that has left it vulnerable to terrorist attacks such as the recent bombings of London's transportation system, according to a briefing paper released early Monday by one of the country's most prominent foreign affairs research groups... Chatham House, also known as the Royal Institute of International Affairs, which has close ties to the government.

See Glenn Frankel, "Ties to U.S. Made Britain Vulnerable, Report Says," *The Washington Post* (July 18, 2005).

[49] See Kevin Baker, "We're All in the Army Now: The G.O.P.'s Plan to Militarize Our Culture," *Harper's Magazine*, Vol. 307, No. 1841 (October 2003), p. 43. For lists of countries with US military presence, see Dana Priest, *The Mission: Waging War and Keeping Peace with America's Military* (New York: W. W. Norton, 2003), p. 187, and *The Military Balance, 2004–2005* (London: Institute for Strategic Studies, Taylor & Francis, 2005), p. 17. The importance of the African continent in American strategic calculations is discussed in Greg Mills, "Africa's New Strategic Significance," *Washington Quarterly*, Vol. 27, Issue 4 (Autumn 2004), pp. 157–169, and for an example of American training of African troops, see Robert D. Kaplan, "America's African Rifles," *The Atlantic Monthly*, Vol. 295, Issue 3 (April 2005), pp. 91–94.

[50] Lyman and Morrison, "The Terrorist Threat in Africa," *Foreign Affairs*, Vol. 83, No. 1 (Jan–Feb 2004), p. 75.

[51] See Peter Riddell and Rosemary Bennett, "More Call for Troops to Pull Out Now Voting is Over," *The Times* (London) (February 9, 2005) and Glenn Frankel, *The Washington Post* (March 28, 2004).

CHAPTER FIVE

THE UNITED NATIONS
AND THE MUSLIM WORLD:
ALLIES OR ADVERSARIES?[1]

Islam and the United Nations were born out of competing concepts of universalism. Islam is a universalistic religion as it seeks to preach to the human race as a whole; the United Nations is a universalist organization as it has sought to represent the human race as a whole. Islam has envisaged a universalism of people, the *Ummah*; the United Nations has envisaged the universalism of nation-states, the international community.

The universalism of Islam was to be based on a shared faith; the universalism of the United Nations was based on a joint contract. The faith of Islam consists of its five pillars, the Qur'an, and the *Sunnah*. The contract of the United Nations is its Charter and subsequent conventions, declarations, and resolutions. A universalism of faith expands by biological reproduction and religious conversion; a universalism of contract expands by signing up new states as members of the world organization.

Since there are fewer than 200 states in the world, and more than five billion people, a universalism of states is achieved more quickly than a universalism of people. At first glance, it might therefore seem that the United Nations has achieved its universalism of states long before Islam has achieved her universalism of people. The UN already has 193 member states.[2]

Today one out of every five human beings is a Muslim. In this twenty-first century, the Muslim community will reach the mark of a quarter (i.e., 25%) of the human race. It will have become the largest concentration of believers in one religion in history. In terms of population, it is now one of the fastest-growing religions in the world.[3]

But the United Nations seems to have already achieved a universalism of states. Or is it only pseudo-universalism? Is the UN universalism still a game of smoke and mirrors?

The "Clash of Civilizations"

In the summer of 1993, Professor Samuel P. Huntington of Harvard University unleashed a debate about the nature of conflict in the post-Cold War era. In an article in the influential American policy journal *Foreign Affairs*, Huntington argued that now that the Cold War was over, future conflicts would not be primarily between states or ideological blocs, but rather they would be between civilizations and cultural coalitions.[4] To use Huntington's own words:

> The fault lines between civilizations will be the battle lines of the future. Conflict between civilizations will be the latest phase in the evolution of conflict in the modern world.[5]

Huntington was at his best when he discussed how the West masquerades as "the world community," and uses the United Nations to give universalist credentials to Western interests. In Huntington's words:

> Global political and security issues are effectively settled by a directorate of the United States, Britain and France, world economic issues by a directorate of the United States, Germany and Japan, all of which maintain extraordinarily close relations with each other, to the exclusion of lesser and largely non-Western countries. Decisions made at the UN Security Council or in the International Monetary Fund that reflects the interests of the West are presented to the world as the desires of the world community. The very phrase "the world community" has become the euphemistic collective noun (replacing "the Free World") to give global legitimacy to actions reflecting the interests of the United States and other Western powers.[6]

We have here a situation where the universalism of the United Nations is far less than it seems. The United Nations has become the collective fig-leaf for rapacious Western interests and actions.

On becoming a member of the *Ummah*, a Muslim must recite the *Shahadah*, saying that "There is no God but Allah." It seems that to remain a member of the United Nations in good standing, all countries must acknowledge that "There is no political god but the West." Only the West has the right to determine when and how force should be used in world politics.

Huntington goes on to show how the West has used the UN Security Council to impose sanctions against Muslim countries or invoke the use of force. After Iraq occupied Kuwait, the West was faced with a choice between saving time and saving lives. The West chose to save time. In Huntington's words:

> Western domination of the UN Security Council and its decisions, tempered only by occasional abstention by China, produced UN legitimation of the West's use of force to drive Iraq out of Kuwait and its elimination of Iraq's sophisticated weapons and capacity to produce such weapons. It also produced the quite unprecedented action by the United States, Britain and France in getting the Security Council to demand that Libya hand over the Pan Am 103 bombing suspects and then to impose sanctions when Libya refused.[7]

At some point, there seemed to be evidence that Libya might not have been the culprit in the Pan American 103 disaster at Lockerbie, Scotland after all. Some other Middle Eastern country might have been implicated and not Libya at all. But the sanctions against Libya were not lifted. Washington, London, and Paris were reluctant to eat their own words even if injustice was being committed.[8] The arrogance of power was at work.

My own thesis in this chapter concurs with Huntington that there is indeed a clash of civilizations, but disagrees with him about the nature of that clash and about how old it is. I believe that the clash of civilizations did not begin with the end of the Cold War but is much older. I also believe that the chief cultural transgressor has been the Western World throughout.

Following the formation of the United Nations in 1945, a strange thing happened. Quite unconsciously, the West adopted an ancient and medieval Islamic view of the world.

Not long after the creation of the United Nations, the West appropriated for itself—almost unconsciously—the tripartite division of the world of ancient Islamic jurists.[9]

Ancient international Islamic law divided the world into *Dar al-Islam* (the Abode of Islam); *Dar al-Harb* (the Abode of War); and *Dar al-'Ahd* or *Dar al-Sulh* (the Abode of Peaceful Co-Existence or Contractual Peace).

Within *Dar al-Islam*, amity and cooperation on Islamic principles were supposed to prevail. Pax Islamica was supposed to be triumphant. It included both Muslims and non-Muslims of the tolerated communities ("People of the Book" or Dhimmis), who enjoyed state protection against internal insecurity and external aggression.[10]

Dar al-Harb, the Abode of War, was not necessarily an arena of direct military confrontation. These were the lands of non-Muslims, often hostile to Islam, constituting the sort of situation which Thomas Hobbes was to describe much later as a condition without a shared sovereign.[11] Centuries before Hobbes, Muslim jurists had evolved the concept of *Dar al-Harb*, a state of war, for cognizance of authorities in countries which did not agree on the sovereignty of God. As Khadduri points out, this recognition was necessitated for the survival of mankind:

> Islam's cognizance of non-Islamic sovereignties merely meant that some form of authority was by nature necessary for the survival of mankind, even when men lived in territories in the state of nature, outside the pale of the Islamic public order.[12]

The third category of countries under ancient international Islamic law was the countries of *Dar al-'Ahd* or *Dar al-Sulh* (the Abode of Contractual Peace or Peaceful Co-Existence). These were the non-Muslim countries which worked out a deal with the Muslim rulers for greater autonomy and peace in exchange for some kind of tribute or collective tax paid to the Muslim treasury. The last-mentioned area was not universally recognized by most jurists, as they felt that "if the inhabitants of the territory concluded a peace treaty and paid tribute, it became part of the *Dar al-Islam* and its people were entitled to the protection of Islam."[13]

Following the formation of the United Nations, the West appropriated this tripartite view of the world of ancient Islamic international law and simply substituted itself for Islam. For much of the second half of the twentieth century, during the period of the Cold War, there were the following categories:

- *Dar al-Maghrib* or *Dar al-Gharb* (the Abode of the West) instead of *Dar al-Islam*
- *Dar al-Harb* (the Abode of War—which was essentially the Communist World)
- *Dar al-'Ahd*—or *Dar al-Sulh* (the Abode of Peaceful Co-Existence which was the Third World). The Third World paid tribute to the West in the form of the debt-burden and other forms of economic exploitation. It was no different from the tribute paid by *Dar al-Sulh* countries to medieval Muslim rulers.

But one major proviso needs to be emphasized in the second half of the twentieth century. While doctrinally the Abode of War for the West was supposed to be the Communist World, in practice the actual military fighting by the West in the second half of the twentieth century has been almost entirely in the Third World, including the World of Islam.[14]

The Korean War was in the Third World but not the Muslim World. In the case of Korea and Vietnam, it was not easy to draw a distinction between the Communist World and the Third World. Several million people perished in the two American-led wars of Korea and Vietnam. Militarily, no member of the Warsaw Pact was hurt directly. The Warsaw Pact and the North Atlantic Treaty Organization (NATO) were basically fighting each other through intermediaries. The doctrinal Abode of War was not necessarily the literal abode of war. The US armed itself to the teeth to fight the communist Second World—and turned on the Third World instead. In Korea, this Western onslaught appropriated the flag of the United Nations.[15]

While Korea and Vietnam might have been cases where it was difficult to determine where the communist Second World ended and the Third World began, the Muslim World poses no such ambivalence. Muslim states have not been communist.[16]

And yet since 1980, at least a million Muslims have been killed by Western armaments. These casualties have included Libyans, Iranians, Lebanese, Palestinians, and Iraqis. The West has been trigger-happy in responding to Muslim political challenges. In the Gulf War of 1991, the West used the flag of the United Nations to give its militarism a universalistic appeal and legitimacy.[17] The human toll in Iraq was a result of the deprivations caused by the Anglo-American economic sanctions, given universalistic legitimacy by the UN Security Council.[18]

The ostensible reason was to make sure that Iraq did not rebuild weapons of mass destruction. And yet each of the permanent members of the Security Council is possessive about its own weapons of mass destruction. Unlike France, Iraq did not have the arrogance of testing nuclear weapons thousands of miles away from its own core population— and endangering the population of other lands. Protests by the militarily-weak Pacific nations have been manifested in the form of street demonstrations, diplomatic downgrading of relations, and boycotts of French goods—like wine.[21] Nor did Iraq have the equivalent of a permanent member of the Security Council to say to it "scratch my nuclear back and I will scratch yours." John Major was scratching Jacques Chirac's back.

The West's doctrinal *Dar al-Harb*, the Abode of War, was supposed to be the Communist World. The West's operational *Dar al-Harb* has been the developing world and the islands of the seas. The United Nations has sometimes provided a universalist umbrella for the West's operations in the Third World.

The UN and the Cultural Counter-Revolution

The UN's universalism represents nation-states and world regions but does not try to represent civilizations. Six out of the last eight Secretaries-General of the UN have come from Christian traditions.[22] The Christian World is about one-fifth of the population of the world. There has been no Hindu, Muslim, or Confucian Secretary-General although together those populations outnumber Christians by more than two to one. There has been one Buddhist Secretary-General—the Burmese U Thant. One Buddhist against six Christians—although there are probably as many Buddhists as Christians in the world.[23] Should the UN system be more sensitive to civilizational representativeness?[24]

Although the world body has never had a Muslim Secretary-General, it has had a Secretary-General who was a national of a major Muslim country. That was Boutros Boutros-Ghali, who was an Arab but not a Muslim. His country of birth and historical ancestry was of course Egypt. Unfortunately, the United States ensured that Boutros-Ghali had only one term, instead of the usual two. His second term was vetoed.

Should peacekeeping in the future be more sensitive to geo-cultural movements? International geocultural organizations like the Organization of the Islamic Conference (OIC) can be relevant in preventative diplomacy or in peacemaking—although the OIC efforts in trying to stop the Iraq–Iran conflict in the 1980s were less than successful.[25] On the other hand, patient efforts by the Economic Community of West African States Monitoring Group (ECOMOG) in Liberia appear to have been more successful.[26]

Then there are intra-civilizational conflicts with extra-civilizational consequences—like movements of Islamic militancy in places like Algeria and Egypt and potentially Saudi Arabia. Consultations have taken place between officials of NATO, and some members of the League of Arab States concerning Islamic militancy. How was the UN involved?

For the time being, the United Nations' system is part of the cultural hegemony of the Western World. In the past, when former Director-General Amadou-Mahtar M'Bow of UNESCO tried to rebel against it, the United States and Great Britain withdrew from UNESCO—and M'Bow was consequently ousted.[27]

The UN was formed primarily by the victors of World War II. Those victors belonged to one civilization-and-a-half: Britain, US, France, USSR. They made themselves permanent members of the UN's powerful Security Council. They made one concession to another civilization—by also making pre-Communist China a permanent member.

Of the five original languages of the UN, four were in origin European languages: English, French, Spanish, and Russian. A concession was made to another civilization—by recognizing the Chinese language.

A kind of bicameral legislature began to emerge—an upper house, which was the more powerful, but less representative, called the Security Council—and a lower house, which was less powerful, but more representative, called the General Assembly. This bicameral concept developed by practice rather than design and was in origin very Western. The upper house was the global House of Lords—warlords! The conception was basically from Western civilization and history.

One of the major functions of the UN was to help keep the peace according to the principles of international law. The Law of Nations was itself a child of European diplomatic history and statecraft. It once used to be:

The Law of Christian Nations, and then became,
The Law of Civilized Nations, and then became,
The Law of Developed Nations[28]

That old International Law used to legitimize the colonization of other countries by Western countries. Intellectual ancestors of Western political thought were marked by an arrogant Eurocentrism. J. S. Mill distinguished between "barbarians and societies worthy of the Law of Nations."[29] What was even more appalling was the approbation of colonialism by early socialists; Karl Marx applauded Britain's colonization of India.[30] Friedrich Engels applauded France's colonization of Algeria.[31] All these were civilizational criteria, accepted by almost the whole White World.

And then the UN began to admit not only more countries, but also more cultures. These included the admission of India and Pakistan in 1947, Myanmar (formerly Burma) and Sri Lanka (formerly Ceylon) in 1948 and later Malaysia and Singapore. From the Arab World, there later followed some additional countries: Morocco, Tunisia, Sudan, Algeria (Egypt was already a member), and subsequently newly-independent Black African countries, beginning with Ghana in 1957. New values were trying to express themselves through a Eurocentric infrastructure.

Later, the UN became the channel through which other countries and cultures began to insist on changes in International Law. When India occupied Goa, thus liberating it from Portuguese rule, Krishna Menon enunciated the principle that "colonialism was permanent aggression"—thus delegitimizing colonialism.[32]

African struggles against apartheid led to the shrinkage of the principle of domestic jurisdiction as applied to South Africa's policy of apartheid. Eventually apartheid was regarded as a matter of relevance to international security and as virtually a 'crime against humanity.' The United Nations began to take a more active role in combating apartheid.[33] Apartheid was worse than a crime against democracy.

In the post-Cold War era, is the UN likely to be used by the dominant civilization (the West) against other civilizations? Was that what happened during the Gulf War? Was the UN hijacked by the West to legitimize massacres in defense of its oil interests? In Bosnia, was the UN being used by the West to make sure there was no viable Muslim state in the middle of Europe?

The UN has sometimes been guilty of sins of omission. Such sins of omission include:

- Standing by while Patrice Lumumba was literally dragged to his death in 1961 in the Congo (now Democratic Republic of the Congo, which was also known as Zaire between 1971 and 1997).[34]
- Standing by while thousands of people were massacred in the bombing of Iraq—euphemistically termed 'collateral damage'—during the Gulf War, and in the aftermath, continuing to ignore the privations of Iraqi individuals due to sanctions.
- Standing by while hundreds of thousands of Bosnians were maimed, murdered, mutilated, or raped in the 1990s. Standing by while hundreds of thousands of Rwandans were killed in the genocide of 1994. Is this a clash of civilizations?

In an earlier work, I had raised the issue of the West, particularly the United States, becoming the defender of the holy places in Islam—Mecca and Medina—during the Gulf War.[35] In 1995, the United States emerged as the peacemaker acceptable to all parties in the Bosnian imbroglio—including Bosnian Muslims. Part of the peace plan envisaged reducing Serbian and Croatian armaments, while increasing Bosnian Muslim arms. The peacekeeping forces were not directly involved with this exercise, but the United States got third parties to undertake the task of arming the Bosnian forces for them to be able to repel any future challenge.[36]

It is striking to note that while the United Nations and the European allies, along with the Clinton Administration, were reluctant to lift the arms embargo so as to allow the Bosnian Muslims to arm themselves, conservative Republicans (like Senator Bob Dole) had long called for allowing Bosnia to arm itself.[37]

In the UN, the temporary omen was in the 1970s. In 1971, there was the euphoric recognition of the People's Republic of China (PRC) by the United Nations.[38] There was also Yasser Arafat's address to the General

Assembly in plenary session virtually as Head of State in the fall of 1974.[39] Third was Algeria's launching of the campaign for a New International Economic Order (NIEO) also in 1974.[40] Fourth was the subsequent recognition of Arabic alongside Chinese as the only non-European languages accepted as official idioms of the world body for some occasions. Did these events portend a Muslim-Confucian coalition?

All these are modest, even if significant, achievements. On the whole, the UN system and the Bretton Woods institutions (World Bank and the IMF), continue to be major disseminators of Western ideas, concepts, and values. In conception, and in much of their operations, the institutions are rooted in the Western Worldview (Weltanschauung). Future Directors-General of UNESCO are unlikely to be as assertive as Amadou-Mahtar M'Bow.[41] And most developing countries have, in any case, been forced to toe the Western party line since the disintegration of the Soviet Union.

At the moment, the UN Security Council is primarily a 'White Man's Club' with White permanent members and non-white visitors. Four of the five permanent members are essentially White countries rooted in a Euro-Christian legacy (US, France, Britain, and Russia). Has the United Nations inevitably become a future arena for a clash of civilizations?

The different conflicts in the Muslim World dictate an agonizing reappraisal. The majority of the victims are Muslims, but there are conflicts where Muslims are the villains.

Has the ancient *Dar al-Islam* (the Abode of Islam) now become the modern *Dar al-Harb* (the Abode of War)? In traditional Islamic international law, *Dar al-Islam* was the land where Muslims were free and secure. But now Muslims are caught up in conflict in different lands.

In this regard, I have three main categories of societies. The first category includes those societies where Muslims are the victims of the violence of others. This has included the wars in Bosnia, Chechnya, Kashmir, southern Lebanon, the Central African Republic, and occupied Palestine. It once included Afghanistan under Soviet occupation.

Second is the category where Muslims are at war with each other. This includes Afghanistan, Syria, Libya, Mali, Somalia, Algeria, the city of Karachi in Pakistan, and Egypt.

Third is the category where Muslims are more culprits than victims— where Muslims victimize others. Although the war in Sudan against South Sudan is not primarily a religious war, its net effect casts Muslims as the greater culprits in the conflict. What about the November 1995 terrorist act in Riyadh, Saudi Arabia against Americans?[42] Is that a case of Muslims against foreigners? Or is it the beginning of something comparable to Algeria and Egypt?

Within the ancient Abode of Islam, where conflict was not supposed to be the order of the day, we now have anguish and discord. The universalism of faith has yet to find a universality of peace.

The United Nations is involved in some of these conflicts affecting Muslims, but not in others. There are UN resolutions about Kashmir, and many more UN resolutions about Palestine. The UN has sometimes attempted to help in the civil war in Afghanistan. The UN kept out of the war in Chechnya. What is heartrending for the Muslim World is how much fratricide, as well as victimization, there is.

While Muslims have failed in maintaining peace towards each other, Westerners have found it among themselves. A whole new body of literature has emerged based on the premise that "democracies do not go to war against each other."[43] The literature is not based on moral wishful thinking, but on what is presented as systemic and scientific analysis of the nature of the democratic process, especially in the liberal West. There is nothing in the democratic process to stop the United States from invading Panama, or to stop Britain and France joining a military coalition against Iraq in the Gulf War. But, the new school of thought asserts that these democratic countries are systemically unlikely to go to war against each other. Huntington captured this sentiment when he said, "Military conflict among Western states is unthinkable."[44] But how much of this peace is due to the presence of economic prosperity and nuclear weapons?

Instead of a situation in which Muslims do not go to war with each other (as the ancient doctrine expected), we have a situation in which Westerners do not go to war with each other (as the new political science asserts). Instead of *Dar al-Islam* triumphant (the Abode of Islam in victory), we have *Dar al-Maghrib* victorious (the Abode of the West in triumph).

And the West controls the United Nations. Islam's universalism of faith has foundered because of the weakness of the Muslims. The United Nations' universalism of states has triumphed because of the power of the West.

Perhaps nowhere in the world was there such a stark confrontation between the universalism of faith and the universalism of nation-states as in Bosnia. The state called Yugoslavia disintegrated—and out of the fragments emerged several states including a country called Bosnia-Herzegovina with a plurality of Muslims. The idea of a Muslim-led government in the middle of Europe, however democratic, raised disturbing specters in some circles. Muslim Turkey was a Middle Eastern country trying to be recognized as European. Muslim Albania was technologically the most backward country in Europe. But relatively advanced Bosnia in the middle of Christian Europe was a disconcerting prospect in a world where influential professors from Harvard University expected 'a clash of civilizations.'

Let us therefore look at Bosnia-Herzegovina as a case study involving the confluence of a number of factors. Bosnia is an intriguing case-study pitting the universalism of faith against the universalism of statehood. It is a case-study of the United Nations in opposition to the aspirations of most of the Muslim World. It is a case-study of a clash of civilizations as Bosnia was gradually led, in the 1990s, towards *de facto* partition.

Bosnia-Herzegovina was originally invaded partly by troops from Serbia and partly by Bosnian Serbs armed by Serbia. The UN imposed an arms embargo on both sides. And yet the UN was wrong to impose the embargo on the Bosnian government. It was wrong for two main reasons:

1. Because Bosnia had the right of self-defense under Article 51 of the UN Charter
2. Because the Serbian side had inherited the bulk of the armory of the former Socialist Republic of Yugoslavia and thus came to acquire undue advantage

A Bosnian equivalent of the Palestine Liberation Organization and a Bosnian equivalent of the Irish Republican Army might have been unnecessarily created tomorrow by the humiliation of the Bosnian Muslims.

The irony is that just when the Muslim World was, in spite of the Hebron mosque massacre perpetrated by a Jewish militant, learning to accept a Jewish state in the midst of a Muslim Middle East, Europeans were reluctant to countenance a Muslim state in a Christian Europe.

In Afghanistan, the West armed the liberation of a Muslim society in order to frustrate Moscow. In Bosnia, the West, through the UN, disarmed a Muslim society, partly in order not to offend Moscow.

The shadow of cultural prejudice persists. Would the West and the UN have been slow to react in Bosnia if it was a case of Muslims slaughtering and raping Christians instead of the other way around? Would the US Administration and the Senate have been slow if the Serbian concentration camps were for Bosnian Jews rather than for Bosnian Muslims? Would the UN not have been forced to respond more robustly and energetically if Jewish women were being raped by Muslim men as an instrument of war instead of Muslim women being raped by Orthodox Christian Serbs?

Indeed, there is reason to believe that if it was Jews who were being subjected to such unspeakable humiliation, Israel would not have waited for either the UN Security Council or the US Senate.[45] Israel would have staged a major international spectacular event to grab the world's attention—even if it meant bombing Belgrade. And Israel would certainly have gotten the world's attention. Fifty Muslim governments, on the other hand, were content to timidly obey the demands of the Security Council, refrain from arming the Bosnian Muslims, or even evacuate refugees. The conclusion to be drawn from all this is that the universalism of states ostensibly achieved by the United Nations is still seriously flawed. The United Nations is still a creature of the Western World—and the West still views the world through the tripartite lenses of medieval Islam duly adapted (by the West).

What to medieval Muslim jurists was *Dar al-Islam* (Abode of Islam) has now become *Dar al-Maghrib* or *Dar al-Gharb*, the Abode of the West. Westerners are the preeminent pioneers.

Until the 1990s, the Abode of War to Westerners was the lands of communism. Has the Abode of War now become the Muslim World in all its complexity?

To some medieval Islamists, there was the Abode of *'Ahd* and/or *Sulh*—the home of contractual coexistence in exchange for tribute. Tribute is what the Western World has been receiving from most of the Third World in profits, interest on the debt burden, and the returns on other forms of exploitation. And the United Nations has sometimes unwittingly provided an umbrella for this tripartite division of the world.

Conclusion

But when all is said and done, under what circumstances is the United Nations ever an ally of the Muslim World?

First, the UN is an ally in the humanitarian role of the world body and its agencies—such as crises of refugees or international responses to famine, draught, and other catastrophes. In such roles, it does not matter whether the immediate beneficiaries are Muslims, as in Somalia and Bangladesh, or non-Muslims, as in Rwanda. The UN is supportive of all such efforts.

Second, the United Nations is an ally when it provides an umbrella for mediation for some of the quarrels between Muslims—as in the effort to resolve the destiny of Western Sahara. The UN in such instances helps the *Ummah* more directly. The UN helped in the quest for peace between Iran and Iraq in their conflict in the 1980s.[46]

Third, the United Nations is an ally to Muslims when the world body provides peacekeeping troops and peacekeeping auspices in conflicts between Muslims and non-Muslims. Over the years, United Nations troops have often been involved in the often thankless task of trying to keep the peace between the Arabs and the Israelis especially prior to the Oslo peace process. The UN's long-drawn role in Cyprus is another example of attempted mediation between Muslims and non-Muslims.

Fourth, the United Nations has been allied to Muslims—when the Western World has been divided! The Muslim World has sometimes had the UN move decisively as an ally in such a situation—as during the Suez War of 1956 when, in spite of the veto by Britain and France in the Security Council, the mood of the world body was opposed to the invasion of Egypt by Britain, France, and Israel. The United Nations joined forces with Muslim Turkey to create an Alliance of Civilizations. They were joined by Spain in promoting inter-civilizational activities, as Spain's socialist government wanted to create an alternative to the Bush administration's War on Terror.

When the Western World was divided, the United Nations was also able to play a major decolonizing role. This is the fifth positive role of the UN. The United States was historically opposed to some of the older varieties of European imperialism. By the second half of the twentieth century, the United States was often on the same side as the Soviet Union among the critics of old-style European colonialism.

Under these conditions, it was indeed easier for the United Nations to become increasingly one of the great arenas for the anticolonial struggle waged by the peoples of Asia, Africa, and the scattered islands of the seas. The anticolonial role of the United Nations encompassed not only the Trusteeship Council but also the General Assembly, especially from the late 1950s onwards. This anticolonial role was often a great service to the Muslim World.

Sixth, the United Nations can be an ally of the Muslim World when it takes seriously the idea of prosecuting war criminals and those who have committed crimes against humanity. Especially relevant for the Muslim World is the prosecution of war criminals in Bosnia and some Serbs in Serbia and many Serbs in Bosnia who have committed crimes against humanity as in the proceedings at The Hague involving war crimes committed in Bosnia in the 1990s.

The United Nations has done well to appoint the relevant tribunal for the task, but has fallen far short of providing the resources for this complicated task.

Seventh, the United Nations has been an ally when the Muslim World was united. It has, at times, been possible to pass through the General Assembly highly contentious points of principle. The state of Israel is based on an ideology which says that a Russian who claims to be descended from Jews, and whose family has had no connection with the Middle East for the last two thousand years, has more right to go and settle in Israel than a Palestinian who ran away from Israel during the 1948 war. Was such discrimination racist?

When Muslims were united in 1975, they managed to persuade the UN General Assembly to pass a resolution affirming that Zionism was a form of racism. But when Muslims were divided in 1991, that resolution was repealed by an overwhelming majority.[47]

When the Muslims were united they could persuade the General Assembly not only to defy the United States but move the Assembly itself out of New York in further defiance. Thus, when in 1988 the United States refused to grant a visa to Yasser Arafat, thereby preventing him from coming to New York to address the UN General Assembly on his declaration of an independent Palestinian state, the General Assembly denounced Washington's action as a violation of the host country's legal obligations under the 1947 Headquarters Agreement. The General Assembly then shifted this December 13–15 session to Geneva, Switzerland, to make it possible to listen to Chairman Arafat. It was the first and only such move in the history of the United Nations. The unity of the Muslim members of the UN helped to persuade others to join their ranks.[48]

Finally, is the UN an ally or an adversary of Islamic values when the UN promotes such mega-conferences as the one in Beijing, China, in 1995 on the issue of women; the one in Copenhagen on the issues of poverty and development in 1994 and the one in Cairo, Egypt, in 1994 on the issue of population?

Muslims themselves are divided as to whether these UN mega-conferences led to the erosion of Islamic values or helped Islamic values find a new historic setting in the twentieth and twenty-first centuries. For example, are Muslim women being helped by new global standards of gender equity which are promoted at these conferences? These mega-conferences have of course been global and have been part of the United Nations' universalism of nation-states. Some tension has at times been created with Islam's universalism of faith.

But it is a tension which can itself be creative; it is a dialectic which can have a human face. At the very minimum, Islam and the UN have one paramount interest in common—to ensure that *Dar al-Harb*, the Abode of War, shrinks further and further into the oblivion of history, and Planet Earth becomes a House of Peace at long last.

Notes

[1] Revised and updated text of Evan Luard Lecture to mark the fiftieth anniversary of the United Nations, sponsored by the United Nations Association at Oxford and the Oxford Centre for Islamic Studies, given at Oxford University on November 14, 1995.

[2] Arthur S. Banks, (ed.), *Political Handbook of the World, 1994–1995*, (Binghamton, NY: CSA Publications, 1995), p. 1107, reports 184 members; the updated figure is drawn from the Internet at http://www.un.org/overviews/unmember.html. This source also provides details on membership accession dates and other relevant details.

[3] On population distribution and trends among Muslims, consult John Weeks, "The Demography of Islamic Nations," *Population Bulletin*, Vol. 43, No. 4 (1988), especially pp. 5–9, and Pew Research Center, Forum on Religion & Public Life, *The Future of the Global Muslim Population: Projections for 2010–2030*, (Washington, DC: Pew Research Center, January 2011).

[4] See Samuel P. Huntington, "The Clash of Civilizations?" *Foreign Affairs*, Vol. 72, No. 3, (Summer 1993), pp. 22–49. Responses by Fouad Ajami, Kishore Mahbubani, Robert L. Bartley, Liu Binyan, and Jeane J. Kirkpatrick, among others, were published in the next issue of *Foreign Affairs*, Volume 72, No. 4 (September/October 1993), pp. 2–22.

[5] Huntington, "The Clash of Civilizations?" p. 22.

[6] Ibid., p. 39.

[7] Ibid., p. 40.

[8] For one account of the Lockerbie investigation that cast a wider net of suspects than Libya alone at the time, see David Leppard, *On the Trail of Terror: The Inside Story of the Lockerbie Investigation* (London: Jonathan Cape, 1991). While Leppard emphasized the Libyan connection, he also pointed to Iranian and Syrian connections in his last chapter. On the sanctions, see footnote 15 in Vera Gowlland-Debbas, "The Relationship Between the International Court of Justice and the Security Council in the Light of the Lockerbie Case," *American Journal of International Law*, Volume 88 (October 1994), p. 646; and *The New York Times*, (March 31, 1995), Section A, p. 3.

[9] Our discussion here is based on Majid Khadduri's introduction to his translation of *The Islamic Law of Nations: Shaybani's Siyar* (Baltimore, MD: Johns Hopkins Press, 1966), pp. 11–13, although he tends to emphasize the dual division.

[10] Ibid., pp. 11–12.

[11] Hobbes describes this condition in his seminal *Leviathan*; for one recent edition, see Edwin Curley, (ed.), *Leviathan; with Selected Variants from the Latin Edition of 1668/Thomas Hobbes* (Indianapolis: Hackett Pub. Co., 1994).

[12] Khadduri, *The Islamic Law of Nations*, p. 13.

[13] As pointed out by Majid Khadduri, ibid., pp. 12–13. However, for our analysis, this distinction will prove useful.

[14] Although international relations scholars concentrated on the US–Soviet connections, some have pointed out that the West, particularly the United States, has had its most problematic international relations headaches in practice in the

Third World. See, for example, Charles W. Maynes, "America's Third World Hang-Ups," *Foreign Policy*, No. 71 (Summer 1988), pp. 117–140, and Steven R. David, "Why the Third World Matters," *International Security*, Vol. 14, No. 1 (Summer 1989), pp. 50–85.

[15] On the UN role in the Korean conflict, consult, for instance, Leon Gordenker, *The United Nations and the Peaceful Unification of Korea: The Politics of Field Operations, 1947–1950* (The Hague: M. Nijhoff, 1959); and for a specific examination of the US moves in the UN regarding Korea, consult Leland M. Goodrich, *Korea: A Study of U.S. Policy in the United Nations* (New York: Council on Foreign Relations, 1956).

[16] Albania is demographically an Islamic country, but the religion was ruthlessly suppressed by the communist authorities.

[17] See, for example, Burns H. Weston, "Security Council Resolution 678 and Persian Gulf Decision Making: Precarious Legitimacy," *American Journal of International Law*, Volume 85 (July 1991), pp. 516–55.

[18] For one analysis of the American stand on sanctions, see Eric Rouleau, "America's Unyielding Policy toward Iraq," *Foreign Affairs*, Vol. 74 (Jan/Feb 1995), pp. 59–72.

[19] In fact, according to one study, the infant mortality rate had increased fivefold since the end of the war in 1991, killing almost 576,000 Iraqi children; see *The New York Times* (December 1, 1995) Section A, p. 9. Also see Bie Kentane, "The Children of Iraq: 'Was the Price Worth It?,'" *Global Research*, February 19, 2013. Kentane estimates that 100 children die daily in Iraq. Available at: www.globalresearch.ca/the-children-of-iraq-was-the-price-worth-it/30760

[20] For critical reports on the sanctions, see the analysis by Haris Gazdar and Jean Dreze, "Hunger and Poverty in Iraq, 1991," *World Development*, Vol. 20 (July 1992), pp. 921–945, and Eric Hoskins, "Killing is Killing—Not Kindness," *New Statesman & Society*, Vol. 5 (January 17, 1992), pp. 12–13. In spite of internal unrest and prominent defections, Saddam Hussein was not hurt by the sanctions, as pointed out, for example by Steve Platt, "Sanctions Don't Harm Saddam," *New Statesman & Society*, Vol. 7 (November 4, 1994), p. 10.

[21] French Beaujolais wine, according to one report in *The New York Times*, lost many markets in a boycott of French products to protest against French nuclear tests in the Pacific. Markets lost included not only the Pacific nations of Japan, Australia, and New Zealand, but also the Netherlands, Scandinavia, and Germany. See *The New York Times*, (November 17, 1995), Section A, p. 10.

[22] The Secretaries-General of the United Nations have been Trygve Lie (of Norway), Dag Hammarskjöld (of Sweden), U Thant (of Burma, now Myanmar), Kurt Waldheim (of Austria), Javier Pérez de Cuéllar (from Peru), Boutros Boutros-Ghali (from Egypt) and Kofi Annan (from Ghana).

[23] See Evan Luard, *The United Nations: How it Works and What it Does* (New York: St. Martin's Press, 1994), pp. 102–125.

[24] Brian Urquhart, "Selecting the World's CEO," *Foreign Affairs*, Vol. 74, No. 3 (May/June 1995) pp. 21–26.

[25] See John Bulloch and Harvey Morris, *The Gulf War: Its Origins, History and Consequences* (London: Methuen, 1989), p. 117 and 119.

[26] On the peace plan and ECOMOG's role, see the following news reports: "Peace Plan is Accepted by Liberians," *The New York Times* (August 20, 1995), Section A, p. 17 and "Eight-Nation African Force is Peacekeeping Model in War-Torn Liberia," *The Washington Post* (April 1, 1994), Section A, p. 26.

[27] For samples of attacks on M'bow in the Western Press, see *The Economist* (October 3, 1987), p. 48, and *Nature* (October 8, 1987), p. 472.

[28] See, for example, Adam Watson, "European International Society and its Expansion," in Hedley Bull and Adam Watson, (eds.), *The Expansion of International Society* (Oxford: Clarendon Press, 1985), pp. 13–32 and Ian Brownlie, "The Expansion of International Society: The Consequences for the Law of Nations," in Hedley Bull and Adam Watson, (eds.), *The Expansion of International Society*, pp. 357–369.

[29] John Stuart Mill, "A Few Words on Non-Intervention," in Mill, *Dissertations and Discussions*, Vol. 3 (London: Longmans Green Reader, 1867), pp. 153–158.

[30] Consult, for example, Karl Marx, *On Colonialism: Articles from the New York Tribune and Other Writings*, by Karl Marx and Friedrich Engels, (New York: International Publishers, 1972), pp. 81–87.

[31] See Karl Marx and Friedrich Engels, *Collected Works*, Vol. 6, (New York: International Publishers, 1976, p. 471.

[32] For a description of Menon's view of the Goa affair and Western reactions to the Indian action, see Michael Brecher, *India and World Politics: Krishna Menon's View of the World* (New York: Praeger, 1968), pp. 121–136.

[33] Guides to the UN's role in combating apartheid may be found in "The UN and Apartheid: A Chronology," *UN Chronicle*, Vol. 31 (September 1994), pp. 9–14; Newell M. Stultz, "Evolution of the United Nations Anti-apartheid Regime, *Human Rights Quarterly*, Vol. 13 (February 1991), pp. 1–23; and Ozdemir A. Ozgur, *Apartheid, the United Nations, & Peaceful Change in South Africa* (Dobbs Ferry, NY: Transnational Publishers, 1982).

[34] See, for example, Michael G. Schatzberg, *Mobutu or Chaos?: The United States and Zaire, 1960–1990* (Lanham, MD: University Presses of America/Foreign Policy Institute, 1991).

[35] See Ali A. Mazrui, "The Resurgence of Islam and the Decline of Communism," *Futures: The Journal of Forecasting and Planning*, Vol. 23 (April 1991), pp. 283–285.

[36] As stated by Vice President Al Gore on *Nightline*, December 1, 1995. Also see *The New York Times* (December 5, 1995), Section A, p. 7.

[37] See, for example, Carroll J. Doherty, "Dole Takes a Political Risk in Crusade to Aid Bosnia," *Congressional Quarterly Weekly Report*, Volume 53 (March 11, 1995), pp. 761–763.

[38] See, Samuel S. Kim, *China, The United Nations, and World Order* (Princeton, NJ: Princeton University Press, 1979).

[39] UN, *Yearbook of the United Nations, 1974* (New York: UN, 1977), pp. 189–251.

[40] On the NIEO, consult, for example, Pradip K. Ghosh, (ed.), *New International Economic Order: A Third World Perspective* (Westport, CT: Greenwood Press, 1984).

[41] See Lawrence S. Finkelstein, "The Political Role of the Director-General of UNESCO," in Finkelstein, (ed.), *Politics in the United Nations System*, pp. 385–423.

[42] On the bombing, see *The New York Times*, (Tuesday, November 14, 1995), Section A, p. 1.

[43] An evaluation of the literature, in the 1990s, may be found in James Lee Ray, *Democracy and International Conflict: An Evaluation of the Democratic Peace Proposition* (Columbia, SC: University of South Carolina Press, 1995). Also, several leading scholars on this subject, such as Bruce Russett, Christopher Layne, David Shapiro, and Michael W. Doyle, assessed the state of the field in their contributions to the *International Security*, Vol. 19 (Spring 1995) issue on this topic.

[44] Huntington, "The Clash of Civilizations?," p. 39.

[45] Witness the airlift of the "Falasha Jews" from Ethiopia, detailed in Ruth Gruber, *Rescue: The Exodus of the Ethiopian Jews* (New York: Atheneum, 1987).

[46] For a critical account of the mediation, see Mohammed H. Malek and Mark F. Imber, "The Security Council and the Gulf War: A Case of Double Standard," Chapter 4 in Mohammed H. Malek, (ed.), *International Mediation and the Gulf War* (Glasgow, Scotland: Royston, 1991).

[47] On the change, see "Zionism No Longer Equated with Racism," *UN Chronicle*, Vol. 29 (March 1992), p. 67.

[48] For a report on this incident, see *The New York Times* (December 3, 1988), Section A, p. 1.

CHAPTER SIX

BETWEEN THE PRE-DEMOCRATIC *UMMAH* AND THE POST-DEMOCRATIC UNITED STATES OF AMERICA

The countries of origin of most Muslim Americans are pre-democratic. Those societies have yet to achieve the following basic principles of democracy:

    i.   Accountable rulers
    ii.   Participatory electorate
    iii. An open society and the transparent economy
    iv. Basic social justice for groups and individuals

If I apply the term pre-democratic to a country like Pakistan, it is because I believe the country has the capacity to evolve into a full-fledged democracy in the years ahead.

On the other hand, a country which appears not to stand a chance of becoming a democratic system either this century or in the foreseeable future may be described simply as undemocratic rather than pre-democratic. Brunei or Saudi Arabia are undemocratic rather than pre-democratic.

Those Muslim countries which are pre-democratic in our special sense are in that condition because of one or more of the following impediments to democratization:

    a. Royalist Muslim States: Such countries have powerful monarchs exercising power. These include Saudi Arabia, Jordan, Brunei, Morocco, and the United Arab Emirates.
    b. Militarized Muslim States: Such countries are under *de facto* military rule either overtly or covertly. Among these are Syria (which is still experiencing armed conflict due to the pro-democracy uprisings), Algeria, and Sudan (from which South Sedan seceded).
    c. Authoritarian Muslim Regimes: These include Mali, Guinea, and possibly Indonesia.

   d. Weak Muslim States: These include Somalia and Afghanistan. Pakistan somewhat belonged to this category but has made a lot of progress recently, including the 2013 election which saw one democratically-elected government transfer power to another, and both Afghanistan and Somalia have made progress.

   e. Experimental Muslim Regimes: These include Malaysia, Senegal, Turkey, and those Emirates of Nigeria which have adopted the Shari'a.

But while most Muslim countries are either undemocratic or pre-democratic, and some Muslim countries are in transition to democracy (such as Egypt and Tunisia, after the Arab Spring), the United States is becoming post-democratic. Of the three branches of the American political system (the executive, the legislative, and the judiciary), only the executive branch has become more democratic in the twenty-first century. The executive branch is now headed by a Black President (something inconceivable in the twentieth century). Because the choice between Barrack Obama and Hillary Clinton as a possible Democratic candidate was so close, the United States gave signs that it was almost ready for a woman President (though long after at least four Muslim countries had had women Prime Ministers or Presidents—Pakistan, Bangladesh, Turkey, and Indonesia).

But while the executive branch of the American system has made progress in democratization in the twenty-first century, the judiciary and the legislative are relapsing into negative post-democracy. The judiciary's behavior in the case of Bush vs. Gore in the year 2000 was worthy of a Third World-style corrupt Supreme Court. Five justices of the US Supreme Court subverted the system so that George W. Bush would win. The justices were so conscious of the subversion that they themselves explicitly declared their decision as not a precedent. This was post-democratic.

Since then, the Supreme Court of the United States has negated decades of precedents which were legally regulating the role of money in elections. The Supreme Court has now legitimized a freewheeling use of money by American corporations and rich individuals to influence elections. This new additional empowerment of the rich is fundamentally post-democratic.

Additionally, Miranda rights were supposed to protect a suspect in the process of law enforcement. The US Supreme Court diluted those rights in the year 2010 and increased the power of the police—again, throwing out decades of established legal practice: "You have the right to remain silent." This is another case of post-democratic deterioration.

But it is not only the judiciary that has been democratically degenerating. The Congress of the United States is more paralyzed by partisanship than it has been for over one hundred years. The requirement of sixty votes instead of a simple majority in the Senate has now become applicable to many decisions—instead of being a rare occurrence.

Studies indicate that since the election of a Black President in the United States, polarization between the two political parties has reached paralyzing proportions reminiscent of America in the nineteenth century. This is another measurement of a post-democratic trend.

While the election of a Black President of the United States has been a major step forward in the process of democratizing the US executive branch, the same election has worsened the democratic quality of the legislature, paralyzing it further. And the US judiciary is moving further and further away from the old Warren Court standard of social justice.

Democracy and Political Decay

In a seminal article entitled "Political Development and Political Decay" published in *World Politics* (Princeton, NJ) in April 1965, the late Samuel Huntington argued that premature political modernization caused political decay rather than political development. Premature modernization included efforts to mobilize the population at election time when the political institutions were still not strong enough to sustain the disproportionate political participation. Networking under the discipline of the clock has not always been efficient.

Modern political institutions are intended to maximize the account-ability of the rulers and to optimize the political involvement of the ruled. Postcolonial enthusiasm and charismatic mobilization put undue stress on weak institutions. Hence Huntington's conclusion that this kind of modernizing the political process resulted in decay rather than development.

Huntington was referring to underdeveloped countries which were essentially (in my lexicon) premodern. Development in their case was definable as capacity-building to sustain a democratic order. Modernization in their case was a quest for greater rationality, greater technical efficiency, and a more knowledge-intensive political process. In the context of Huntington's model, a premature quest for either greater rationality, greater efficiency, or greater knowledge-intensity could make it more difficult to sustain the pursuit of a stable democracy.

Political decay in developing societies occurs when the process of democratization is stalled, interrupted, or even reversed. What Huntington never addressed in that seminal article was whether a society which had already been democratic for generations, if not centuries, could still be liable to political decay. Was democracy in advanced countries reversible or subject to a serious relapse?

I am addressing here the possibility of advanced countries becoming not only postmodern, but also (in my lexicon) post-democratic. Negative post-democracy is when an advanced political system does indeed relapse normatively or decay institutionally. Positive post- democracy arrives when there are signs of innovative governance superior in ethics and performance to liberal democracy as I have known it so far. It could also be a new moral stride forward superior to social democracy, indeed, as I have known it so far.

In his own influential article entitled "The End of History" published in 1989, Francis Fukuyama argued that the capitalist and democratic standards that the human race had already achieved were, to all intents and purposes, the final stage of the whole history of political economy. Those of us who rejected Fukuyama's notion of the end of history were, in fact, insisting that humanity's capacity to innovate and even reinvent itself should not be presumed to have dried up.

Winston Churchill had argued that democracy was the worst form of government, except for all the others.[1] But Winston Churchill did not know yet what "all the others" were. Nor are we as yet knowledgeable as to what new and superior methods of human governance may be around the corner in the march of global history.

What we do know already is that fully mature and well established democracies are subject to relapses and even potential reversals. Even if positive post-democracy (entailing an improved social order) has not yet arrived, we know that negative post-democracy (a declining ability to maintain modern democratic standards) is already at hand.

Political decay in developing countries is usually caused by factors in the wider civil society—such as disproportionate networking and political activism. But political decay in advanced countries is more often caused by excesses of those in power—civilian or military—rather than by civil society as a whole.

Ends and Means in Democracy

Let us now examine more fully the basics of modern democracy. Are the basics universal or culturally relative? It would make sense for the Muslim World to distinguish between fundamental rights and instrumental rights.[2] The right to vote, for example, is an instrumental right designed to help us achieve the fundamental right of government by consent. The right to a free press is an instrumental right designed to help us achieve the open society and freedom of information.

By the same token, I can distinguish in modern terms between democracy as means and democracy as goals. The most fundamental of the goals of democracy are probably four in number. Let us recapitulate. First, to make the rulers accountable and answerable for their actions and policies. Secondly, to make the citizens effective participants in choosing those rulers and in regulating their actions. Thirdly, to make the society as open and the economy as transparent as possible. And fourthly, to make the social order fundamentally just and equitable to the greatest number possible.[3] This is not the democracy of ancient Greece, but is an approximation of democracy married to modernity.

Accountable rulers, actively participating citizens, an open society, a transparent economy, and social justice—those are the most fundamental ends of democracy.

How to achieve these goals has elicited different means. In making the rulers more accountable, some democracies (like the United States) have chosen separation of powers (executive, legislative, and judiciary), and checks and balances, while other democracies (like the United Kingdom) have chosen the more concentrated notion of sovereignty of parliament. These are different means towards making the executive branch more accountable and answerable in its use of power. Is this democratic picture still valid? Is it alive and well?

In May 2010, the British Broadcasting Corporation (BBC) did a series of radio programs about whether democracy was out of date. Was democracy a system of values and institutions which had been overtaken by events? The BBC involved me in the project. I reflected on the fact that the 1970s witnessed an eruption of publications on postmodernism. The spectacular rise of Barack Obama raised the question of whether we had entered a post-racial age. The BBC and I wondered together whether we had now entered the post-democratic age.

As I mentioned earlier, current democratic problems include the massive partisan polarization in the United States, often paralyzing Congress; the excesses of the Tea Party intolerance and their denunciation of Barack Obama as Hitler and Stalin rolled into one; Greece as the mother of democracy is now reduced to being the mother of political extravagance and corruption, becoming the biggest of all threats to the Euro; England as the mother of Parliaments now was reduced to a coalition of opposites, Liberal Democrats and the Tories; Islamophobia has emerged as a child of Western democratic populism; Switzerland has banned minarets in a country which so far has a total of barely six minarets; France considers outlawing the Muslim veil and the hijab because such anti-democratic measures are nationally popular; the United States has come closer to tolerating torture than at any time in the last one hundred years; the United States is more comfortable with imprisoning suspects for years at Guantanamo Bay without access to their own lawyers and often without hope of early release.

Are all these factors part and parcel of a post-democratic Western World? Indeed, the Supreme Court of the United States, as I indicated, is in danger of becoming a post-democracy institution. The Supreme Court's decision of the year 2000 in favor of Bush and against Gore could have been made by a cynical Third World court. No wonder the Supreme Court was, as I mentioned earlier, embarrassed enough to declare its decision as not constituting a legal precedent.

The Supreme Court's decision in 2010 allowing unlimited use of money by companies in elections, and its decision in 2014 to give individuals the right to contribute money among several different candidates, is also (in our lexicon) post-democratic,

But while the Western World may be drifting towards a post-democracy era, most of the Muslim World, the *Ummah*, is still in a pre-democracy stage. Many Muslim elections are notoriously rigged. Muslim losers in national elections are seldom gracious.

I personally believe that the majority of Muslim countries—though still pre-democratic—stand a good chance of getting democratized. Most recently, Malaysia has led the *Ummah* in relatively successful democratization. But the real test is when an incumbent President, or an incumbent political party, allows itself to be voted out of office—not once, but at least twice. Turkey has met that requirement. Malaysia is still working its way towards democratic inclusiveness in a plural society.

Democracy Resistant Countries

But there are Muslim countries which are unlikely to be democratized before the second half of the twenty-first century, at the earliest, and more likely in the twenty-second century.

Particularly vulnerable are dual societies—countries where two rival ethnic groups account for the majority of the population. Such vulnerable countries include Iraq, which is ethnically dual between Arab and Kurd, and religiously dual between the Sunni and the Shi'a.

Another vulnerable category which may find democracy elusive is a country which has a long history of a nomadic lifestyle, and one which, in precolonial times, was a case of ordered anarchy. Ordered anarchy is a form of governance which relies more on consensus than on state coercion, and relies on rules rather than rulers. The best illustration of a precolonial ordered anarchy is, of course, Somalia. A combination of precolonial, colonial and postcolonial factors has made Somalia the worst case of a failed Muslim state.

Another undemocratic category of countries is almost the opposite of ordered anarchy. These are countries which were already states in precolonial times, and were often cases of ordered tyranny rather than ordered anarchy. They may have been dictatorial for centuries.

African countries of today which are mentioned by the same name in the Old Testament are Ethiopia, Egypt, and Libya—countries with a Biblical history of indigenous dictatorship long before European colonial rule. In the postcolonial era, it is almost certain that the pharaohic legacy of Egypt, and the dynastic legacy of Ethiopia has slowed down the democratization of these Old Testament states.

As for the relations between Christianity and Islam in Africa of today, both religions are expanding in numbers, and growing in influence. But can they coexist democratically and peacefully? Is this a threat to Nigeria's democratization?

On the other hand, Muslims in Senegal soon after independence repeatedly voted for a Christian President. This degree of ecumenical democracy has not been achieved in the Western World. No major Western democracy has ever elected either a Jew or Muslim for President. Joseph Lieberman, a distinguished Jewish Senator in the United States, trailed far behind in his bid for the Democratic Presidential nomination in the 2003–2004 primaries.

As for the distinguished nineteenth century British Tory Benjamin Disraeli, there is a general consensus that he would never have become Prime Minister of Great Britain in the nineteenth century had his dad, Isaac D'Israeli, not quarreled with his Synagogue of Bevis Marks, and then decided to have his children baptized as Christians.[4] After all, until 1858, Jews by religion were not allowed even to run for parliamentary elections in Britain, let alone become ministers.

Pre-democratic Nigeria has not yet developed a religiously rotating presidency like experimentalist Tanzania, as I have discussed in an earlier chapter. But there are some party advocates of a regionally rotating Nigerian presidency, alternating between the North and the South. Such regional alternation could, *de facto*, be a religious alternation of the Nigerian presidency.

Africa had no religious wars before the arrival of Islam and Christianity. But now that Africa has embraced its own Islam and Christianity, and in spite of being pre-democratic, some Africans are developing ecumenical attitudes toward religion which are far ahead of the rest of the world. The ecumenical spirit of Africa is a plus for democratization.

Most of the global *Ummah* did not have secular ideological wars either until the Cold War. The Cold War favored Muslim states whose foreign policies were either pro-Soviet or pro-Western. The Cold War was bad news for democracy even in the United States. Fear of communism after World War II made the United States almost pre-democratic.

Now the US fosters a war against terrorism. On the whole, this "war on terror" is also bad news for American democracy. The worsening American tilt to the right has unleashed post-democratic trends in the American experience.

Political Dualism: Ethnic and Regional

Let us now return to the dialectic between dual and plural societies. In the new sociology of underdevelopment, the real contrast to the plural society as a threat to the state is the dual society. The plural society endangers the state by having more sociological diversity than the political process can accommodate. Paradoxically, the dual society endangers the state by having less sociological differentiation than is needed for the politics of compromise. Democracy is caught in-between. It is to this understudied and even unrecognized category of the dual society that I must now turn.

As I grapple with new levels of identity disputes and ideological conflicts in the Muslim World, from Dacca to Dakar, from Baghdad to Beirut, I ought to, at least, try to identify which sociopolitical situations are particularly conflict-prone.

Quite a good deal of work has been done on the plural society in the Third World—the types of societies like Malaysia and Pakistan, which have a multiplicity of ethnic and linguistic groups and a plurality of political allegiances. What has yet to be explored adequately is the phenomenon of the dual society—a country whose fundamental divide is between two groups or two geographical areas. The state in a dual society is vulnerable in a different way from the state in a plural society. In a dual society, two ethnic groups may account for more than three quarters of the population.

Algeria is a dual society. So was the old Sudan. But they are dual societies in very different senses. Algeria is an ethnically dual society whose potentially fatal cleavage is between the majority Arab and the minority Berber. As I mentioned, Iraq is religiously dual between Sunni and Shi'a, as well as linguistically dual between Arabs and Kurds.

However, old Sudan is a regionally dual society divided between a more Arabized northern Sudan and a Christian-led South Sudan. But although Sudan is regionally dual, it is ethnically plural. Both Sudan and South Sudan are culturally diverse within themselves. Indeed, Darfur is a miniature dual society within the north.

Outside Africa, Cyprus is both regionally and ethnically dual between Christian Greeks and Muslim Turks. There is a stalemate hovering between partition and confederation, with the United Nations still trying to mediate. Czechoslovakia was also both ethnically and regionally dual between Czechs and Slovaks. In the post-communist era, the country has indeed partitioned itself into separate Czech and Slovak Republics. In effect, the state of the old Czechoslovakia has collapsed and split into two. Was this comparable to the Bengali-led East Pakistan and the Urdu-led West Pakistan between 1967 and 1971? The two halves of old Pakistan collapsed long before Czechoslovakia.

The most risky situations are not those involving a convergence of ethnic duality and regional (territorial) duality, as in Cyprus or Czechoslovakia. It is true that when the two ethnic groups are concentrated in separate regions, it increases the risk of territorial or political separatism and secession. But, in human terms, that may not be the worst scenario. This is still pre-democratic, but not fundamentally undemocratic.

The most risky form of duality is that of pure ethnic differentiation without territorial differentiation. This can be dangerously undemocratic. These would be two groups physically intermingled. The religious inter-mingling of Sunni and Shi'a in Iraq is one example. It means that there is no prospect of a Cyprus stalemate, keeping the ethnic groups separate but peaceful. It also means that there is no prospect of Czechoslovakia's "gracious parting of the ways"—creating separate countries. Rather, the two groups are so intermingled in neighborhoods, at times so intermarried, (like Shi'a and Sunni in Iraq) that a soured ethnic relationship is an explosive relationship. Such political dualism can be more than a condition: it can be an agony. Can such a country be democratized?

Although only minority Muslim, Rwanda and Burundi fall into that category—ethnic duality without regional duality. The two groups are intermingled from village to village, certainly from street to street. Rwanda also happens to be the most densely populated country on the African continent (estimated 210 persons per square kilometer before the genocide in 1994—or, about 540 persons per square mile). Can Rwanda ever be truly democratized? Is it pre-democratic or fundamentally undemocratic?

Ethnic duality without regional separation can be a prescription for hate in close quarters. Algeria combines Arab intermingling with some territorial Berber areas. Rwanda's and Burundi's tragedies are a combination of ethnic duality, population density, geographic intermingling, and the legacies of colonial and precolonial relationships.

Northern Ireland is also a case of ethnic duality (Protestant and Catholic) with considerable intermingling within the North. There is no question of partitioning the North itself into a Catholic sector to be united with the Irish Republic and a Protestant section loyal to the United Kingdom. A second Irish partition is not in the cards, not least because the population of the North is too geographically intermingled for another partition. Intercommunal hate is therefore immediate and at close range, in spite of hundreds of years of Irish liberalism.

Is Sri Lanka on the Indian Ocean also a dual society, with the two biggest groups being the majority Sinhalese and the minority Tamils? The population is intermingled to a substantial extent—but the Tamil Tigers rebel group waged a long war for a separate Tamil homeland in pre-dominantly Tamil areas. Militarily, the country faced a stalemate until 2009. Has Sri Lanka now become democratizable?

Ethnically dual societies are vulnerable to the risk of polarization. This includes Nilotic and Great Lakes countries in Eastern Africa. The absence of potential mediating coalitions through other groups makes the Rwandas and Burundis of this world more vulnerable than ever to periodic ethnic convulsions. These societies have cultural frontiers without territorial frontiers—a dual identity within a single country, a society at war with itself. Democratization becomes more elusive than ever.

Sudan was also a country at war with itself, but its duality was regional rather than ethnic, which resulted in the secession of the South in 2011. As I indicated, both northern and southern Sudan are multiethnic, but the South is distinctive by being culturally more indigenous, less Islamized, and led in the main by Christianized Sudanese. There was a civil war between the two regions between 1955 and 1972, ending with the Addis Ababa accords of the latter year. In 1983, a second Sudanese civil war broke out, and raged for almost two more decades. Both civil wars created hundreds of thousands of refugees and displaced persons. Underdevelopment was more deeply aggravated in terror and tears. More recently, there has been the more localized civil war in Darfur. There is also the wider paradox that while the Sudanese South is more Christianized than the North, the North is more modernized than the South—if only infrastructually!

The First Sudanese Civil War (1955–1972) was more clearly secessionist. The Southern rebels wanted to pull out of Sudan and form a separate country (the Bangladeshi solution of outright secession). The Second Sudanese Civil War had been more ambivalent about secession. Indeed, a southern military leader, the late Colonel John Garang, had emphasized that he stood for a democratization of the whole of Sudan rather than for southern secession. The South chose to secede early in 2011 in a referendum. There may continue to be some nation-wide intermingling between southerners and northerners even after separation, but on a more modest scale.

Muslims in Rwanda tried to remain out of the 1994 conflict. Nevertheless, the speed of killing in Rwanda in April and May 1994 was much faster than almost anything witnessed in the Sudanese civil wars— some two hundred thousand people were killed in Rwanda within barely a two-week period. "There are no devils left in Hell," declared the cover title to the May 1994 issue of the American news magazine *Time*, "They are all in Rwanda."[5] More were killed later. A third of the population of the country was subsequently displaced or dislocated.

Of course, the state has not collapsed in Khartoum, though at times it has had no control over parts of the South or the West. Secondly, unlike the Rwandan national army, the Khartoum national army had not been seeking out helpless civilians for slaughter from refugee camps to hospitals. However, over the long run, both civil wars have indeed been very costly in human lives and human suffering. Sudan has more or less found a solution to its violent dualism. Its split cultural personality between north and south has so far been more divisive than its split ethic personality among diverse tribes and clans. Was Sudan pre-democratic? Or was it hopelessly undemocratic? The answer hangs in the balance.

The dual society continues to cast its shadow over the Muslim World—from Lebanon (Shi'a vs. Sunni) to Algeria (Arab vs. Berber), from Nigeria (north vs. south) to the tensions of Karachi and Khartoum. The sociology of underdevelopment continues to express itself in a split personality.

While the Pakistan of 1947 was a case of both ethnic and territorial dualism (Bengali vs. Others) and Burundi as well as Rwanda are cases of ethnic dualism (Tutsi vs. Hutu) without territorial dualism, Yemen has been a case of territorial dualism (north vs. south) without significant ethnic dualism. Is the distinction between the self-styled Republic of Somaliland and the rest of Somalia a case of territorial dualism without ethnic dualism (as in the case of Yemen)? Or is there sub-ethnic dualism between the two parts of Somalia which make it more like the case of Cyprus (Greek–Cypriot vs. Turkish–Cypriot), both ethnically distinct and territorially differentiated? Alternatively, the two parts of Somalia may be an intermediate category of dualism, equally prone to internecine conflict. The question continues to persist whether such dual societies are truly democratizable. Somaliland may be pre-democratic, but the rest of Somalia is hopelessly undemocratic.

The shadow of the United States is cast over all these Muslim states— sometimes for the better, but often for the worse. As America becomes more post-democratic, its international power may become even more dangerous. The struggle continues between the largely pre-democratic *Ummah* and the ominously post-democratic United States of America.

Conclusion

I have tried to demonstrate that while most of approximately fifty Muslim countries in the world are politically pre-democratic, the United States is deteriorating into a post-democratic condition. A Muslim country is pre-democratic if it has never been a full democracy, but stands a good chance of evolving into one. On the other hand, the United States is drifting towards a post-democratic condition after generations of relatively stable, even if flawed, democratic order.

But how can the United States be said to be democratically deteriorating when it has elected its first Black President—Barack Obama—and came nearer to having a woman Presidential candidate—Hillary Clinton—of a major party than at any time in history?

I acknowledge that the executive branch of the American system has become almost post-racial rather than post-democratic. The election of Barack Obama to the US Presidency was a significant step forward in democratic inclusiveness.

On the other hand, the other two branches of American government (the legislative and the judiciary) have become less and less democratic. Congress is more paralyzed today than it has been for more than a hundred years. Partisanship is almost at an all-time high, and the filibuster has almost totally replaced the principle of majority vote in the US Senate. The growth of the so-called Tea Party has introduced forms of fanaticism which sometimes threaten armed revolution against the Obama administration. Political candidates have openly threatened "Second Amendment Methods"—the use of guns—if they lose future elections. This rhetorical extremism has been indirectly supported by the insensitivity of the current Supreme Court which has further legitimized possession of guns as a Constitutional right more than ever before in the history of the Second Amendment.

Although eligibility for being elected to the US Presidency has been deracialized and heavily degenderized, what the executive branch concretely does in actual policy remains painfully post-democratic. Barack Obama has not closed down the Guantanamo Gulag, nor has he released dozens of suspects who have been languishing without trial for years.

Again, in spite of Obama's rhetoric, there is reason to believe that torture is still occurring under US jurisdiction or with American complicity in Third World countries.

Obama's use of unmanned flying machines (drones) to bomb areas of Pakistan has become much worse than such technological acts of terrorism perpetrated under George W. Bush. Dozens of innocent people have been killed. This method of warfare has been entrusted to the Central Intelligence Agency (CIA) rather than to the US Armed Forces directly. This unmanned covert warfare has not been subject to the democratic oversight of any Congressional committee whatsoever. It is a form of an unsupervised system of technological assassinations committed by the Obama Administration in a blood-letting form of post-democratic foreign policy. The Obama Administration is, indeed, still fundamentally militaristic in foreign policy.

The US executive branch has become democratic at the time of election but has continued to be tyrannical in some of its actions in office after the election.

With regard to the countries constituting the Muslim *Ummah*, a few are almost inherently undemocratic rather than pre-democratic. The latter stand a chance of self-democratization; but the almost inherently undemocratic are unlikely to be democratizable for at least another hundred years.

The different Muslim regimes which are resistant to democratization include those which are still monarchical, for example, Saudi Arabia, those which are under some kind of military rule, for example, Sudan, Libya, and Syria, those which culturally come from a tradition of little or no government, for example, Somalia and Afghanistan, those which are as old as the Biblical Old Testament and have had centuries of dictatorship, for example ex-pharaohic Egypt and post-dynastic Ethiopia, and those which have been experimenting with alternative models of democracy, for example, Turkey and Malaysia.

All these have experienced impediments to democratization stemming from the history of governance in those countries—pre-democratization at the elite level. But there are also societal (rather than elite) obstacles to democratization. I have paid special attention to Muslim societies which are ethnically or linguistically dual (Arab vs. Kurd), or religiously dual (Shi'a vs. Sunni, or Muslim vs. Christian) and, thirdly, Muslim countries which are regionally dual (like East and West Pakistan from 1947 to 1971; or North and South Sudan). These are societal rather than elite impediments.

Finally, I have distinguished between negative post-democracy (when a long-established democracy tolerates more and more injustice, as the United States has been doing) and positive post-democracy (when the human mind at last succeeds in inventing a more ethical moral order than either liberal democracy or social democracy).

One scenario is a future evolution of the best that Islam has to offer to the human condition in terms of values, on one side, and, on the other side, the best that democracy in the West and in the rest of the liberalized world has demonstrated in terms of the ethics of politics and of public order.

Perhaps much of the Muslim World will succeed this century in evolving from pre-democracy to full-fledged democratic standards. And perhaps the United States will put the brakes on the drift towards post-democracy and return to its historic role as a beacon of high expectations and wide democratic inclusiveness.

Notes

[1] See Winston Churchill's House of Commons Speech of November 11, 1947.
[2] For a discussion on fundamental rights, see Milton R. Konvitz, *Fundamental Rights: History of a Constitutional Doctrine* (New Brunswick, NJ: Transaction Publishers/Rutgers University, 2001).
[3] For a historical overview of democracy, consult Roland N. Stromberg, *Democracy: A Short, Analytical History* (Armonk, NY: M. E. Sharpe, 1996) and for a contemporary view, see Anthony H. Birch, *Concepts and Theories of Modern Democracy*, 2nd ed. (London and New York: Routledge, 2001 Edition). For more specific comments on African democracy, consult Obioma M. Iheduru, (ed.), *Contending Issues in African Development: Advances, Challenges and the Future* (Westport, CT: Greenwood Press, 2001), and Teodros Kiros, with a Preface by K. Anthony Appiah, *Explorations in African Political Thought: Identity, Community, Ethics* (New York: Routledge, 2001), and for a cultural approach, see Daniel T. Osabu-Kle, *Compatible Cultural Democracy: The Key to Development in Africa* (Peterborough, Ont. and Orchard Park, NY: Broadview Press, 2000), a chapter on Kenya may be found on pp. 149–162.
[4] See Todd M. Endelmann, "Benjamin Disraeli and the Myth of Sephardic Superiority," in Todd M. Endelman and Tony Kushner, (eds.), *Disraeli's Jewishness* (London; Portland, OR: Vallentine Mitchell, 2002), p. 34, and Bernard

Glassman, *Benjamin Disraeli: The Fabricated Jew in Myth and Memory* (Lanham, MD: University Press of America), pp. 35–36.

[5] This was a quote from a Christian missionary who witnessed the carnage in the Central African country which *Time* decided to use over a picture of a Rwandese mother holding her baby at a refugee camp near Ngara, Tanzania. See *Time*, Vol. 143, No. 20, May 16, 1994, cover page and pp. 56–63. See also "Rwanda Civilian Slaughter" *Africa Confidential*, Vol. 35, No. 9 (6 May 1994), pp. 5–6, and "Rwanda: A Double Agenda" *Africa Confidential*, Vol. 35, No. 10 (20 May 1994), p. 8, and "Rwanda: From Coup to Carnage," *Africa Confidential*, Vol. 35, No. 8 (15 April 1994), p. 8, and "Streets of Slaughter," *Time*, Vol. 143, No. 17 (April 25, 1994), pp. 45–46, and "Rwanda: All the Hatred in the World," *Time*, Vol. 143, No. 24 (June 13, 1994), pp. 36–37.

CHAPTER SEVEN

IS ISTANBUL A SECULAR JERUSALEM?
LESSONS FROM ATATÜRK
AND TAHRIR SQUARE

The pro-democracy crisis in Syria has drawn attention not only to the Syrian version of The Arab Spring, but also to Syria's neighbors. Turkey has been particularly important not only as a refuge for Syria's opposition on the run, but also as a base for democratic forces in the region.

The Turkish city which has been most relevant for these democratic trends has been Istanbul. For a long time Istanbul has been a center for region-wide civilizing forces. What has happened more recently is the emergence of Istanbul as a center for region-wide democratizing forces, as well as civilizing influences.

A Tale of Two Centers of Civilization

Istanbul is a particularly appropriate city to host architects of change in global values. Diverse civilizations have interacted with each other in Istanbul across the centuries. Greeks, Romans, Byzantines, and the Ottomans held sway in Istanbul across different centuries. The Atatürk Revolution between the two world wars weakened Islamic civilization, but planted the seeds for democratization.

If Jerusalem is a point of convergence of different religions, Istanbul is a point of convergence of different civilizations. It may be too early for Jerusalem to assume the role of peacemaker among religions, but it is not too early for Istanbul to become a force for peace among civilizations. Has Istanbul already become a secular Jerusalem? The new democratic forces in Istanbul have added to the progressive agenda of the city.

The histories of the two cities have points in common. Historically, Jerusalem had been a sacred ground of rivalry and contestation between and among the three Abrahamic traditions.

The Crusades sometimes united Muslims and Jews on one side against European Christians on the other. On their way back from one of the Crusades, some Western Christians invaded fellow Christians in Constantinople—and devastated life, limb, and lands. The Orthodox Church of Byzantine nursed a grievance against the Roman Catholic Church right into the twentieth century.

Under the Ottoman Empire, conflict in the Holy Land declined dramatically and the Ottoman millet system permitted considerable autonomy to Jews and Christians as they lived under Muslim jurisdiction.

Jerusalem has continued to be a sacred city to followers of Moses, of Jesus, and of Muhammad. Unfortunately, the creation of the state of Israel, and the Israeli conquest of Jerusalem in the 1967 War, have reactivated the role of Jerusalem as a trigger of conflict rather than a symbol of peace.

Like Jerusalem, Constantinople (alias Istanbul) has in the past been the headquarters of major religious traditions. Under Byzantine and under the Ottomans, Constantinople had a special status for Orthodox Christianity. The Ottomans also hosted the Caliphate until Mustafa Kemal Atatürk unilaterally abolished it in the 1920s.

Even under the Turkish Republic, Istanbul has been the headquarters of the Greek Orthodox Church, though relations between church and state have not always been smooth.

Like Jerusalem, Istanbul (or Constantinople) has in the past been a sacred trigger of contestation and war. Western books refer to the fall of Constantinople to the Muslim conquerors in the fifteenth century (1453). Muslims refer to the same conquest as the spiritual liberation of Constantinople.

But in recent centuries, Istanbul has become less and less a trigger of religious conflict and more and more a meeting point of both sacred and secular cultures.

Fifty years after the death of Mustafa Kemal Atatürk, Istanbul had become more peaceful than Israeli-occupied Jerusalem. Istanbul had become a secular Jerusalem but more peaceful. Istanbul is a synthesis of civilizations, while occupied Jerusalem remains a tense convergence of religions. When Lawrence of Arabia published his book *Seven Pillars of Wisdom*, Ottoman-friendly Turks were disgusted by Lawrence's prejudices. But Lawrence did not coin the phrase "Seven Pillars of Wisdom." T. E. Lawrence was aware of the words in the Book of Proverbs (IX: i):

Wisdom hath builded a house; she has hewn out her seven pillars.

Towards Modern Wisdom

We now need new modern pillars whether they be seven or ten, or fewer than either. But modern pillars of wisdom may simply entail reinterpreting ancient lessons. When the Prophet Muhammad conquered Mecca from the ruling Quraysh in the year 630 CE, the Prophet showed magnanimity in triumph. He and thousands of his followers entered Mecca without shedding any blood. He did not issue cards of the fifty most wanted Quraysh. He did not imprison thousands as some conquerors have done. The Prophet Muhammad conquered Mecca, granted amnesty to all Meccans who entered the sacred mosque for asylum, stayed peacefully in their homes, or found their way to the home of the paramount Quraysh leader, Abu Sufyan—Muhammad's former enemy. This was magnanimity in triumph.

And the Qur'an urged Muslims not to nurse ancient grievances even if Muslims had been unjustly robbed in the past. In chapter two, Surat al Baqara, the Qur'an recommends compensation and forgiveness as a better alternative to revenge or collective punishment. Surah 2, verse 149, asserts the following:

> Kind words and the forgiving of faults are better than charity followed by injury.

The Islamic calendar, *Hijrah*, subsequently was determined to start not when Muhammad was born in 570 CE, nor when he first received sacred revelation in 610 CE, nor when he died in 632 CE, but when he migrated from Mecca to Medina in 622 CE. The whole Islamic calendar is therefore a celebration of asylum as a gesture of territorial magnanimity.

Another pillar of ancient wisdom worthy of modern interpretation is the Qur'an's salute to ethnic diversity and the spirit of internationalism.

> Oh people!
> We have created you from male and female, and fashioned you into nations and tribes, that you may know each other, and learn from each other. Surely the best among you are [not that tribe or that nation], but the best are the most pious among you.

Muhammad embraced a black man of Ethiopian origin—Bilal bin Rabah—into one of his closest disciples, and the first muaddhin, muezzin, to call believers to prayer upon the spiritual conquest of Mecca by the Muslims.

Was Muhammad thinking of Bilal when, upon Muhammad's farewell pilgrimage, the Prophet reaffirmed the following: "An Arab is not superior to a non-Arab, nor a red man to a black man except through piety and virtue."

Lawrence of Arabia did not do justice to the concept of Seven Pillars of Wisdom. But modern Istanbul could reformulate modern pillars of wisdom, partially based on ancient insights and sacred values.

Although Istanbul is a secular Jerusalem, it should be ready to borrow wisdom from both science and religion, from both Einstein of yesterday and Abraham of ancient times.

Finally, a word about gender issues as well as ethnicity in the context of democratization. If Turkey has had a woman Prime Minister long before the Arab World has broken through that ultimate gender-barrier, does that mean that Turkey is ahead of the Arab World in gender democracy and civilized gender relations?

On the other hand, if the Arab World has had Black Presidents and Black Prime Ministers long before Turkey has broken through that ultimate racial barrier, does that mean that the Arab World is ahead of Turkey in pursuit of a post-racial social order?

Both Egypt and the Arabian Peninsula have produced rulers who are parentally 'black' in the Barack Obama sense—a ruler whose one parent is a black African, as in the case of Anwar Sadat.

In reality, both Turkey and the Arab World need more scientific measurements of both interracial democratic performance and intergender democratic performance than can be provided by an isolated Turkish woman ruler like Tansu Çiller, or by an isolated Afro-Arab President like Anwar Sadat. Nevertheless, Istanbul as a convergence of civilizations will have observed contradictions as well as similarities between civilizations.

Should the fact be more advertised that five Muslim countries have produced five women Presidents or Prime Ministers long before the United States has elected a woman President, before Italy has elected a woman Prime Minister, or before modern Russia has produced a woman Head of State? Turkey has now joined the ranks of Pakistan, Bangladesh, Senegal, and Indonesia as Muslim countries which have permitted women to reach the pinnacle of power.

Ancient Jerusalem is already in the shadow of one great lady of the past who is revered in the sacred scriptures of both Christianity and Islam. This great lady who breathed the air of Jerusalem was, of course, the Virgin Mary. Israel more recently has a record of a woman Prime Minister, Golda Meir.

Istanbul as the new secular Jerusalem is already in the process of producing great female Istanbulis. The men are conceding space for them.

The stream of civilization meanders on
In the vast expanse of the valley of Time
The new is come, the old is joined,
And people abide a changing clime.

Lessons from Atatürk and Tahrir Square

The most spectacular example of democratizing a Muslim society from above is still the case of the Atatürk Revolution of the 1920s and 1930s. On the other hand, the most spectacular twin cases of trying to democratize a Muslim society from below are, firstly, the popular uprising which overthrew President Zein al-Abidine Ben Ali in Tunisia in January 2011 and, secondly, the popular Tahrir Square Revolution in Cairo which succeeded in ousting President Mohammed Hosni Mubarak of Egypt by February 11, 2011.

Mustafa Kemal Atatürk asked himself in the interwar years "Can we liberally democratize without culturally Westernizing?" Mustafa Kemal regarded it as a trade-off. For all intents and purposes, Kemalism regarded cultural Westernization as a precondition for liberal democratization and scientific modernization.[1]

One of the greatest paradoxes of the Atatürk Revolution was that Atatürk brilliantly saved the political independence of Turkey, and then proceeded to sacrifice the cultural authenticity of his country. Kemalism had reached the conclusion that there had to be a trade-off between political autonomy and cultural authenticity.

Atatürk was not ashamed of acknowledging that liberal democracy was a Western invention. Turkey therefore had to become as Western as possible in its way of life if it was to be democratic in terms of politics and governance.

The most obvious step towards Kemalist Democracy was first and foremost the abolition of the monarchy or sultanate, which occurred in 1922.[2] The Sultan fled the country on board a British vessel.[3] The Turkish Republic was established a year later towards the end of October 1923.[4]

An opportunity was missed for creating a sovereign Muslim Vatican in a small territory, as the Ottoman Empire disintegrated. The Caliphate had been the nearest approximation to a Muslim Papacy. A small territory could have been created with absolute sovereignty of its own, and a new method could have been devised for electing a new Caliph when the previous incumbent died—the equivalent of a Council of Cardinals in the Roman Catholic Church.

Unfortunately, this supreme opportunity of creating a sovereign Muslim Vatican was squandered away in the 1920s. The Caliphate was abolished on March 3rd, 1924.[5]

Just as Italy has been a secular state in spite of having a sovereign Vatican next to Rome, Turkey could have been a secular state even if it saved the Caliphate with its own separate jurisdiction. But it was not to be. Mustafa Kemal saved the sovereign independence of Turkey but terminated the Caliphate once and for all.

Turkey's democratization from above was simultaneously Turkey's Westernization from above. It was also Turkey's secularization and democratization. These three processes were undertaken step-by-step—Westernization, secularization, and democratization.

The year after the abolition of the Caliphate was also the year when public activities of religious sects were banned.[6] The dress culture of Turks was compulsorily secularized.[7] Wearing religious attire in 1924 was restricted to sanctuaries, monasteries, and Mosques.[8]

Steps were also taken to make secular law and jurisprudence supreme from 1926, thus marginalizing much of the Shari'a in the lives of ordinary Turks, in spite of their being Muslim.[9]

Dress culture of ordinary folks was also directly affected in 1926 when the Turkish Fez was discouraged and the European hat promoted.[10] It continued to be believed that democracy needed the soil of Westernization. In reference to individual names of Turks, Atatürk did not make the mistake of African societies. He avoided adopting Euro-Christian and Jewish names at the expense of indigenous Turkish ones.

However, Turkish nicknames were abolished—as were personal titles and Ottoman decorations like *Bey* and *Pasha*.[11] The Surname Law was also passed in 1934 in imitation of the European sequence of names, rather than imitating actual European names.[12] On November 24, 1934, Mustafa Kemal himself was given the surname of Atatürk—the father of the Turks.[13] The new name was supposed to be a gift from the Turkish people.

The Kemalist belief that liberal democracy needed the soil of the wider Western culture in order to thrive persisted. Turkey adopted the Western calendar in 1925[14] and the international metric system as early as 1931.[15]

The Kemalist Revolution tried to de-Arabize the Turkish language in vocabulary and alphabet as far as possible.[16] But with regard to numerals, the process of Europeanization was indistinguishable from Arabization.

After all, the numerals which Europeans use are called "Arabic numerals." Turkey Euro-Arabized its numerate culture in 1928.

Atatürk also invited the American Grand *Mufti* of liberal progressive education, John Dewey, to help reform Turkish schools in major cities and establish linkages between education and preparation for democracy.[17]

More directly relevant to democratization were Atatürk's ideas about empowering women in the political process. From 1926, the Kemalist Revolution started addressing the gender question—including the newly recognized eligibility of women to run for parliamentary elections and be elected to the national legislature.[18]

The belief persisted that liberal democratization required wider cultural Westernization. In 1928, the Roman alphabet for the Turkish language was introduced to replace the Arabic alphabet.[19] Institutions were also established to address the national history of Turkey rather than the history of the Ottoman Empire.[20] An institution was also established to monitor desired changes in the Turkish language.[21]

Because of the influence of the Qur'an, the Arabic language has been stabilized over a period of fourteen centuries.[22] On the other hand, because of the influence of the Kemalist Revolution, the Turkish language has changed beyond all recognition in less than a century.[23] Ottoman Turkish is almost a different language from the modern Turkish of the Republic.[24]

One big advantage of democratization from above is the fact that those who have abolished the old order are still there to create the new political order. Atatürk saved the sovereignty of the country, abolished the Sultanate, ended the Caliphate, and then introduced wide-ranging cultural changes in preparation for secularization, Westernization, and democratization. Mustafa Kemal Atatürk was President of Turkey from 1923 to 1938.[25] He died in office after fifteen years of neo-democratic and secular changes in Turkey.[26]

On the other hand, democratization from below is more effective in ending the old than in shaping the new one. The protesters in Tunisia in January 2011 and in Tahrir Square in Cairo in February 2011 ousted two Presidents who had been in power for decades. It was a dramatic achievement. But we still do not know how effective the protesters of Tunisia and Egypt will be in shaping the new future.

The major disadvantage of democratization from above is that even if the changes are genuinely democratic, it is often a case of guided democracy at best—and a case of imposed democracy at worst. Democratization from above begins by being an elitist democracy.

In the Turkish experience, a second disadvantage was appointing the Turkish army as the trustee and guardian of both Turkey's secularism and democracy.[27] For decades, the Turkish military held veto-power in both the general elections and on legislation.[28]

For the first time in the history of the Middle East, at least ten Arab countries have witnessed pro-democracy demonstrations in varying degrees of intensity.[29] The uprisings in Tunisia and Egypt have already resulted in ousting dictators who had been entrenched in power for decades. Libya witnessed a foreign intervention in its civil war for the favor of rebels against Muammar Gaddafi. In Syria, a fourth dictator's future is on the line. Other Arab countries may have to avert political collapse with preemptive reforms. Never in the history of the Arabs have there been so many popular uprisings which seem to be inspired neither by Islam nor by anti-imperialism but in the quest for liberal reforms.

Research institutes in Turkey should join the scholarly effort to try to understand both the probable causes and the likely consequences of the most remarkable democratizing political contagion since the collapse of the Soviet Union and the collapse of communism in Eastern Europe in the final decade of the twentieth century. A symposium in Istanbul "The Pro-democracy Arab Uprising of 2011" will almost certainly be followed by further research and publications, probably in both English and Arabic.

In recent years, political scientists have increasingly examined the hypothesis that mature democracies do not go to war against each other.[30] A future war between Germany and France or between Britain and Italy, is now inconceivable. The question therefore arises whether successful democratization in the Middle East would reduce the propensity for warfare in this volatile region of the world in future decades.

In the 1920s and 1930s, Mustafa Kemal Atatürk embarked on a long-term project of democratizing a Muslim society (post-Ottoman Turkey) from above. What the Arab World in the present day is struggling to achieve is the goal of democratizing Muslim societies from below. The long-term consequences may be of vital importance in relations between Israel and the Arabs, between the Muslim World and the United States, and between Islam and Western civilization.

Institutes in Istanbul are well-placed to participate in the relevant research and scholarship. This tradition has produced not only authors of relevant books and articles, it has also produced leaders in the Study of Islam and Democracy in Turkey, Presidents of Associations of Muslim Social Studies worldwide, and scholars who have been to almost every Arab country and met some of their leaders.

Istanbul's credentials are strong in the effort to promote greater understanding of this new phase in Arab history. Initiatives from Turkey are likely to be an important step forward.

Notes

[1] See B. Baskan, What Made Atatürk's Reforms Possible? *Islam and Christian-Muslim Relations*, Vol. 21, No. 2 (2010), p. 145.

[2] Ibid., p. 144.

[3] See E. J. Brill, *E. J. Brill's First Encyclopaedia of Islam: 1913–1936*. (E. J. Brill's First Encyclopaedia of Islam, 5–6.) (Leiden: E. J. Brill, 1993), p. 662.

[4] See D. A. Rustow, Atatürk as Founder of a State. *Daedalus*, Vol. 97, No. 3 (1968), p. 826.

[5] See J. Teitelbaum, "'Taking Back' the Caliphate: Sharīf Husayn Ibn 'Alī, Mustafa Kemal and the Ottoman Caliphate," *Die Welt Des Islams*, Vol. 40, No. 3 (2000), p. 423.

[6] See Baskan, (2010), p. 145.

[7] Ibid.

[8] See Y. Doğaner, "The Law on Headdress and Regulations on Dressing in the Turkish Modernization," *Bilig*, No. 51 (2009), p. 36.

[9] See Baskan, (2010), p. 145.

[10] See Doğaner, (2009), pp. 38–39.

[11] See R. L. Bayrer, *Free People, Free Markets: Their Evolutionary Origins* (Washington, DC: New Academia Pub. 2010), p. 352.

[12] See R. F. Spencer, "The Social Context of Modern Turkish Names," *Southwestern Journal of Anthropology*, Vol. 17, No. 3 (1961), pp. 205–207.

[13] Ibid., p. 206.

[14] See N. Berkes, *The Development of Secularism in Turkey* (Montreal: McGill University Press, 1964), p. vii.

[15] See S. Gopalan, A. Kavas, & R. Nelson, "Gaining a Perspective on Turkish Value Orientations: Implications for Expatriate Managers," in B. Maniam, (ed.), *Journal of International Business Research*, Vol. 4, No. 2 (2005), p. 46.

[16] See S. Ayata, "Patronage, Party, and State: The Politicization of Islam in Turkey," *The Middle East Journal*, Vol. 50, No. 1 (1996), p. 41.

[17] See J. Martin, *The Education of John Dewey: A Biography* (New York: Columbia University Press, 2002), p. 337.

[18] See Gopalan et al., (2005), p. 46.

[19] Ibid.

[20] G. S. Tahir, *The Politics and Poetics of Translation in Turkey, 1923–1960* (Amsterdam: Rodopi, 2008), especially pp. 57–58.

[21] Ibid., p. 57.

[22] As cited in the Encyclopedia Britannica, the Prophet Muhammad received the revelations in Arabic (from Allah through the angel Jibril) that formed the Qur'an in the cave of *Hira* from 610 to 629 CE; additionally, in 632 CE, the Prophet Muhammad died. Therefore, nearly fourteen centuries have traversed between this early period in the seventh century and the twenty-first century during which the Arabic language has been preserved and stabilized. Retrieved in 2011 from http://www.britannica.com/EB checked/topic/396226/ Muhammad

[23] For further reading on the Kemalist Revolution language reforms see F. Tachau, "Language and Politics: Turkish Language Reform," *The Review of Politics*, Vol. 26, No. 2 (1964), pp. 191–204; and Baskan, (2010), p. 147.

[24] Ibid.

[25] For further reading about the Presidential tenure of Mustafa Kemal Atatürk see Rustow, (1968), pp. 793–828.

[26] Ibid.

[27] For further reading on the role of the Turkish military as established during the Kemalist Revolution, see F. Tachau & M. Heper, "The State, Politics, and the Military in Turkey," *Comparative Politics*, Vol. 16, No. 1 (1983), pp. 17–33; and A. Perlmutter, "The Praetorian State and the Praetorian Army: Toward a Taxonomy of Civil-Military Relations in Developing Polities," *Comparative Politics*, Vol. 1, No. 3 (1969), p. 392.

[28] Ibid.

[29] These prodemocracy demonstration country sites include: Tunisia, Egypt, Libya, Syria, Yemen, Bahrain, Saudi Arabia, Algeria, Lebanon, and Jordan (others include: Iraq, Morocco, and Oman). For one compilation on the 2010–2011 prodemocracy demonstrations in Arab and non-Arab majority countries see CNN special "Unrest in the Middle," February 18, 2011.

[30] See S. P. Huntington, "Democracy for the Long Haul," *Journal of Democracy*, Vol. 7, No. 2 (1996), p. 6, and James Lee Ray's evaluation of the thesis in his *Democracy and International Conflict: An Evaluation of the Democratic Peace Proposition* (Columbia, SC: University of South Carolina Press, 1995). Also, several leading scholars on this subject, such as Bruce Russett, Christopher Layne, David Shapiro, and Michael W. Doyle, assessed the state of the field in their contributions to the International Security, Vol. 19 (Spring 1995) issue on this topic.

CHAPTER EIGHT

FROM BANDUNG TO BENGHAZI:
MUSLIM NATIONALISTS
IN COMPARATIVE PERSPECTIVE[1]

Although Indonesia is the most populous Muslim country in the world today, the country is seldom remembered for any major global event. However, one of its cities gave its name to what is arguably the most important conference of Afro-Asian solidarity in the twentieth century.

It was in April 1955 that Indonesia hosted the Bandung Conference, held in that beautiful city in the West Java Province. The three most populous Muslim countries at the time were Indonesia, Pakistan (which included what later became Bangladesh) and, paradoxically, India. These three countries were the major organizers of the Bandung Conference. As organizers, they were supported by Burma (later Myanmar) and Ceylon (now Sri Lanka).

The Bandung Conference as a whole was attended by twenty-nine countries, with a total population of more than half the inhabitants of planet-earth. The countries with large Muslim populations at Bandung accounted also for more than half of the global *Ummah*.

Africa at Bandung was represented primarily by Muslim Africa (Egypt, Libya, and Sudan). Much of the rest of Africa was still under colonial rule. Algeria was already at war with France in the struggle for independence. Nigeria was approaching independence more peacefully, but was surprisingly not invited to Bandung. Although the Gold Coast (later Ghana) did not become independent until two years after Bandung, Kwame Nkrumah was indeed invited to represent Sub-Saharan Africa at this Afro-Asian conference. Ethiopia and Liberia were also in attendance at Bandung.

The passionate debates at the conference focused on anticolonialism and global North–South relations at large. Indeed, when does "foreign rule" become "colonialism?" The conference even debated whether the Soviet Union was an imperialist power, and whether Soviet control of Eastern Europe and Central Asia was a form of colonialism.

Indonesia sought support in its dispute with The Netherlands. There were islands which were claimed by Jakarta, but which the Dutch regarded as neither ethnically Malay nor religiously Muslim. The Netherlands wanted those islands to be prepared for separate independence from Indonesia.

The Bandung Conference was silent about whether some of Indonesia's own territorial ambitions were themselves imperialistic. The Bandung participants did manage to reach consensus in a shared condemnation of colonialism in all its forms.

Was Communist China a threat to the independence of some of its neighbors? Prime Minister Chou En-Lai at the Bandung Conference was conciliatory towards the anti-communist countries. He assured them that China was an ally to the oppressed of the world, and did not covet other people's territory.

Bandung as a name became a symbol of Afro-Asian solidarity. A ten-point declaration was adopted at the end of the conference. The declaration encompassed some of the principles of the United Nation's Charter, as well as Jawaharlal Nehru's five principles of peaceful coexistence (Panchsheel). Krishna Menon, India's Foreign Minister, was later to be credited with the immortal formulation that "colonialism is permanent aggression."

In global stature, Muslim peers to Jawaharlal Nehru included Egypt's Gamal Abdul Nasser (prior to his nationalization of the Suez Canal) and Indonesia's own President Sukarno (with his new philosophy of guided democracy).

The international Muslim populations represented at Bandung were later to produce the first modern female rulers in Muslim history before the end of the twentieth century. Pakistan subsequently produced Prime Minister Benazir Bhutto, Indonesia itself produced Megawati Sukarnoputri, and what later became Bangladesh produced Begum Khaleda Zia and Sheikh Hasina Wajed. Turkey did produce a woman Prime Minister also, Tansu Çiller, in approximately the same period, but Turkey was not represented at Bandung.

Muslims in Regional Wars

Was the Bandung Conference of 1955 the antithesis of the Berlin Conference of 1885? The Berlin Conference of 1885, hosted by Bismarck, was an assembly of imperial powers of the West scheming on ways to colonize Africa. The Bandung Conference of 1955 (70 years after Berlin) was an assembly of the colonized countries and formerly colonized, scheming on how to defeat the remnants of colonialism.

A distinguished German figure—Otto von Bismarck—hosted the assembly of colonizers on the eve of the partition of Africa late in the nineteenth century. In 1955, a distinguished Indonesian figure—Sukarno —hosted the assembly of the colonized on the eve of the decolonization of Africa.

In 1855, most of Africa was still free—but about to be subjected to colonialism. In 1955, most of Africa was subjugated—but about to experience the winds of liberation.

The five years—1953 to 1957—were pregnant with great formative events concerning relations between the West and the developing world. 1953 witnessed the end of the Korean War—with a stalemate between the mighty power of the United States leading a United Nations "coalition of the willing," on one side, and communist North Korea supported by so-called "volunteers" from the People's Republic of China.

That the Korean War ended in a stalemate and a ceasefire rather than the defeat of North Korea was one of the early shifts in power between the mighty Northern Hemisphere and the much less developed Southern. The United Nations side in the Korean War included many Muslim soldiers.

The following year witnessed another great indicator that developing countries need not necessarily be on the losing side of global North–South conflicts. Events were unfolding which would constitute more than just a wind of change. A benign hurricane was about to shift the course of history.

The French colonizers of Vietnam were defeated by the Vietnamese in the Battle of Dien Bien Phu in 1954. The days of a French Empire in Asia were coming to an end. The Vietnamese militarily defeated the French twenty years before they defeated the Americans.

1954 was also the year when the Algerian War of Independence broke out. The same France which had been humiliated by the Vietnamese now faced the challenge of Muslim nationalists in Algeria.

But 1954 was also a year pregnant with fundamental changes for the African Diaspora. In Washington, DC, the US Supreme Court handed down its momentous decision regarding Brown vs. the Board of Education. The old racial doctrine of separate but equal was abandoned. Ironically, the Nation of Islam under Elijah Muhammad was expanding as a Black separatist movement.

But these different winds or hurricanes of change in 1954 had divergent consequences.

In the US, Brown vs. Board of Education of Topeka signified the beginning of the end of overt racial segregation in the country. The changes which followed not only made Black people freer but also made the United States more democratic. This favored the new Muslim immigrants, as well as others.

For Algeria, 1954 turned out to be truly ironic. The Algerian struggle for independence (1954–1962) not only helped Algeria to attain sovereignty but also helped France achieve greater stability.

Three years after Bandung (in 1958), France faced the risk of a civil war in the streets of Paris—not because Muslim nationalists from Algeria had come to France, but because the war in Algeria had precipitated a colossal crisis. The crisis eventually had the following consequences:

(a)   Charles de Gaulle ascended to power once again.
(b)   There was a constitutional change from unstable Fourth Republic to a more stable Fifth Republic.
(c)   De Gaulle asserted greater French independence from US leadership in the North Atlantic Treaty Organization (NATO).
(d)   De Gaulle accelerated the march of France into a nuclear power.
(e)   De Gaulle strengthened French power and influence in the European Economic Community (now European Union).

By fighting for their independence, Algerians transformed more than the history of Algeria—they impacted the history of France, Europe, and the world. North African Muslims were changing the history of the twentieth century.

The Vietnamese triumph at Dien Bien Phu in 1954 defeated France, but did not reunite Vietnam. The American phase of the war in Vietnam cost at least three million Vietnamese lives and nearly sixty thousand American lives. But Vietnam in the end illustrated that a poor and underdeveloped Asian country could militarily defeat a super power—the United States.

A decade later, a Muslim country illustrated that an even poorer underdeveloped country could defeat another superpower—the Soviet Union. Indeed the defeat of the USSR in poverty-stricken Afghanistan may have been the most important cause of the collapse of the Soviet Union.

The peoples of the Bandung legacy, when struggling for their independence, could dramatically change the course of global history. Another illustration was the anti-colonial struggle in Angola, Mozambique, Guinea-Bissau against Portuguese imperialism. By 1970, Portugal had become the most backward European country after Albania.

Throughout its modern history, Portugal had turned its back on every progressive force in European history.

Portugal resisted the Renaissance, the Enlightenment, the Reformation, the Industrial Revolution and the French and American Revolutions.

And then Africans fighting for their independence led to the collapse of the old Fascist order in Lisbon. These nationalists included the Muslims of Guinea (Bissau). Portugal lost the colonies and gained democracy, modernity, and European identity.

It remains to be seen whether the Taliban insurgency in Afghanistan will one day defeat the Americans in the same way as the North Vietnamese communists defeated the United States. After all, the Mujahideen in Afghanistan had defeated the old Soviet Union.

But what some of the descendants of Bandung have already demonstrated is yet another fundamental change. In the past when developing countries fought the West militarily, the blood was spilled on the soil of the developing countries.

As I indicated in a previous chapter, in Kenya, Mau Mau fought the British on Kenyan soil. Not a single Mau Mau shot was fired in London. Similarly, Angolans and Mozambicans fought the Portuguese—but blood was not spilled in Lisbon. Vietnamese fought the French in Dien Bien Phu—not in the Port of Marseilles. Malay communists fought against the British in the 1950s—but in the jungles of Malaya rather than the streets of Manchester.

In 1956, Britain and France invaded Port Said in Egypt and Israel invaded the Sinai. Once again, it was on the soil of the victim that blood was spilled. Indeed, Indonesian Muslims in the 1940s had fought the Dutch imperialists—but inevitably on Indonesian soil.

The Mujahideen in Afghanistan engaged the Soviets in the hills of Afghanistan—not in Leningrad or Moscow. The Americans killed and were killed in the jungles of Vietnam—not in the alleyways of Chicago or Washington, DC.

Again, what was remarkable about September 11, 2001, was that militants from the Third World had brought the battle into the heartland of the most powerful Western country in history. At the World Trade Center and at the Pentagon, the Empire was struck back in the capital of the Empire itself. Muslim militants under Al-Qaeda had declared war on a superpower.

In July 2005, the Pakistani Diaspora in London struck at the British railway infrastructure and killed people. Later in the same month, the Diaspora of the Horn of Africa also struck at London. Muslims from different geographical areas were counter-penetrating the citadels of power.

In Spain in 2004, the railway system in Madrid was hit seemingly by North African Muslims. The Moors—who had been expelled from Spain in the fifteenth century—were back in Madrid not as conquerors but as fighters. Between the global North and the global South a new equilibrium had been inaugurated—an equilibrium of mutual vulnerability.

But Africans, Asians, and the Diaspora have not always fought for their rights with lethal weapons. Other forms of resistance have been tried out by descendants of the Bandung Conference. The historian E. H. Carr was wrong in bracketing Gandhism and Christianity together as "doctrines of non-resistance."[2] What Gandhi provided to Black Nationalism was the element of resistance to the passivity of imperial Christianity. Carr was certainly wrong in extending the description of "boycott of politics" to Gandhism as well as to Christianity. If politics is an activity between groups rather than between individuals, then Gandhism was almost a politicization of Christian doctrine. As Martin Luther King, Jr., the African-American leader, put it:

> Prior to reading Gandhi, I had about concluded that the ethics of Jesus were only effective in individual relationships. The "turn the other cheek" philosophy and the "love your enemies" philosophy were only valid, I felt, when individuals were in conflict with other individuals... Gandhi was probably the first person in history to lift the love ethic of Jesus above mere interaction between individuals to a powerful and effective social force on a large scale...[3]

The Reverend Dr. King came to feel that Gandhism was "the only morally and practically sound method open to oppressed people in their struggle for freedom."[4] Gandhism in the 1940s had even been used to protect the Muslim minority of India.

It is, in fact, one of the curious things of history that, outside India itself, the torch of Gandhism came to be passed not to his fellow Asians, but to Blacks both in the New World and in Africa. It is not without significance that the first non-white winners of the Nobel Prize for Peace were Ralph Bunche, Chief Albert Luthuli, Martin Luther King, Jr., and Archbishop Desmond Tutu—two Black Americans and two Black South Africans. Later Black Nobel Laureates were Nelson Mandela, Wangari Maathai, Kofi Annan, Ellen Johnson Sirleaf, and Leymah Gbowee.

Perhaps Gandhi himself would not have been surprised. Quite early in his life he saw nonviolent resistance as a method which would be well-suited for the African as well as the Indian. In 1924, Gandhi said that if the Black people "caught the spirit of the Indian movement their progress must be rapid."[5]

In 1936, Gandhi went even further. And to understand his claim, one should perhaps link it up with something which was later said by his disciple, Jawaharlal Nehru. Nehru said: "Reading through history I think the agony of the African continent ... has not been equaled anywhere."[6]

But Africa includes Arab Africa. The first Muslim peace laureates in Africa were Egyptians—Anwar Sadat and Mohammed ElBaradei. They were peace-lovers but not passive resisters.

However, to the extent that the black man had more to be angry about than other men, he would need greater self-discipline than others to be 'passive' in his resistance. But by the same token, to the extent that the Black people in the last three centuries had suffered more than any other, passive but purposeful self-sacrifice for the cause should come easier to them. And to the extent that the Black people had more to forgive the rest of the world for, that forgiveness when it came should be all the more weighty. Perhaps in response to adding up these considerations, Gandhi came to the conclusion, by 1936, that it may be through the Negroes that the unadulterated message of nonviolence will be delivered to the world.[7]

In fact, it was not the torch of nonviolence which Africa has inherited: Africa has independently manifested a short memory of hate. Kenyatta proclaimed suffering without bitterness; Ian Smith in Zimbabwe was forgiven by his Black victims; Gowon pacified the Nigerian Civil War; and, finally, Nelson Mandela was magnanimous in South Africa. But what do I mean by Africa's short memory of hate? Hate-retention varies by culture. Armenians against Turks, the Irish against the English, and the Jews against Germans have long memories of grievance. Africa's short memory of hate has gone to the extent of trivializing its own entitlement to reparations for centuries of humiliation.

The Cooperative Factor:
From Afro-Asianism to Nonalignment

Almost all Muslim countries are either in Africa or Asia. Four interrelated political forces helped to bring Africa and Asia closer together in the twentieth century, at least for a while. One was the bond of being fellow victims of European racial and pigmentational arrogance (racial solidarity). Second was the bond of being fellow victims of European cultural and civilizational arrogance (cultural solidarity). Third was the bond of being fellow victims of actual and direct Western imperialism and colonization (anti-imperial solidarity). And fourth was the bond of attempted disengagement from the Cold War while it lasted (the solidarity of nonalignment).

The first two bonds (those of racial and cultural solidarities) resulted in historic Afro-Asian movements. The most famous indeed was the Bandung Conference in Indonesia in 1955 which brought together emerging leaders of the two continents in a shared struggle against Western hegemony.[8] More than half of the human race, and more than half the global *Ummah*, were represented at Bandung.

Clearly, racial and cultural solidarity were closely linked to the struggle against imperialism—the third of foundation of Afro-Asian solidarity. But, in time, imperialism was defined not simply as old-style territorial colonization and annexation by Europe, but also as continuing Western hegemony and control, including the powerful and ominous shadow of the United States on other countries. Other civilizations were threatened by Western hegemony, not least Islamic values and traditions.

But by this extended definition of imperialism, it was not merely Asia and Africa which had been dominated by the West. It was also Latin America. The concept of "the Third World" entered the vocabulary of international politics in the 1960s. The First World was the world of technologically-advanced capitalist countries economically led by the United States, Germany, and Japan. The First World was politically led by the United States, Britain, and France. The Second World, in much of the twentieth century, was the world of technologically-advanced socialist countries, led or dominated by the Soviet Union at the time, but encompassing also such healthier economies as that of Hungary and Czechoslovakia. (The Soviet Union has since disintegrated, and Czechoslovakia has split into Czech and Slovak Republics). The Soviet-dominated Second World included many millions more Muslims than did the First World.

The Third World was the world of developing counties in Africa, Asia, and Latin America—ranging from Brazil to Botswana, from Pakistan to Paraguay, from China to Chad. The People's Republic of China insisted on being regarded as part of the developing world rather than being associated with either the Warsaw Pact or with the status of a potential superpower. About fifty countries in this Third World were Muslim societies.

The extension of Afro-Asian solidarity to include Latin America had wide ramifications for the whole emerging paradigm of North–South relations in the global domain. It affected alliances in such United Nations fora as the United Nations Conference on Trade and Development (UNCTAD) and cooperation in the Uruguay Round, General Agreement on Tariffs and Trade (GATT) and the successor to GATT, the World Trade Organization.[9]

The expansion of Afro-Asian solidarity to encompass Latin America was also part of the foundation of the Non-Aligned Movement (NAM). However, it is worth remembering that the Non-Aligned Movement included a European component right from the start. Its first conference was indeed held in Belgrade, Yugoslavia, September 1–6, 1961. Other European members since then have included Cyprus and Malta.[10]

The purposes of the Non-Alignment Movement were originally inspired by a concern about the arms race between the North Atlantic Treaty Organization (NATO) and the Warsaw Pact. The original 25 members of the movement aspired to influence the world towards both disarmament and increasing decolonization. The original Muslim leaders of NAM included Sukarno of Indonesia, Gamal Abdel Nasser of Egypt, and others.

Over the decades, the Movement retained the ambition of pursuing "peace, achievement of disarmament, and settlement of disputes by peaceful means." It also remained committed to self-determination and independence "for all peoples living under colonial or alien domination and foreign occupation." But the Non-Aligned Movement also increasingly emphasized "sustainable and environmentally-sound development," the promotion of "fundamental rights and freedom" and the quest for strengthening "the role and effectiveness of the United Nations."[11]

Above all, the Non-Aligned Movement advocated "a transition from the old world order based on domination to a new order based on freedom, equality and social justice and the well-being of all."[12]

Africa and Asia remained the senior continents in the Movement and hosted most of the conferences to date. Indeed, until the mid-1990s only one conference had been hosted in Latin America—and that was the conference in Havana, Cuba, in 1979. Moreover, the largest country in Latin America, Brazil, had not been a member of the Non-Aligned Movement. On the other hand, in June 1994 the Movement admitted Africa's most industrialized and potentially most influential state on the world stage—the Republic of South Africa. Nigeria had also been a member since its independence in 1960. Nigeria had the largest concentration of Muslims in Africa.

Just as the Afro-Asian solidarity movement suffered from a crisis of *raison d'être* as old-style European colonialism came to an end, the Non-Aligned Movement started suffering from a similar crisis of ultimate purpose in the wake of the end of the Cold War. Some members went as far as to recommend the dissolution of the Movement now that the world is no longer endangered by East–West tensions. Other members, in response, have championed a refocus on North–South relations at the global level—asking the movement to seek three paramount objectives. These are, first, greater and healthier economic cooperation between North and South; second, greater and more self-reliant cooperation between South and South; and, third, a more general reform of the world system towards greater social justice and international equity.

From Bandung to Barack: A Conclusion

If the Bandung Conference of 1955 helped to establish solidarity between African and Asian countries, and if the Non-Aligned Movement extended that solidarity to Latin America and the Caribbean, what impact did the end of the Cold War have on such pan-nationalist movements?

There is, of course, a debate as to whether the Cold War has really ended. However, there is no doubt that the collapse of the Soviet Union and the new independence of Eastern Europe killed the Warsaw Pact and ended the old East–West rivalry.

That part of the Soviet Empire which had incorporated a number of Asian republics had included millions of Muslims. The break-up of this old Czarist empire produced such new Muslim countries as Uzbekistan, Tajikistan, and others. The collapse of the post-World War II Soviet Empire (incorporating such countries as Hungary, Czechoslovakia, Poland, Romania, and Bulgaria) produced new Christian countries, with some Muslim minorities here and there.

Some of these changes created paradoxical situations. The North Atlantic Treaty Organization (NATO), which had been heatedly discussed at the Bandung Conference, and which had been widely distrusted by Muslim nationalists everywhere, became an ally of Muslim causes in some parts of the world. NATO intervention in Kosovo in the 1990s (1998–1999) saved the lives of thousands of Muslims at the hands of ethnic Serbs. Kosovo had been part of Yugoslavia, and the Serbs regarded it as part of their ancestral heritage. They were prepared to suppress the aspirations of Kosovo Muslims with genocidal ferocity. NATO intervened on the side of the Muslims against their Christian tormentors. This intervention laid the foundations of the subsequent Kosovo secession into an independent country.

NATO also intervened in a more purely Muslim civil war. This was the Libyan Crisis of 2011 when NATO militarily helped the rebels from Benghazi against the regime of Muammar Gaddafi in Tripoli. For about two decades, Gaddafi had decided he was an African first and an Arab second—almost the first North African ruler ever to define himself more as an African than an Arab. Gaddafi used his money accordingly, investing in such enterprises as hotels and colleges in Black Africa. Mali (overwhelmingly Muslim) was a major beneficiary of Gaddafi's largesse. The best hotels in Mali were owned by Gaddafi's Libya. The former Grand Regency Hotel in Nairobi, Kenya, was also taken over by Gaddafi's Libya. His African economic partners were both Muslims and non-Muslims. He also allowed thousands of neighboring Black Africans to get hired as workers in his Libya—sometimes to the chagrin of indigenous Libyans. He also funded some Pan-African conferences.

Unfortunately, Gaddafi paid heavily for divesting himself of Arab identity. His fellow Arabs threw him under the bus. They virtually encouraged NATO to attack Libya as a way of helping the rebels. The Security Council of the United Nations joined the anti-Gaddafi conspiracy.

Black Africans working in Libya also paid heavily in the Civil War—whether or not they picked up arms to defend his regime. Even Libyan nationals from the South of the country, who were dark in color, were brutalized and killed. The Libyan revolution of 2011 was the most racist Afro-Arab revolution since the upheaval in the Sultanate of Zanzibar in 1964. In the Zanzibar Revolution, Arabs and people descended from Arabs were the victims, as Black people stormed the armory and turned on the old Zanzibari Arab aristocracy.

In Benghazi and other Libyan cities, Black people later suffered as victims, often subjected to summary executions in the War of 2011.

When American Jews offered to fight for Israel when there was an Arab-Israeli war, they were called "volunteers." But when Black Africans participated in the defense of Gaddafi, they were called "mercenaries."

The United States, Britain, and France claimed that their bombardment of Libya enjoyed what was called "regional support." But what "region?" NATO and the United States regarded the Arab World as the only 'region' to which Libya belonged—in spite of the fact that Gaddafi regarded his primary 'region' to be Africa instead.

The first United States' President of African ancestry in history showed supreme indifference to what the African region thought about the Libyan crisis. The African Union sent Heads of State to Libya to try to negotiate a settlement between Gaddafi and the Rebels. The primary reason for the rebel refusal to negotiate was because the rebels already had the support of NATO and Barack Obama.

The Bandung Conference took place only a year after the Supreme Court of the United States gave its ruling against racial segregation in American educational institutions. That decision was discussed in

Bandung as a milestone in the liberation of Black Americans. Nine years after Bandung, Martin Luther King, Jr. won the Nobel Prize for Peace. By the first decade of the twenty-first century, the United States of America was served by two Black Secretaries of State in succession—Colin Powell and Condoleezza Rice. By 2008, Barack Obama was elected the first Black President in the Western World.

Indonesia, the country which had hosted the Bandung Conference, was also the country which briefly nurtured young Barack Obama. Indonesia had also produced Obama's step-father and half-siblings. Many of the participants at Bandung regarded the United States at the time as the most hegemonic racist country in the world. Little did the Bandung Conference imagine that in less than sixty years the United States would elect a man of color as President—thus making Barack Obama the most militarily powerful black person in the entire history of civilization.

The biggest Muslim country in population had hosted the Bandung Conference in 1955. By 2008–2009, the United States had created the most powerful son of a Muslim father since Harun al-Rashid of the ancient Abbasid Dynasty in Baghdad. History had played its ironic role—from ancient Baghdad to modern Washington, DC, and from Bandung to Barack's impact on Benghazi. The Bandung Conference had launched Afro-Asian solidarity. In their different ways Kwame Nkrumah and Muammar Gaddafi tried to promote Afro-Arab solidarity. So did Gamal Abdel Nasser earlier. There have been setbacks to those ambitions. The struggle continues.

Notes

[1] Partly based on the keynote address at an international conference on "Fifty Years beyond Bandung: Linkages Between Africa, Asia, and the Diaspora," sponsored by Cleveland State University, Cleveland, Ohio, April 21–22, 2006.
[2] E. H. Carr, *The Twenty-Years Crisis*.
[3] *Stride Towards Freedom*, pp. 76–77.
[4] Ibid.
[5] *Young India*, 1924–1926 (madras: S. Ganesan, 1927), pp. 839–840. Consult also Pyarelal, "Gandhiji and the African Question," *Africa Quarterly*, Vol. II, No. 2, July–September 1962. See as well the selection from Gandhi entitled "Mahatma Gandhi on Freedom in Africa," *Africa Quarterly*, Vol. I, No. 2, July–September 1961. For a more extensive discussion by Gandhi on nonviolence consult Gandhi, *Nonviolence in Peace and War* (2nd ed.) (Ahmedabad: Navajivan Publishing House, 1944).
[6] Jawaharlal Nehru, "Portuguese Colonialism: An Anachronism," *Africa Quarterly*, Vol. I, No. 3, October–December, 1961, p. 9. See also Nehru, "Emergent Africa," *Africa Quarterly*, Vol. I, No. I, April–June, 1961, pp. 7–9.

[7] *Harijan*, 14 March 1936.
[8] On the Bandung Conference, see Richard Wright, *The Color Curtain: A Report on the Bandung Conference* (Cleveland, OH: World Pub. Co., 1956).
[9] Relatedly, consult Robert A. Mortimer, *The Third World in International Politics*, Second, updated edition, (Boulder: Westview, 1984); Marc Williams, *Third World Cooperation: The Group of 77 in UNCTAD* (London and New York: Pinter and St. Martin's Press, 1991); and Frans N. Stokman, *Roll Calls and Sponsorship: A Methodological Analysis of Third World Group Formation in the United Nations* (Leyden: A. W. Sijthoff, 1977).
[10] A dated but still useful guide to the Nonaligned Movement may be found in D. R. Goyal (ed.), *Non-Alignment: Concept and Concerns* (Delhi: Ajanta Books International, 1986).
[11] For an examination of the relationship between the United Nations and the Non-Aligned Movement, see M. S. Rajan, V. S. Mani and C. S. R. Murthy (eds.), *The Nonaligned and the United Nations* (New York and New Delhi: Oceana and South Asian Publishers, 1987).
[12] See *Final Declaration*, Non-Aligned Movement, Belgrade Conference, 1989.

CHAPTER NINE

THE ARAB SPRING AND FEMALE
EMPOWERMENT

Why did the 2011 Arab awakening begin in Tunisia? In population, Tunisia is basically the smallest Arabic-speaking country on the continent of Africa. In national resources, it is much poorer than either Libya or Algeria. The latter are the leading oil-producing Arab countries in Africa. In cultural and political influence across the Arab World, Tunisia is behind the cultural and diplomatic leverage of Egypt and Morocco—in spite of the fact that Tunisia was the first country in Africa to be called "Africa" in history. However, if Tunisia is small in population, relatively poor in natural resources, modest in international influence, why did the Arab Awakening of 2011 begin in Tunisia?

Another paramount question hanging over the current tumultuous changes in the Middle East is whether the Arab Spring will end the female winter of discontent. Will the push towards the democratization of the Arab World include not only greater liberation of women but also greater female empowerment?

It is too early to be sure how durable are the current liberal trends are in Tunisia, Egypt, Libya and elsewhere. It is certainly much too early to draw conclusions about prospects for the greater empowerment of Arab women. But we can begin to raise questions about the participation of women in the current Arab Awakening. We can also explore progress in female liberation before the Arab Spring. What impact did that prior progress on gender relations have on the events of the year 2011?

Tunisia's Gender Experience

What has now been called "the Arab awakening" or "the Arab Spring" was indeed triggered by the uprising in Tunisia in January 2011 against the regime of Zein al-Abidine Ben Ali.

Was it merely a coincidence that in the twentieth century Tunisia as a country led the whole of the Arab World in women's liberation? The seed of Tunisia's liberation of women goes back to the early years of the twentieth century.

By the 1920s, Tunisia had produced an outstanding Islamic reformer who belonged to the Great Mosque of the Zaitouna. The man's name was Tahar Haddad who championed the liberation of women from the shackles of what he regarded as un-Islamic customs and taboos. In 1930, he published his influential book *Our Women in the Sharia and Society*— arguing that Islamic teachings had been distorted to the disadvantage of women.

Tunisian women were inspired by Haddad but initially decided to join the national struggle against French colonialism rather than fight feminist battles. Women patriots started being arrested by French colonialists as early as 1938. By 1950, the leading Neo-Destour Party opened its first women's section. Many women agitators against France were from time to time arrested and imprisoned.

On attainment of independence on March 20, 1956, women's credentials as Tunisian patriots were so strong that the first postcolonial Tunisian President, Habib Bourguiba, leader of the Neo-Destour Party, declared within months of independence (on August 13, 1956) that Tunisia owed its women a debt of gratitude not only for their roles as mothers, wives, daughters, and sisters, but also for their roles as nationalists and patriots.

Tunisia led the Arab World by promulgating a Code of Personal Status "removing all injustices against women" and "conferring upon women their full rights." Such ideas were echoed by both the African National Congress and the Pan-African Congress in South Africa.

Tunisia was the first Arab country to outlaw polygamy—but not the first Muslim country. Turkey under Mustafa Kemal Atatürk had led the way in improving the status of women in marriage, inheritance, and dress culture. Much later Turkey became the first Muslim country in the Middle East to elect a female Prime Minister—Tansu Çiller.

In Tunisia, women in the year 2011 were significant participants in the pro-democracy uprising. They were protestors rather than rebels. It remains to be seen if Tunisia will become the first Arab country to elect a woman Prime Minister or a woman President.

Although there have already been at least four Muslim countries (Pakistan, Bangladesh, Indonesia and Turkey) which have produced women Prime Ministers and one President, none of them was an Arab country.

If Tunisia in 2011 led the Arab pro-democratic awakening, was it partly because it had led the Arabs half a century earlier in women's liberation? The immediate trigger of the Tunisian uprising was the self-immolation of a young trader who was victimized by bureaucrats at the expense of his livelihood. Mohamed Bouazizi set himself aflame in protest. Although politically inspired self-immolation is much rarer in Muslim countries than among Hindus and Buddhists elsewhere, the Tunisian suicide of a food cart vendor in January 2011 was widely regarded by Tunisians as a case of heroic martyrdom. The physical flames which consumed the young man became a political flame which helped to light a revolution. Tunisian mothers were reportedly particularly moved by the young man's rage.

The Egyptian Precedents

The Egyptian uprising of 2011 against Hosni Mubarak finally succeeded in ousting Mubarak on February 11, 2011. Women were very visible participants in the protests of Tahrir Square. Egyptian women—though among the best educated in Africa and the Muslim World—were not as liberated as the women of Tunisia and Turkey. But historically, Egypt has led the way in female empowerment in other ways. Did Egypt invent the phenomenon of a female Head of State? The first great female ruler in recorded history was probably the Egyptian Hatshepsut who reigned from 1479 to 1458 (BCE).

Because Pharaohs were supposed to be male, Hatshepsut was represented in statues with a false beard! But she was a strong ruler—and is widely regarded as a forerunner of such tough future female rulers as Catherine the Great, Elizabeth I and Indira Gandhi. Other great women rulers of Egypt itself included Pharaoh Akhenaton's co-Regent, Queen Nefertiti, and Cleopatra VII, arguably the last Pharaoh of ancient Egypt, though less indigenous than either Hatshepsut or Nefertiti. Cleopatra was North Africa's great woman ruler. Her life was from 69 BCE to 30 BCE. Her reign was from 51 BCE to 30 BCE.

Egypt has always been the northern extension of Sub-Saharan Africa, the Southern extension of Mediterranean Europe, and later became the Eastern extension of Arabia. These influences probably eventually helped the relative liberation of Egyptian women. They have been much freer than the women of the Arabian Peninsula. Did this empower them in Tahrir Square as protestors in February 2011?

Yearnings of Yemen

An Arab country outside Africa which had been drifting towards a civil war was Yemen, under President Ali Abdullah Saleh. Yemen's links to Africa included their own settlements in East Africa and the Horn of Africa—especially from the Yemeni sub-region of Hadhramaut. Such Hadhrami settlers were highly visible in Mombasa as shopkeepers, merchants, intellectuals, and Muslim missionaries. Many became assimilated and Swahilized.

On the gender question, this is partly neutralized by the Yemeni equivalent of the right to bear arms. Yemen is the most heavily armed of all Arab countries at the level of individuals and families. It has been estimated that most adult males not only own, but often wear arms in Yemen. Some families even own a tank or two, often marked "Private"—though this may be a hyperbole.

This culture of militarized manhood (macho) has contributed to the extra marginalization of women. Yemen is also the poorest Arab country. However, it is worth remembering the more eminent of Yemeni's female leaders, such as the executive editor of *The Yemeni Times*.

The most famous woman in the history of Yemen is the Queen of Sheba. Jewish, Biblical, and Qur'anic versions of the Queen of Sheba place her in a kingdom called Sarba in Yemen instead of in Ethiopia. So Yemen competes with Ethiopia in claiming Sheba.

But Ethiopia is taking the legacy of Sheba much more energetically than do the Yemenis. Emperor Menelik I is supposed to have been the offspring of Solomon and Sheba. Indeed, Ethiopians believe that King Solomon's Ark of the Covenant is protected today in St. Mary's Church in Aksum. The divine right of the Emperor is traced to the Covenant.

To top it all, modern Ethiopia produced the first Empress of today's history of Black Africa. This was Queen Zewditu I, daughter of Menelik II (1844–1913). Zewditu reigned from 1916 to 1930. More than half a century later, Liberia produced Africa's first elected female Head of State—Ellen Johnson Sirleaf. The Muslim World had five major female political leaders (two of them in Bangladesh). Will the Arab Spring of 2011 fill in the gap in the Arab World's gender experience?

From Khartoum to Tahrir Square

Sudan set the precedent of civilian nonviolent demonstrations against military rule. Nonviolent popular eruptions occurred against General

Ibrahim Abboud in the Sudan in 1964 and against General Gaafar Nimeiry in 1985.

The two Sudanese uprisings did not trigger imitation either in Sub-Saharan Africa or in the Arab World—in spite of the fact that old Sudan shared borders with nine other countries.

But why were Sudanese women less evident in the uprising against General Ibrahim Abboud in 1964 than in the uprising against General Gaafar Nimeiry in 1985? The trend was towards greater political awareness among women. South Africa had led the way with female protesters in both Sharpeville and Soweto.

Women in Khartoum were outraged by Nimeiry's decision to execute Mahmoud Mohammed Taha, an old man who was radically reinterpreting Islam in a more liberal direction. Taha's book in the English language was published under the title of *The Second Message of Islam* (Evanston: Northwestern University Press, 1987).

But there was another reason why Sudanese women were less evident in the uprising against General Ibrahim Abboud in 1964 than in the uprising against General Gaafar Nimeiry in 1985. Sudanese Universities had far fewer women students in the 1960s than they did in the 1980s. Female students enhanced the numbers of those who protested against Nimeiry more noticeably than they did in the outburst against Abboud twenty years earlier.

In the 2011 uprising in the Arab World, women have had a pronounced presence in situations in which the opposition has engaged in protest but not in situations when the opposition has resorted to rebellion. Tunisia and Egypt were cases where the opposition had consisted of protesters, but in Libya the opposition rapidly turned into rebels.

But what is the difference between protest and rebellion? The difference is where the opposition is armed. While Tahrir Square in Cairo in 2011 was nonviolent, the Libyan opposition turned to weapons and transformed the conflict into a civil war in less than a week.

But will the experience of a civil war nevertheless liberate women faster than otherwise? Is the female winter of discontent likely to end sooner in post-Gaddafi Libya than it would have done with Gaddafi still in power? The new Libya does stand a chance of empowering its women in the years ahead.

But it is more likely that the first female Head of State in modern Arab history will be either an Egyptian or a Tunisian. While Tunisia awaits a female Bourguiba, Egypt may yet produce a new and more indigenous Cleopatra, or a reincarnation of Hatshepsut.

Only then will we begin to celebrate the female spring and complete the Arab Spring in Middle Eastern history. Amen.

CHAPTER TEN

POLITICAL ISLAM:
PIETY, PATRIARCHY AND PETROLEUM
IN AFRICAN AND COMPARATIVE EXPERIENCE

Does a resource-rich Muslim country find it easier or more difficult to stabilize democracy? Libya has, of course, been an oil-rich country almost throughout its life since the fall of King Idris in 1969. Has Libya's oil wealth helped or hindered its prospects for democratization?

I plan to demonstrate that if the natural resources are discovered after democracy has started maturing, the new wealth would help stabilize the democracy. But if the mineral wealth comes before democratization, it could delay the democratizing process.

Lessons from Europe and Africa

A positive example outside Africa is the discovery of oil resources in the waters of Norway and Scotland. This was a case of economic enrichment of already mature democracies. In the case of Norway, the oil has strengthened the welfare state and stabilized democratic governance.

In the case of Scotland, petroleum initially deepened Scottish nationalism and aggravated separatist sentiment for a while. But the longer term consequences have given Scotland a regional legislature and more solid influence within the United Kingdom. The arrival of economic enrichment after substantial democratization has stabilized the democratic order in both Norway and Scotland.

With a developing country like Libya or Algeria, on the other hand, the petro-wealth preceded stable democratization. The countries became independent with huge economic and political problems which made the postcolonial era inherently unsustainable for long. The oil wealth of Nigeria posed comparable challenges. Nigeria's petroleum was mainly in the Eastern region. The debatable point was whether the petro-wealth contributed to the level of self-confidence of Eastern Nigeria. Did this trigger the Eastern-led military coup of January 1966? Did the East seek to control more effectively the petroleum located in their region? And when Eastern Nigerians later became victims of the Northern counter-coup, and the genocidal anti-Igbo massacres, did the petroleum in the East strengthen the late Ojukwu's resolve to attempt secession from Nigeria? Pre-democratic petro-wealth had created impediments to Nigeria's democratic progress.

Another African example of natural wealth before national democratization was the former Belgian Congo upon attaining independence in 1960. Eastern Congo at the time was almost as well-endowed as Eastern Nigeria—but the Congo had Katanga minerals rather than petroleum. Just as oil-wealth later triggered separation and attempted secession in Eastern Nigeria, copper and other mineral wealth inspired Moïse Tshombe to attempt the secession of Katanga from the former Belgian Congo. In the second half of the twentieth century, both Nigeria and Congo Kinshasa illustrated the proposition that natural resources before the stabilization of democracy was likely to militate against further democratization.

On the other hand, the Republic of South Africa had selective democracy for White people a century and a half before extending the full franchise to Black people and other South Africans of color. Whites had free and fair elections for themselves but not for the rest of the population. The country had a working parliamentary system, and a judiciary which had relative independence within the constraints of a racial political order. Even at the height of apartheid, South Africa was acquiring democratically relevant experience. Did the fact that South Africa had a racially selective democracy, alongside prior mineral wealth, help post-apartheid South Africa to enhance its democratic order?

While the Congo had seen its democracy collapse within a year of attaining independence, and Nigeria had a military coup in less than six years of attaining sovereign status, South Africa continues to have the most liberal constitution in Africa's entire history nearly two decades after the end of apartheid.

Post-apartheid South Africa had not only extended the franchise to citizens of color, but had also abolished the death penalty, enhanced Press freedom, freely elected three different Presidents since 1994, recognized gay rights, and legalized same-sex marriage and civil unions. Even selective democracy, combined with simultaneous mineral wealth, provided subsequent opportunities for further democratization.

However, all three well-endowed countries (Nigeria, the Democratic Republic of the Congo and the Republic of South Africa) had to confront a shared threat to democracy—the threat of plutocracy. Substantial mineral and petro-wealth in these three countries created potential rivalry between rule by the wealthy and rule by the people. Let us turn to these dilemmas more fully.

Democracy vs. Plutocracy?

Oil-rich Third World countries are indeed caught between the reality of plutocracy (rule by the rich) and the aspiration towards democracy (rule by the people). The wealth of petroleum creates great disparities in income and major differences in economic power. On the other hand, the population as a whole can become restless for a greater say in how the wealth of the nation is distributed.

In addition to the choice between plutocracy (the power of wealth) and democracy (the power of votes), Algeria was for a while disrupted by militocracy (the power of soldiers and the military). Indeed, during much of the second half of the twentieth century, Algeria was controlled more by soldiers than by either the economically rich or by people's power. Nevertheless, the country's petro-wealth created additional motivation for the military to control the economy.

Here, it is worth distinguishing between coup-prone Muslim countries like Pakistan, Mali, Niger, Algeria, and Libya, and coup-proof Muslim states which have never experienced military governments since independence. Coup-proof Muslim states include Saudi Arabia, Senegal, the United Arab Emirates, Malaysia, and the Kingdom of Morocco.

Indonesia also used to be coup-prone. Even before the twenty-first century, Indonesia had become less coup-prone by demonstrating how an incumbent ruling party can be outvoted and be peacefully replaced. When such a change occurs though the ballot box more than once (as it has in Indonesia) the prospects of becoming a coup-proof country improve.

In the case of Iraq and Bangladesh, the twenty-first century seems to have made those two states less and less coup-prone but unfortunately more and more conflict-prone. Nigeria has also been repeatedly disrupted by conflict and terrorism. And the tensions between Christians and Muslims have often exploded into violence—including terrorism against such foreigners, as United Nations personnel. Pakistan has been both coup-prone and conflict-prone.

In addition to plutocracy, democracy, and militocracy, the Muslim World has been struggling with meritocracy (rule by the learned and the skilled). The world has viewed the Ayatollahs of Iran primarily as a religious class. What has been ignored is that the Ayatollahs are also a learned class. Iran is both a theocracy and a meritocracy. Indeed, the

Supreme Leader of Iran is one of the three or four best educated political leaders in the world. Of course, the education of the Iranian leadership is Islamic rather than Western. This educated revolution in Iran can be contrasted with the Congo which in 1960 had only a handful of college graduates in Western terms. Unfortunately, the military coup in Lagos in January 1966 interrupted the merit-symphony in Nigeria. Southern leaders in Nigeria in 1960 were educated in the Western tradition. Northern leaders of Nigeria in 1960 were educated in the Islamic tradition.

Ironically, the Nigerian Civil War (1967–1970) reactivated elements of meritocracy within the separatist Eastern Region (Biafra). The Igbo had revealed technological skills in the second half of the twentieth century. Indeed, their triumphant economic skills in Northern Nigeria in the 1950s and 1960s contributed to their vulnerability as a people in 1966. For a while, Eastern Nigeria was well-endowed in education as well as in petroleum. The East was both skill-intensive and resource-intensive.

During the Nigerian Civil War, the innovative inclinations among the Igbo produced Black Africa's first locally-made gun-vehicles. During that Biafran conflict, the Igbo displayed levels of innovation which were unprecedented in postcolonial African history. The Igbo created rough-and-ready armed militarized vehicles as well as the beginnings of Africa's industrial revolution. This renaissance was aborted by the oil bonanza from 1997 onwards.

Although warfare is inherently destructive, it also often releases inventiveness. During the Biafran War, Nigeria was more internally innovative than externally prosperous. The Nigerian Civil War produced some of the high points of Nigeria's experience with technological innovation. Meritocracy manifested itself. However, the Nigerian oil bonanza after the 1973 OPEC price escalation created disincentives to Nigerian enterprise.

In Iran, the Ayatollahs were not only educated in the Islamic tradition. The Ayatollahs were ironically also patrons of advanced Western science. Hence Iran's relentless pursuit of nuclear physics and atomic expertise for the land of the Ayatollahs.

On the Shores of Tripoli

A fourth resource-rich country which has been instructive was Libya under the late Muammar Gaddafi. Libya was oil-rich long before it could even experiment with democratization. Gaddafi was definitely not ideologically a democrat, but he did have some egalitarian tendencies. As a *de facto* Head of State, he declined such ostentatious titles as "President" and "His Excellency." His Green Book was not a manual for democracy, but it was a manual for a more participatory society and a more inclusive world system.

Gaddafi used his petro-wealth partly to assert that a small country can be a player on the world stage, and not merely a pawn in the hands of the Big Powers. Over the decades, Gaddafi was involved in such international conflicts as supporting the Irish Republican Army, funding the Palestinians, financing Muslim rebels in the Philippines, subsidizing Louis Farrakhan of the Nation of Islam in America, and trying to defend Idi Amin from both his domestic and international adversaries.

Gaddafi also increasingly used his petro-wealth in support of Pan-Africanism and the solidarity of African states. He helped finance some of the liberation movements in Southern Africa before the collapse of apartheid. He subsidized some of the meetings of the Organization of African Unity (OAU) and the African Union (AU) and some of the projects of Afro-Arab solidarity under UNESCO in Paris, France.

He also allowed citizens of some neighboring Sub-Saharan African countries to find varied kinds of jobs in Libya. He invested in development projects in such countries as Mali, Niger, and even Kenya. Gaddafi's Libya owned multiple hotels in other African countries.

With Libya, as with Nigeria and the Congo, resource-wealth before democratization was an impediment to genuine maturation of democracy. But Gaddafi did try to promote a more egalitarian society, a more inclusive global system, and African solidarity.

On the whole, Gaddafi, in the last two or three decades in office, had been a good African but a bad Libyan. He had been a bad Libyan by being intolerant of dissent, and being too long in power. Although he rejected titles like President or His Excellency, and preferred to live in a tent, he did suppress critics uncompromisingly.

But if he was a bad Libyan, in what sense was he a good African? He had invested in African countries often at a great loss and with limited returns for himself. He had financed expensive African conferences from his own resources. He supported the very expensive Arabic translation of the eight-volume UNESCO General History of Africa.

Black Africans had jobs in Libya when they were rejected elsewhere. Young Malians who recently enlisted to fight for Gaddafi did so out of sentimental attachment to the Libyan leader. Black faces fighting for Gaddafi were not mercenaries necessarily. Gaddafi's money could have bought better skilled mercenaries than the peasants of Mali and Burkina Faso. East European mercenaries would have been better trained.

Over dinner in Gaddafi's tent as his guest some years ago, I found myself defending the Arabs against Gaddafi's hostility. I was also astonished when Gaddafi asked me to send him a copy of my father's book, *The Mazrui Dynasty of Mombasa*. It was part of his fascination with Afrabia. The book was published by Oxford University press in the 1990s.

By early January 2011, Gaddafi had paid a price for preferring his African identity. He had alienated fellow Arabs to a disastrous extent. The Arab League virtually gave the green light to the Security Council and the Western powers to bomb Gaddafi's Libya. His fellow Arabs threw him under the bus!

On the other hand, Gaddafi's Libyan adversaries in Benghazi had been stimulated by the pro-democracy uprisings in Tunisia and Egypt—the Arab Spring. Petro-wealth had not prepared Libyans for democracy, but the fall of Hosni Mubarak opened up new democratic possibilities. What Libya's oil could not achieve, Libyan revolutionaries tried to accomplish with the help of the North Atlantic Treaty Organization and American air power.

It is not clear how far Gaddafi allowed himself to be constrained by Islamic law both as a leader and as treasurer of his country's wealth. He might have found a way of paying *Zakat* (Islamic tax). But he was certainly unsure whether Islamic banking, with its distrust of interest, was appropriate for the billions of petro-dollars generated by Libya's oil industry.

How much of the petroleum of both Africa and the Middle East comes from countries which are subject to the Shari'a. The biggest Shari'a producers of petroleum are of course Saudi Arabia, Iran, Kuwait, the United Arab Emirates. Their national systems of law are partly informed by Islamic law.

There are other oil-producers which are selectively subject to the Shari'a either in chosen portions of law (such as personal law) or chosen provinces of the country (such as the Shari'a states of Nigeria). Such partial Shari'a oil-producers also include Iraq, Bahrain, Algeria, and the contested area bordering Sudan and the Republic of South Sudan.

Shari'a Lessons from Nigeria

It used to be said in the twentieth century that, "Where there was sand, and there were Muslims, there might be oil." This coincidence was because the deserts of the Middle East had yielded billions of gallons of petroleum.

But although Nigeria has the largest concentration of Muslims on the African continent, the Nigerian oil is not located primarily in Muslim areas. Similarly the oil in the two Sudans may indeed coincide with a lot of sand, but not necessarily with a lot of Muslims.

In the Old Sudan, a combination of the Shari'a in the North and the discovery of oil in the South crystallized separatist demands from the South.

In Nigeria, the concentration of both petro-wealth and political power in the South helped to trigger Islamic nationalism in the North. Aspects of Shari'acracy illustrated what was exceptional about Nigeria while other aspects of the Shari'a manifested what was typical of postcolonial Africa as a whole.

Shari'acracy between Typicality and Exceptionalism

TYPICALITY	EXCEPTIONALISM
Nigeria inherited a legal system based primarily on British law, but with minor amendments to suit local conditions in each colony. Typical of other colonies.	Nigeria is the only African country outside Arab Africa which has seriously debated an alternative to the Western constitutional and legal option.
Both constitutional arrangements and criminal law were primarily based on western systems of order.	That is what the debate about the Shari'a is partly about.
The language of interpreting the constitution and interpreting the laws was the imperial language, English. In Nigeria, as in most former colonies, this imperial, and legal, order was seriously flawed and did not deliver constitutional stability or respect for law.	Exceptionalism includes the fact that Nigeria has the largest concentration of Muslims on the African continent. Exceptionalism therefore includes the fact that Nigeria has more Muslims than any Arab country, including Egypt. But can exceptionalism support Shari'a at the State level combined with secularism at the federal level?

Between Lingo-Constitutionalism and Religio-Constitutionalism

TYPICALITY	EXCEPTIONALISM
Whether or not a federal system should permit cultural self-determination for its constituent parts has been faced by other federations before.	Initially, Nigeria's federation allowed cultural self-determination for neither language nor religion.
Switzerland concedes cultural self-determination in terms of language but not religion. Some cantons are officially French-speaking, some German-speaking, some Italian-speaking.	What the Shari'a debate has opened up is whether religion, rather than language, should be the basis of the cultural self-determination for constituent units in Nigeria.
India concedes cultural self-determination in terms of language—different states have a lot of say on the official language of the state.	In Quebec, English-speaking Canadians have no choice but to put up with Francophone state schools and Francophone road signs.
Canada is coming to terms with a Quebec which insists on making French the sole language. The English-speaking minority in Quebec is disadvantaged.	In Zanfara, should non-Muslim Nigerians similarly have to accept their minority status and conform? Or is that undemocratic?
	Is an imposed lingo-cultural policy any different from an imposed religio-cultural policy for the relevant minorities?

The Gender Question in Oil-Rich Africa

Let us return to the late Gaddafi before he was lynched by his own people. Muammar Gaddafi had ruled Libya since the military coup of 1969. He had been less important as a social or religious reformer domestically than in his efforts to be a political player globally. How far did Islam affect his attitude to women and the gender question?

On the gender question, Gaddafi used symbolism. Far from regarding women as unsuited for military roles, or incapable of using firearms efficiently, Gaddafi theoretically entrusted his life to female bodyguards. These were often referred to as "the Amazons." Women in oil-rich Libya were more liberated than in oil-rich Saudi Arabia. Was Gaddafi influenced by the memory of the widow of the Prophet Muhammad—Aisha? She participated in the Battle of the Camel during the Caliphate rivalry. She rode in the middle of the battle.

The Pope in history has had the physical protection of the Swiss guards and the spiritual protection of the Virgin Mary. Gaddafi had women body guards who were spiritually required to be virgins.

On the link between virginity and military effectiveness, Gaddafi in North Africa in the twenty-first century had shared a characteristic with Shaka Zulu of South Africa in the eighteenth century. Shaka wanted his male soldiers to be celibate, totally denying themselves sex. Gaddafi had wanted his female guards as virgins from the start—and committed to celibacy until military retirement.

But since the 2011 Libyan War erupted in the second half of February 2011, there had been no evidence of female soldiers protecting Gaddafi. Actually, there had been more female warriors in the opposition in Benghazi than among Gaddafi's forces in Tripoli.

Black Women in the Crossfire

Much more interesting was Gaddafi's decision from the 1990s that he was an African first and an Arab second. He got disenchanted with fellow Arabs—having first begun as a Pan-Arabist. His gender policy was perhaps more African than Arab. And in his last twenty years in office, he had put his money more in Pan-African ventures than in Pan-Arabist projects. He saw himself less and less as heir to Gamal Abdel Nasser of Egypt and more and more as heir to Kwame Nkrumah of Ghana. His foreign policy was less informed by Islam than by anti-imperialism. His colorful dress culture was more reminiscent of West Africa than of the Arabian Peninsula.

Let us now look at the gender question more broadly in postcolonial Africa. Uganda had gold mines before it prospected for oil. Did this affect gender? Uganda has had a woman for Vice President under Yoweri Museveni (on and off) since the 1990s, but Uganda had a woman Foreign Minister as far back as the regime of Idi Amin in the 1970s. This female empowerment occurred during the only period when Uganda had a Muslim Head of State—Idi Amin Dada.

Both Liberia and Kenya have repeatedly had women Presidential candidates who had campaigned hard for the ultimate political office. Ellen Johnson Sirleaf in Liberia did lose to Charles Taylor and Charity Ngilu in Kenya did lose to Daniel arap Moi. But both women put up a spirited fight and had substantial support. Since then Ellen Johnson Sirleaf has served as the first elected woman President in Africa's history. She has since shared the Nobel Prize for Peace of 2011 with two other women, one Christian (a Liberian) and one Muslim (a Yemeni). The Yemeni was the first Arab woman to win the Nobel Prize for Peace.

In the 1980s, Winnie Mandela was the most famous African woman in the world. She was of course a South African. Albertina Sisulu was another high ranking South African woman. Frene Ginwala served as Speaker of the post-apartheid parliament in the Republic of South Africa before the United States had a female Speaker in the House, Nancy Pelosi.

In Nigeria's public sphere, the strongest Muslim men since independence have been disproportionately Northerners, but the strongest Muslim women have been in the South. But even in the South, Christian women in Nigeria have led the way.

For quite a while, Nigeria was at the level of having its highest-ranking woman as a Minister for women's affairs. Nigeria has since moved up to have full Cabinet level female Ministers as well as Ministers of State. Female empowerment has since included a brilliant woman-Minister of the economy. This may be significantly better than a number of other African countries. Female Nigerian talent has included reciprocal transfer between the Nigerian Government and the World Bank in Washington, DC. Ngozi Okonjo-Iweala has served both as Director of the World Bank and Nigeria's Finance Minister. In 2012, she was even nominated as a candidate for President of the World Bank. She had considerable international support, but she did not win.

On the other hand, Nigerian women are among the most economically independent in the whole of Africa. Regardless of religion, they are assertive individuals, and many of them know how to play the market. In some cities, a female plutocracy is in the making.

As for Nigerian women in scholarship and science, Christian women compare better with men. It is true that Liberia had a woman President of a university long before Nigeria had a woman Vice-Chancellor, but as a country, Liberia has since been led by a woman Nobel Laureate. And now Nigeria is catching up—first with a woman Vice-Chancellor at the University of Benin and later with another female Chief Executive at the University of Abuja. Lagos State also started early with female academic leadership. Female academic leaders have become widespread.

Nigerian educational institutions are in dire financial straits, but within these constraints there is optimism that Nigerian women professors will not be left too far behind Nigerian men in the arts and, hopefully, in the sciences and engineering. Muslim women naturally excel in Islamic and Qur'anic studies, but they are entering secular studies in larger and larger numbers in this new century.

How does the gender divide relate to the digital divide? And what indeed is the digital divide? The digital divide arises out of either unequal access to the computer and the Internet or unequal skill in utilizing them. I have repeatedly raised the issue of whether there is a digital divide between different ethnic groups in Nigeria. Were certain ethnic groups in Southern Nigeria more computer literate than certain ones in the North? Were the reasons cultural or due to different degrees of economic access to computers? Does that mean that in Nigeria, Muslims of either gender are less computer-competent than Christians? The evidence suggests that.

On this occasion, I would like to relate the digital divide to gender rather than to ethnicity. Among Africans in the diaspora, there is strong evidence that African women are almost keeping pace with African men in computer literacy. At a conference at the Ohio State University at the beginning of June 2000 on "The Internet and Culture Change," about half of the paper presenters were African women, complete with computer demonstrations and illustrations in the course of the conference, operated by the women themselves. Computer-literate women have since multiplied. A female meritocracy is in the making.

All this is quite apart from the phenomenon of African American women (as distinct from women directly from Africa). It is even clearer among African Americans that the women are keeping pace with the men in computer skills. Indeed, African American women may already be outstripping African American men in those skills, as well as in education more generally. Indeed, a high proportion of young Black males are in prison cells at the same time as females are in classrooms. Women are getting computerized; men are getting convicted. The gender divide is being widened by an inter-Black digital divide. The first Black First Lady in the White House (Michelle Obama) is probably the most computer literate First Lady in US history. That is at least as remarkable as the fact that the United States has elected the first President whose father was born a Muslim, and the first American Head of State with a Muslim middle name, Hussein.

Towards the Future

One additional unresolved question is whether petro-abundance in a developing country aggravates male dominance. At least four Muslim countries have produced a female President or female Prime Minister—Pakistan, Bangladesh, Turkey, and Indonesia. Together those four countries have produced five female Heads of Government or Heads of State. None of those four countries are abundantly rich in oil, although Indonesia is a member of the Organization of Petroleum Exporting Countries (OPEC).

The Muslim World has produced two female leaders in one of the poorest countries, Bangladesh; a female leader in the most Westernized Muslim country, Turkey; a female leader in the only Muslim country which is a nuclear power, Pakistan; and a female leader in the most populous Muslim country in history and on planet Earth, Indonesia.

What the Muslim World has not produced is a female leader from any of the richest of the oil-producing countries. Saudi Arabia, Iraq, Iran, and Kuwait are petro-abundant but rather limited in the empowerment of women. Muslim female leaders have come from states that are lacking resources and are poor or middle-income countries.[1]

Kuwaiti's petro-wealth also laid the foundations of a plutocracy—rule by the wealthy. Kuwaiti women participated in the plutocratic bonanza, but way behind Kuwaiti male beneficiaries.

Women as voters were slow to wield their influence in Iraq. However, women as parliamentarians have increased in this era after Saddam Hussein, and some have served as Cabinet Ministers in the Executive Branch. A woman Head of State in Iraq was inconceivable during the era of militocracy (rule by soldiers). But a female President in the Arab Spring is conceivable as part of democratization before the middle of the twenty-first century. What Pakistan and Bangladesh achieved may be repeated by an Arab woman in the years ahead.

Women as part of the new meritocracy may soon be winning more Nobel Prizes in different fields in the Arab World.

Oil-wealth had been an impediment to democratization in the first fifty years of post-Ottoman Arab independence. As the twenty-first century unfolds further, will the empowerment of women be the vanguard of wide democratic change? Will petro-wealth, at last, be the mother of government by the people rather than government by the affluent? The answer lies in the womb of history.

Conclusion

I have attempted to illustrate how resource-richness before democratization reduces the motivation for democratic reforms. Wealth which is not created but only mined produces an affluent elite of leisure rather than an elite of labor. The system which emerges is closer to a plutocracy (rule by rich) rather than democracy (rule by the people). I have used examples from oil-producing countries (Nigeria, Algeria, and Libya) and two resource-rich but not oil-based economies (South Africa and the Democratic Republic of the Congo). Other countries were also mentioned to sharpen points of comparison and contrast.

The Muslim World has experienced a rich systemic diversification since independence. The *Ummah* has experimented with federalism, militarism, liberal democracy, meritocracy, and Islamic Law (the Shari'a). But the *Ummah* still needs an architecture of governance which is solidly institutionalized.

While pre-democratic petro-wealth slows down democratization, it does produce opportunities for a welfare state. Gaddafi's Libya was a kind of welfare state—affording medical, educational, residential, and other forms of subsidies to the citizens. Saudi Arabia is a welfare state for Saudi citizens but not for the millions of foreign workers. Are the Emirates similar?

Nigeria's petro-wealth did not result in a welfare state to serve all Nigerians but resulted in a local oil market which was subsidized. Until recently, Nigerians would get their petrol below market-value. There were also many occasions when poor Nigerians helped themselves to oil outside the constraints of the law.

The dilemma for an oil-rich developing country is between using the national resources to create a welfare state and allowing its citizens to have subsidized access to the commodity without a welfare state.

In the case of Nigeria, subsidized oil and cheaper petroleum reduced the cost of energy locally, but without a national health service or subsidized housing. Gaddafi's Libya, on the other hand, had provided elaborate welfare services without necessarily subsidizing the local energy-market.

Subsidizing petroleum does help those who own cars, and promotes cheaper electricity. But such subsidies are more elitist and more selective than is a full-scale welfare state.

Abundant oil-wealth may not necessarily help political democratization but it can enhance economic rights and promote welfare opportunities for the citizenry.

In the case of Algeria, subsidized energy was one of the benefits of petro-wealth. While in the first fifty years of independence Algeria was very coup-prone, the new political horizons have reduced the frequency of military rule but have aggravated conflict situations. Both Algeria and Bangladesh have become less coup-prone but unfortunately still highly vulnerable to conflicts. Pakistan is both coup-prone and subject to terror, but without oil-wealth.

The struggle for democracy and the struggle for peace have become conjoined. It is still an open question when the abundant resources of each country will become a force for stability rather than a trigger of discord. The struggle continues.

Note

[1] Prime Minister Benazir Bhutto (Pakistan), Prime Minister Khaleda Zia (Bangladesh), Prime Minister Hasina Rahman Wazed (Bangladesh), Prime Ministers Mame Madior Boye and Aminata Toure (Senegal), Prime Minister Tansu Çiller (Turkey) and President Megawati Sukarnoputri (Indonesia).

CHAPTER ELEVEN

FROM THE OLD POLITICS OF RACE TO THE NEW POLITICS OF CULTURE: PREJUDICE IN TRANSITION

At the beginning of the twentieth century, W.E.B. Du Bois, the great African American thinker and leader, predicted that the central problem of the twentieth century was going to be the problem of the color line. Du Bois saw the century engulfed by racism, lynching, the white man's burden, and what came to be known as apartheid. The twentieth century was overwhelmed by refugees on the run from racially and nationalistically instigated conflicts.[1]

Now that we are in the twenty-first century, the question has arisen whether or not the central problem of the twenty-first century was going to be the problem of the culture line. Has a transition occurred between a clash of identities (such as races) to a clash of values (such as cultural norms) in conflict? Are refugees of the twenty-first century already disproportionately cultural refugees?

Samuel Huntington is not, of course, a latter-day W.E.B. Du Bois, but on the eve of the twenty-first century Huntington forecasted that the twenty-first century was headed for a clash of civilizations. He argued that now that the Cold War was over, future conflicts in the world would be less and less between states and ideological blocs and more between civilizations and cultural coalitions. Huntington launched this debate with his article in *Foreign Affairs*, New York, in 1993—an article which reverberated around the world. He followed this up with a major book on the same subject.[2]

While another African American distinguished scholar at the University of Chicago, William Julius Wilson, had predicted earlier the declining significance of race,[3] as race was increasingly overshadowed by class and economics, Huntington predicted the rising salience of culture, overshadowing both race and class. Wilson, once a Chicago professor, and an African American, has since also moved to Harvard.

Worldwide there was evidence in the last years of the twentieth century that the salience of race was on the decline. There was also evidence that the salience of culture was on the rise. However, today this balance varies from country to country. South Africa is a less racist society than it was in the 1980s. But the Netherlands and Norway may be more racist now than twenty years ago.

Overt discrimination is ending in Africa and the United States; Black folks have had the vote and have influenced outcomes. In the US, the House of Representatives has had multiple Black members, but the Senate has had only five Black members in 200 years.[4]

Old style race-based European colonialism has ended in Africa. Political apartheid has collapsed in South Africa.

Overt racism is on the defensive, in spite of rear guard action in Great Britain, Germany, France, the United States, and indeed the law-enforcement system in Norway. At the global level there is more Islamophobia than Negrophobia. But there are a few countries where Negrophobia is increasing rather than diminishing.

Globalization has generated an international migration. And these migratory patterns in the short run continue to trigger racist challenges and responses. But, over the long haul, migration is eroding prejudice based on skin color and increasing prejudice based on conflicting values. But in what sense is this rise in culture-conflict threatening to erode Africa's ecumenical spirit?

A major area of the salience of culture is the confrontation between political Islam, on one side, and the American anti-terrorist alliance, on the other. Since the end of the Cold War and the collapse of apartheid, far more Muslims than Blacks have perished in conflicts with White folks. The natural enemy of the white man is now perceived to be less and less a person with a different skin color, and more and more a person with a different religion and values. The salience of culture continues to rise.

Interracial wars of Black versus White have almost disappeared. But intercultural and interreligious wars are raging in Iraq, Afghanistan, Kosovo, and Chechnya between Israelis and Palestinians—and between Al-Qaeda and its enemies in Africa and the world. On the whole, these conflicts are producing cultural refugees rather than racial asylum-seekers. Africa is caught in the crossfire.

The worst terrorist acts in Sub-Saharan Africa in recent years have not been between races, but between civilizations. These include the 1998 bombing of the US Embassies in Nairobi and Dar es Salaam and the 2002 suicide bombing of the Israeli-owned hotel in Mombasa, Kenya.

In order to kill twelve Americans, Arab militants killed over 200 Kenyans in the Embassy atrocity in Nairobi. The Kenyans were caught in the crossfire in 1998.[5] And the number of Kenyans who were killed at the Paradise Hotel in Mombasa was three times the number of Israeli casualties.[6]

In confrontations between antagonistic cultures, many cultural bystanders are often annihilated by default.

The jails of the United States are still full of Black people in disproportionate members.[7] But Black prisoners have been convicted for violating the civil code and are in jail for such alleged offenses as robbery, rape, murder, assault, and drug abuse.[8]

But the overwhelming political prisoners under American jurisdiction are culturally distinct. They are Muslims suspected of terrorist intent— whether the suspicions are validated or not.[9] Many of those come from African members of the Muslim World. Most have never had access to a lawyer, or been told of the evidence against them.

As for the extraordinary rendition by which the United States sends terrorist suspects for interrogation in countries with a history of torture, unfortunately many of those receiving countries are in Africa—both north of the Sahara and in the Horn of Africa. African countries inhabited by both Muslims and Christians are reportedly doing America's dirty work. Good relations between Africa's own Christians and Muslims are endangered by the policy of extraordinary rendition.

From Triple Heritage to Globalization

It is not often realized that the globalization of Pan-Africanism has also been, almost unconsciously, a transition from a solidarity based on skin color to a new solidarity based on shared cultural experience. The founders of Pan-Africanism were almost unaware of this remarkable transition. By a strange twist of destiny, Pan-Africanism was in the lead from the politics of color identity to the politics of the identity of shared cultural experience.

It began with the ultimate contradiction of W.E.B. Du Bois. He was a man whose family name was French, whose actual physical appearance was virtually white, but whose allegiance was indisputably African. He was the reverse of William Blake's poem about the African child. For Blake (1757–1827) the child was black, but "O! his soul was white." For W.E.B. Du Bois one could proclaim the reverse—that this man was white, but O! his soul was black. In reality Du Bois' actual skin color defied his real cultural allegiance. What the Du Bois paradox taught us was that 'Blackness' could be a cultural identity rather than a physical appearance.

Then there was the phenomenon of George Padmore's fascination with Marxism, alongside W.E.B. Du Bois' response to historical materialism. Here were two major Pan-African thinkers who were involved in the politics of Black identity and were at the same time drawn towards the ideas of an ethnic German Jew called Karl Marx. Padmore's most influential book was indeed originally titled *Pan-Africanism or Communism: The Coming Struggle in Africa*. It was an illustration of a huge ideological ambivalence between the politics of Blackness, on the one hand, and the politics of class, regardless of race, on the other.

On the whole, almost without realizing it, W.E.B. Du Bois and George Padmore were products of the dual heritage (two converging civilizations). These Pan-Africanists were products of left wing Western civilization, on the one hand, and left wing Pan-Africanism on the other. Without fully realizing it, Du Bois and Padmore constituted a transition from the politics of Black identity to the politics of multicultural ideologies.

Then came Kwame Nkrumah. He constituted the next stage of transition from the dual heritage of leftist Westernism and leftist Africanism to the new triple heritage of Africanity, Islam, and Western civilization. Kwame Nkrumah called this convergence consciencism—identifying it as a synthesis of African tradition, Islamic heritage, and what Nkrumah called 'Euro-Christian values.'

The concept of "Africa's Triple Heritage" came with Mazrui in the 1980s. But the fusion of three civilizations originated with Edward Blyden's *Christianity, Islam and the Negro Race* in the 19th century. It was then reincorporated in Kwame Nkrumah's Consciencism, and was consummated in Mazrui's *The Africans: A Triple Heritage*.

Obviously this was a transition from the politics of color to the politics of culture. Kwame Nkrumah reconfirmed it in his marriage to a white-skinned Egyptian woman, Fathiyya. The bride was Arab linguistically, Christian religiously, and fair-skinned in color. Nkramah's Pan-Africanism had gone multicultural and multiracial.

While W.E.B. Du Bois's forecast of the color line was indeed vindicated for the twentieth century, there were longer-term prophetic indications of the culture line which had begun to manifest themselves long before the twenty-first century. Globalization as a planetary phenomenon had been preceded by the globalization of Africa itself.

Comparative Apartheid: Cultural and Racial

As we mentioned earlier, the imperial legacy of Europe gave birth to apartheid in South Africa, the most institutionalized form of racism in human history. These were the tensions of identity. But has the new clash of cultures given rise to its own version of apartheid? Are we witnessing the tensions of values? Let us look more closely at normative apartheid, national and global.

Has the risk of South Africa being dominated by White values increased? When South Africa devised the most liberal constitution in the world, it was on its way towards embracing the West through its own civilization.

South Africa has abolished the death penalty long before the United States has. And the homosexual community has received more civil rights in South Africa than in much of the rest of the world.[10] If racism had previously been the ugly face of Western civilization in South Africa, the open society is now the more attractive legacy of the West.

And now the South African Parliament has passed legislation legalizing same sex civil unions. South Africa is the first African country to do so—but the fifth in the world, after the Western countries of Belgium, Canada, The Netherlands, and Spain.[11]

The dictatorship of the White man has ended in South Africa, but has the dictatorship of White values triumphed?

In reality, apartheid as a system has moved from South Africa to the global level.[12] At the global level, countries are ranked by development, rather than race. And development is either fostered or inhibited by culture.[13] The rank order of the world is now based less on who owns what and more on the new principle of who knows what. This latter imperative is the imperative of skill, rather than income. And skills are often culturally relative.

Petro-rich Arabs have much bigger incomes than Israelis. But in one war after another, Arabs have been outskilled by Israelis. The skills are partly products of culture.

For decades, White South Africans dominated millions of Blacks, mainly because Whites out-skilled Blacks. White culture was organizationally more efficient.

In the global system of apartheid, the main economic casualties are still Africans and Black people generally. African peoples have been slow to respond positively to globalization. The politics of identity are still inhibiting Black folks.

However, the main military victims of global apartheid are Muslims. Hundreds of thousands of Muslims have been killed in recent years by Westerners in Iraq, Kuwait, Palestine, Afghanistan, and even Libya. There was also a civilian Iranian airliner which was shot down by an American battleship. The politics of cultural differentiation are now more deadly than the politics of racial segregation.

Even Darfur poses the question of whether it is a cultural civil war or a racial one. Both sides of the Darfur Conflict are in fact Black and both are Muslim. Ironically, the difference between the two sides is linguistic. The Darfurians are not native speakers of the Arabic language, whereas their tormentors are. Are Darfurian refugees cultural or racial?[14]

The North-South civil war in Sudan had been more clearly a racial war at least partially—but that particular conflict has now virtually ended.[15] On the other hand, the Darfur civil war is still raging—and the two sides are divided by language and rivalry over resources.

The case of Somalia poses other cultural variations. In the precolonial period, governance among the Somali was based on rules rather than rulers. This was characterized as ordered anarchy.

Then came colonial rule under the Italians, the British, and the French. The Somalis fell under imperial control. On attainment of independence in 1960, the Somali Republic experimented with what was called a "pastoral democracy." But, although the pastoralists loved liberty and were free-spirited, they were not good in operating a democratic system. The pastoral democracy collapsed and was replaced by an arbitrary military regime. With Siad Barre, the Somalis had a ruler, but almost no rules. Military arbitrariness prevailed.

When Siad Barre was overthrown in 1991, the former Italian Somaliland descended into anarchy without the precolonial order. Former Italian Somaliland became devoid of both rulers and rules.[16] But former British Somaliland seceded into a separate country–much more stable internally than former Italian Somaliland, but much less recognized internationally.[17]

Then came the Islamic Courts into the anarchic part of greater Somalia. Under the Islamic Courts, Mogadishu, the capital, was gradually finding its way back to its precolonial state of rules without rulers. The concept of courts emphasized this distinction of rules and laws instead of Sultans and Emirs. The Islamic Courts were potentially a stabilizing force for the country as a whole. Contrary to American propaganda, those courts were not the equivalent of the Taliban,[18] nor were the Somali women the equivalent of the more submissive Afghan women. On the contrary, in the 1980s and 1990s, Somali women even served in the armed forces—

carrying guns and wearing uniforms. This was a very different history from that of Afghan women.

But the Somali Courts have now been destroyed by the proxy war waged by the United States in the Horn of Africa, in a *de facto* alliance with Ethiopia.[19] Conflict between Ethiopians and the Somali people, both within Ethiopia and in Somalia, is not racial but ethnocultural.[20]

Conflicts in the Middle East have often spilled over into Eastern Africa. Militarized global apartheid is inevitably intercontinental. The hottest is the conflict between Al-Qaeda and the US allies. Similarly, moral debates in the Western World have often spilled over into Africa. The oldest is the debate about women's rights and female empowerment. Does Al-Qaeda break the code of a just war? Does feminism break the code of African tradition? Al-Qaeda represents a clash of civilizations; the role of women represents a clash of cultures. Once again, Africa is caught in the crossfire all the way from Mogadishu to Maiduguri, from Cape Town to Port Said.

With regard to Al-Qaeda, one of the issues of debate is whether their kind of warfare is illegitimate. If the United States can unleash a war which has so far cost close to 600,000 Iraqis and still avoid being called a terrorist power, why should non-state actors be pursued as terrorists for killing three thousand lives in the United States?

Part of the issue is whether killers who wear uniforms as representatives of the state have a more solid license to kill than underground killers like Al-Qaeda and Islamic Jihad.

A related question is whether killing innocent civilians in the vicinity of a suspect is more defensible than killing innocent civilians on the assumption that a number of them are probably collaborators. When the United States targeted Southern Somali villages for an air raid in January 2007 on the assumption that there were three Al-Qaeda suspects,[21] was that really different from Hamas targeting an Israeli bus on the assumption that the bus included Israeli soldiers out of uniform?

Globalization between Othello and Shylock

Finally, a word about two plays by William Shakespeare—*Othello* and *The Merchant of Venice*, both plays set in Venice. It is arguable that there is more anti-Semitism in *The Merchant of Venice* than color prejudice in *Othello*.[22] On the contrary, Othello as a character emerges as a tragic hero in spite of his marrying a white woman and killing her.[23] In the centuries which followed Shakespeare, interracial sexual mating became repugnant to mainstream British and Anglo-Saxon culture. It culminated in

Jim Crow and apartheid. Yet in *Othello,* we have a Black man addressed as "My Lord" by a White woman in the bedroom. We see him kissing her after murdering her. Yet the play's villain is Iago, a scheming White man who succeeded in transforming Othello's tender love for Desdemona into a murderous jealous rage. This became Shakespeare's most memorable portrayal of domestic violence. Yet we pity Othello, rather than hate him. And we admire his decisiveness when he kills himself as soon as he discovers his monumental injustice to Desdemona. He says to her dead body:

> I kiss'd thee ere I kill'd thee: no way but this;
> Killing myself, to die upon a kiss.

Before he dies, Othello also calls upon the rest of us:

> When you shall these unlucky deeds relate,
> Speak of me as I am; nothing extenuate,
> Nor set down aught in malice: then must you speak
> Of one that loved not wisely, but too well…
> [Act V, Scene II]

Shakespeare even makes Othello more prejudiced against another culture than against another race. Here is a black man who is not against White people, but against Muslims. In Shakespeare's day, Islam was almost equated with the Ottoman Empire. The words "Turk" and "Muslim" were almost interchangeable.

The last words uttered by Othello before he stabs himself are essentially Islomophobic. Othello tells us about a man he killed in Aleppo (Syria). He described the victim as a "turbaned Turk." Othello also knew Muslims were circumcised. He even used the circumcision as a term of Islomophobic abuse:

> *… in Aleppo once,*
> *Where a malignant and turban'd Turk*
> *Beat a Venetian and traduced the state,*
> *I took him by th' throat the circumcised dog*
> *And smote him, thus.*
> *[Othello stabs himself.]*

Othello is clearly much more culture-conscious than color-conscious. The skin of the Turk was probably white, but Othello is more offended by the Turk's culture—turban, circumcision, and all. We are back to the

Shakespearean rank order of prejudice. We are witnessing culture prejudice in Othello, rather than color bias.

In contrast to this sympathetic treatment of the Moor of Venice, Othello, Shakespeare is fundamentally unsympathetic to the Jew of Venice called Shylock. He is portrayed stereotypically as a greedy Jewish money-lender constantly worried about ducats rather than dignity. Ducats were the Venetian bottom line in Shakespeare's day.

Shylock is also portrayed as almost literally blood-thirsty as he insists on getting the literal pound of flesh from a fellow human being. Demanding a literal pound of flesh is horrid, but as a crime, it is far less horrid than Othello's strangulation of his innocent wife. Yet Othello emerges as, at worst, a foolish but tragic hero—whereas Shylock is portrayed as being obsessed with gruesome greed. Once again, we see in Shakespeare a greater aversion to a man from a different culture (Shylock) than to a man of a different color (Othello).

But doesn't Shakespeare assign great lines of defense of racial and cultural equality to Shylock? Was Shakespeare ambivalent about the Jew? Was he torn between the apartheid of color and the apartheid of culture?

It is indeed true that one of the great speeches in *The Merchant of Venice* is Shylock's eloquent assertion that Jews were no less human than Christians. Julius K. Nyerere of Tanzania loved that speech when he was translating it into Kiswahili for publication by Oxford University Press in the 1960s:

... I am a Jew. Hath not a Jew eyes? Hath not a Jew hands, organs, dimensions, senses, affections, passions? Fed with the same food, hurt with the same weapons, subject to the same diseases, healed by the same means, warmed and cooled by the same winter and summer as a Christian is? If you prick us, do we not bleed? If you tickle us, do we not laugh? If you poison us, do we not die?

But Shylock soon disappoints us about his real motives. As Shylock continues, it becomes clear that he is not using a shared humanity as a reason for tolerance, but as a reason for revenge. When wronged by somebody else, a Christian may at least consider turning the other cheek. But Shylock says instead:

And if you wrong us, shall we not revenge?... If a Christian wrongs a Jew, what should his sufferance be by Christian example? Why, revenge! The villainy you teach me, I will execute...[24]

The conclusion to be drawn regarding Shylock and Othello is that in Shakespeare's era, culture prejudice (such as anti-Semitism) was much stronger than color prejudice (such as Negrophobia). The apartheid of values overshadowed the apartheid of race.

However, in the succeeding centuries, the English people and their overseas descendants became more and more averse to Blackness and less and less hostile toward Jewishness. Among Anglo-Saxon prejudices, color eventually overshadowed culture decisively for several centuries.

Conclusion

Globalization has helped to reduce prejudice based on skin color. The question which our own twenty-first century now poses is whether we are returning to a kind of Shakespearean scale of values at the global level. Of course, color racism is still alive and well, but is it losing salience in human behavior? Culture conflict goes back to the Crusades and further back to tribal societies, but are we witnessing a resurgence of cultural belligerence in human affairs in the wake of globalization and unprecedented intercontinental migratory patterns?

W.E.B. Du Bois was right about the vital significance of the color line for the twentieth century. Ironically, he himself was a product of a convergence of cultures. In the twenty-first century, culture is once again overshadowing color in most countries, and civilization is overshadowing race—for better or for worse. Is Shylock back as culture-prejudice incarnate? Is this culture line slowly superseding the color line as the dominant foundation of intergroup prejudice? The forces of globalization are indeed redefining clashes of identity in human affairs, for better or for worse.

Notes

[1] There are more than forty two million asylum seekers, refugees, and others of concern to the UN High Commissioner for Refugees in 2011, according to UNHCR, Global Trends 2011 (Geneva, Switzerland: UNHCR, June 2012), p. 3. Africa and Asia accounted for over twenty-five millions of these people (Ibid., p. 46).

[2] For the relevant article and early responses, consult Samuel P. Huntington, et al., "The Clash of Civilizations: The Debate," (New York: Foreign Affairs, 1993).The book-length expansion of Huntington's argument may be found in *The Clash of Civilizations and the Remaking of World Order* (New York: Simon & Schuster, 1996).

[3] Consult William Julius Wilson, *The Declining Significance of Race: Blacks and Changing American Institutions* (Chicago: University of Chicago Press, 1978).

[4] The list of Blacks who have served (or are serving) in the US Senate is remarkably short for a population that is 12 percent of the US population. They are: Hiram Revels and Blanche Bruce (both from Mississippi), Edward Brooke and Mo Cowan (Massachusetts), Carol Moseley Braun, Barack Obama, and Roland Burris (both from Illinois), Tim Scott (South Carolina) and Cory Booker (New Jersey).

[5] Reports lamenting the end of the African safe haven, may be found in *New African*, 367 (October 1998), pp. 16–17 and also "Now for Africa," *The Economist* (July 5, 2003), p. 9.

[6] Beth Potter, "No Vacation From Terror's Reach," *U.S. News & World Report* (December 9, 2002).

[7] According to the National Urban League's *State of Black America 2007* Report, Black men are nearly seven times more likely to be jailed than White men; see "State of Black America," *The Washington Post* (April 21, 2007).

[8] There is an epidemic of Black-on-Black violence. A study by the Bureau of Justice Statistics, found that almost half the people murdered in the US annually were Black; between 2001 and 2005, nine of ten Black murder victims were killed by other Blacks; and Blacks—who comprise 13 percent of the population—were victims in 15 percent of nonfatal violent crimes. For a report, consult Dan Eggen, "Study: Almost Half of Murder Victims Black," *The Washington Post* (August 10, 2007).

[9] For instance, even an insider—Lt. Col. Stephen E. Abraham of the Army Reserve—who had been involved with the military hearings at Guantanamo to determine if the detainees were "enemy combatants"—has called some of the evidence at these hearings "garbage," in testimony to Congress; see William Glaberson, "Critic and Ex-Boss Testify on Guantánamo Hearings," *The New York Times* (July 27, 2007).

[10] South Africa's constitution is the first in the world to protect the rights of homosexuals, as Mark F. Massoud points out in his "The Evolution of Gay Rights in South Africa," *Peace Review* (September 2003), Volume 15, Number 3, p. 301.

[11] Clare Nullis, (*Associated Press*), "Same-Sex Marriage Law Takes Effect in S. Africa," *The Washington Post* (December 1, 2006).

[12] See Ali A. Mazrui, "Global Apartheid? Race and Religion in the New World Order," chapter commissioned by the Nobel Foundation (Oslo, Norway) in Geir Lundestad and Odd Arne Westad, (eds.), *Beyond the Cold War: New Dimensions in International Relations,* (Stockholm: Scandinavian University Press, 1993) pp. 85–98.

[13] For discussions on the linkage between culture and development, see, for instance, Volker Bornschier, *Culture and Politics in Economic Development* (London; New York: Routledge, 2005); Vijayendra Rao and Michael Walton, (eds.), *Culture and Public Action* (Stanford, CA: Stanford University Press, 2004); Lawrence E. Harrison, Samuel P. Huntington, (eds.), *Culture Matters: How Values Shape Human Progress;* and David S. Landes, *The Wealth and Poverty of Nations: Why Some Are So Rich and Some So Poor* (New York: W.W. Norton, 1998).

[14] On the various dimensions of the Darfur Conflict, consult Mahmood Mamdani, "The Politics of Naming: Genocide, Civil War, Insurgency," *London Review of Books* (March 8, 2007), Volume 29, Number 5; Julie Flint, "The Arabs are Victims Too," *The Washington Post* (November 19, 2006); Sam Dealey, "Misreading the Truth in Sudan," *New York Times* (August 8, 2004); and Scott Anderson, "How Did Darfur Happen?" *New York Times Magazine* (October 17, 2004).

[15] Consult Douglas H. Johnson, *The Root Causes of Sudan's Civil Wars* (Oxford; Bloomington, IN; and Kampala: James Currey; Indiana University Press; and Fountain Publishers, 2003); and Catherine Jendia, *The Sudanese Civil Conflict, 1969–1985* (New York: Peter Lang, 2002) for recent overviews of the Sudan conflicts. Also see Dunstan M. Wai, *The African-Arab Conflict in the Sudan* (New York and London: Africana Publishing Co, 1981) and M. O. Beshir, *The South Sudan: Background to Conflict* (New York and London: C. Hurst and Company, 1968).

[16] An overview of Somalia's history may be found in Maria H. Brons, *Society, Security, Sovereignty and the State in Somalia: From Statelessness to Statelessness?* (Utrecht: International Books, 2001).

[17] Consult, relatedly M. Bradbury, A. Y. Abokor, and H. A. Yusuf, "Somaliland: Choosing Politics Over Violence," *Review of African Political* Economy (September 2003), Vol. 30, No. 97, pp. 455–478 and Asteris Huliaras, "The Viability of Somaliland: Internal Constraints and Regional Geopolitics," *Journal of Contemporary African Studies* (July 2002), Vol. 20, No. 2, pp. 157–182.

[18] See, for instance, the report by Jeffrey Gettleman, "Islamists Calm Somali Capital With Restraint," *New York Times* (September 24, 2006).

[19] Mark Mazetti, "US Signals Backing for Ethiopian Incursion Into Somalia," *New York Times* (December 27, 2006).

[20] See Stephanie McCrummen, "Ethiopia Finds Itself Ensnared in Somalia," *The Washington Post* (April 27, 2007).

[21] A report on the strikes may be found in Michael R. Gordon and Mark Mazetti, "U.S. Used Base in Ethiopia to Hunt Al Qaeda," *New York Times* (February 23, 2007).

[22] For discussions of anti-Semitism in Shakespeare's plays, see, for instance, Thomas Cartelli, "Shakespeare's Merchant, Marlowe's Jew: The Problem of Cultural Difference," *Shakespeare Studies* (1988), Vol. 20, pp. 255–260; and Marion D. Perret, "Shakespeare's Jew: Preconception and Performance," *Shakespeare Studies* (1988), Vol. 20, pp. 261–268.

[23] Shakespeare's treatment of the racial aspects of Othello is discussed in, for example, J. Adelman, "Iago's Alter Ego: Race as Projection in 'thello,'" *Shakespeare Quarterly* (Summer 1997), Vol. 48, No. 2, pp. 125–144, and M. Neill, "Unproper Beds: Race, Adultery and the Hideous in 'Othello,'" *Shakespeare Quarterly* (Winter 1989), Vol. 40, No. 4, pp. 383–412.

[24] *The Merchant of Venice*, Act III, Scene 1.

CHAPTER TWELVE

THE AFRABIAN AWAKENING
IN COMPARATIVE PERSPECTIVE

An Interview with Ali A. Mazrui
conducted by Nirvana Tanoukhi[1]

NIRVANA TANOUKHI: As a political scientist of the continent, what do you think is the significance of the location of the Arab Spring uprisings in North Africa? That is, to what extent can we say that the Tunisian, Egyptian, and Libyan revolutions occurred in a particularly African setting?

ALI A. MAZRUI: Among the most interesting aspects is that this is liberal pro-democracy uprising, rather than either nationalist or socialist or Islamic. Most of the values that are articulated are values connected with liberty, open society, and objection to detention without trial. So it's almost as if we were having our first really liberal revolutions, at least in Tunisia and Egypt. And we don't know yet whether this revolution will consolidate itself. But it is different from nationalism as an inspiration, or Islam as an inspiration, or indeed socialism. And that's one of the distinctive aspects of the situation. So far the only Arab uprisings which succeeded in removing a dictator have been in Arab Africa.

TANOUKHI: Having said that though, to what extent do you think Islamist, socialist, and various nationalist groups will be able to integrate into whatever order comes about in the post-revolutionary period?

MAZRUI: It's definitely a fragile situation. And it could be captured by others. For example, we weren't sure with the Iranian Revolution in 1979 how it would go. There were nationalists there, Marxists, Islamists. And then the country was captured by the Islamists within them. This current situation is more clearly liberal than the Iranian one. But it could still be captured by other groups. And we're having our fingers crossed that whoever captures it is concerned about the welfare of the people. And if we look at the Egyptian Revolution of 1952 that was definitely inspired by nationalism and brought into being, not as the most significant Arab nationalists of the second half of the twentieth century. But in this present case, the nationalism is not as yet manifested in North Africa.

TANOUKHI: What is the particular advantage of the revolution in Egypt, for example, not having a primarily nationalist undertone?

MAZRUI: The values are different really, because many of the nationalist uprisings, not just in the Muslim World, but indeed in the Third World have tended to be focused on anti-imperialism and anticolonialism. And that is an issue of liberation rather than an issue of liberty, if I can make that kind of distinction. So in general, what's happening in the North African part of the Arab World is not primarily anti-imperialist. Of course, Gaddafi, because of the participation of the North Atlantic Treaty Organization, has fair grounds to invoke the anti-imperialist theme. But in general, the revolution was very different from the 1979 Revolution in Iran and the 1952 Revolution in Egypt. The Egyptian one included an anti-Israeli element as well as a general anti-imperialist tone.

TANOUKHI: What do you think has been and will be the impact of North African revolutions on Black Arabs and North–South relations on this African continent, perhaps as reflected in the African Union's position on Libya?

MAZRUI: With regard to North Africa proper rather than the upper Nile Valley, it's been relatively bad news for African–Arab relations. In both Libya and Sudan, Afro-Arab solidarity couldn't be sustained in the end. And so, a divorce has taken place. And that's a major setback in relations between Arab and non-Arab Africans more generally. On the other hand, the Libyan situation almost compensates for the disaster in Sudan, because Gaddafi is the first major leader of an Arab-African country who regarded himself as an African first and an Arab second. And this was ages ago. This is not just what has happened just now. I've had opportunities to chat with him about issues of this kind, and I sometimes found myself defending the Arabs against this Arab leader. So Gaddafi did in general (though it was fifteen years ago) regard his African constituency as more sincere and carrying greater promise for fulfillment than his solidarity with the Arabs. And he regarded himself eventually as a successor to Kwame Nkrumah of Ghana and the Pan-Africanists rather than a successor to

Gamal Abdel Nasser as a Pan-Arab. That is why so many of his residual friends in the world have been disproportionately Africans. Fellow Arabs just threw him under the bus and invited the West and the North Atlantic Treaty Organization to do what they liked with him. He was betrayed by the Arabs, but it is not surprising that his residual friends have been Black Africans.

TANOUKHI: Can you comment further on the position on Gaddafi and the Libyan Revolt by African leaders in general, but also, if you like, more specifically on the response of the African Union?

MAZRUI: Fifteen years ago when I had conversations with him, Gaddafi indicated greater Pan-Africanism. But more recently, he wanted to be part of the vanguard of speeding up Pan-African unification. And he was elected as chairman of the African Union and he chaired and financed one or two major conferences in pursuit of rapid regional unification towards continental unity. Much of the dream, as in the case of Kwame Nkrumah, was excessively optimistic. And, of course, you can't distinguish between the dream which is primarily for self-promotion and the dream which is genuinely part of patriotism. But that's not unique to Gaddafi or any leader from Napoleon to George Washington. You always wonder how much is self-promotion and how much is patriotism. In the last few years, I have seen Gaddafi move towards trying to speed up regional African unification, but on terms which were relatively unrealistic in their optimism.

TANOUKHI: So does this Africanist part of Gaddafi's career or his Pan-Africanism in particular, position African leaders from the sub-continent differently towards what is going on in Libya versus what has been happening elsewhere?

MAZRUI: African leaders are focused on the African part of the Arab World for the moment, and do not handle Arab countries outside Africa. It is clear that the only two successful uprisings so far among a dozen Arab uprisings in the Arab World as a whole have been in Africa. Those in Tunisia and Egypt have been successful in ending the old regime, but not yet successful in opening up a new era. Only the African part of the Arab World has succeeded in, for the time being, destroying the old order. But it's still uncertain what kind of new order would replace it. In the case of Libya, the Libyan opponents of Gaddafi moved very rapidly towards becoming an armed insurrection rather than a protest movement. That's one of the things which people keep forgetting as to why the Libyan uprising didn't work out as smoothly. The Egyptian phenomenon of February 2011 was protest; it wasn't rebellion. It was protest. And even when the protestors were provoked by misbehavior of the security forces and some injuries and killings that took place both in Cairo and in Alexandria, they maintained a nonviolent nature of protesting. And this is also true of the Tunisian uprising. There were victims of the security forces, but the people who were in revolt were mainly unharmed and articulated values that did not require weapons. The unfortunate part of the Libyan situation is that the opponents of Gaddafi moved rapidly towards turning it into an armed rebellion. So the protestors became more than just protestors. They became rebels or insurrectionists, and armed. And then the fact that they sought military support from outside their own country increased the difference between Egypt and Tunisia, on one side, and Libya, on the other. So the Libyan situation became more clearly a civil war, whereas Tunisia and Egypt were primarily civil conflicts but not full scale civil war.

TANOUKHI: So let's move on to the issue of Islam in Africa more generally. What do you think is the future of Muslim–Christian relations in Africa after the end of "larger" Sudan (Sudan as it existed from January 1, 1956 until July 9, 2011), both within countries that have significant representation of both groups like Nigeria and Kenya, and between states that are largely made up of members from only one of these religions?

MAZRUI: The Sudanese part is definitely a sad divorce. And the government in Khartoum has not been trying to find ways of creating good neighborly relations apart from accepting the secession. They should have attempted a little more to make it easier for southern Sudanese who might have voted for separation, but are caught up in this situation of having invested so many of their years in northern Sudan. The British allowed the Irish, after conceding Irish autonomy and later independence, considerable free movement into the United Kingdom and back. And I don't mean just Northern Ireland; I mean the Irish Republic. The citizens of that country, long before the European Union, enjoyed considerable freedom of movement into the United Kingdom. And I was hoping that the northern Sudanese authorities would have similar generosity, giving the southern Sudanese some freedom of movement and not just treating them as foreigners. At the moment, unfortunately, General al-Bashir is not leaning in that direction. He's been very reluctant to consider the dual-nationality concept, and he's been very protective of monopolizing the Sudanese currency exclusively for the north. So it's a very different attitude from that of the British when they had to engage in the divorce with the Irish. The Irish were very angry with the English for centuries of domination. But when the separation came, there was a greater readiness to accept generosity. And I hope the northern Sudanese will move in that direction later. The initial reaction has been relatively ungenerous towards southern Sudanese.

And then in general, there is another country with regard to Muslim–Christian relations whose solution is different from Sudan. And that is in Côte d'Ivoire, the Ivory Coast. Not many commentators refer to the sectarian divide in the conflict which has taken place there. In general, Côte d'Ivoire has had a slight majority of Muslims since independence. And yet it has been ruled since independence almost exclusively by Christians, at least at the very top. Now in the case of Ouattara who is now President and a Muslim, he was allowed by the founding President of independent Ivory Coast to hold a high position. When Ouattara was elected President at last, there was a Christian revolt. But French intervention in 2011 favored the Muslim Ouattara. So in Côte d'Ivoire, I see a more interesting and optimistic situation than that in Sudan.

Then, Tanzania has as many Muslims as Christians and has had a remarkable rotation of the presidency due to a combination of term limits and an emphasis on religious rotation. The founding President, Julius Nyerere, was of course a Christian. He was very popular, genuinely popular. And then Ali Hassan Mwinyi, a Muslim, succeeded him. In his case, he just accepted his two terms of five years each, and was followed by Benjamin Mkapa, who was again a Christian. And now there is another Muslim in office. It's not in the constitution. There is a pragmatic rotation of the presidency in Tanzania, given the nature of the divide of the country between Muslims and Christians. And the divide is much closer than many people realize.

Finally, I might add something else which started off very well, but has slightly deteriorated in the smaller country of Senegal. The country has an overwhelming majority of Muslims, nearly 95 percent. But for the first twenty years of its postcolonial experience, it had a Roman Catholic President without cries of "jihad" and "down with infidels," in a relatively open African society. And then after twenty years of Léopold Senghor, he was followed by a Muslim President, Abdou Diouf. And then once again, this was a rather unusual situation, the first lady of Senegal in the next twenty years was a Christian first lady in a presidency headed by a Muslim. So in general, there were four decades of remarkable ecumenical politics in Senegal. Now, things are not as smooth as they were in those

first four decades. But precedents were set which will probably help
Senegal to recover some of that spirit of cooperation between Christians
and Muslims.

TANOUKHI: Do you find the tension that has arisen recently around
Coptic identity in Egypt worrisome? Or do you see it as relatively minor,
despite concerns raised by some about the possibility of religious/ethnic
conflict in post-revolutionary Egypt?

MAZRUI: It's serious. The country as a whole was overwhelmingly Coptic
before the Arab conquest of the seventh century. And it is quite
remarkable that there is still a significant Christian presence, although the
percentage is quite small. But that they have survived for fourteen
centuries of coexistence with Muslim authorities is an interesting
phenomenon. And most of the time, they worked quite well. Recently
things are turning for the worse. Boutros Boutros-Ghali would never have
become Secretary-General of the United Nations if he, as a Coptic, didn't
rise within Muslim Egyptian society and become a kind of Secretary of
State within Egypt before he became eligible for consideration as
Secretary-General of the UN. So this was a Christian Egyptian married to
a Jew in a society which is overwhelmingly Muslim and was permitted by
the realities of the situation to rise so high. Indeed, he would not, of
course, have become Secretary-General if the Egyptian government had
rejected him. The United Nations insists that whoever is nominated for
Secretary-General must begin with the support of their own government.
And there have been cases of a Ugandan who was rejected by his
government in Kampala and never made it for that job. So that was a plus
sign in Egypt. The administrations of both Anwar Sadat and Hosni
Mubarak favored good relations with Coptic Christians. But,
unfortunately, things are sometimes difficult if countries have populations
which are expanding too rapidly, have generational imbalances between
the youth and the elders, have inadequate jobs for young people emerging
from colleges. It poisons wider relations in the society.

TANOUKHI: In your remarks, you generally seem hopeful about what has
happened in Tunisia and Egypt. However, it could be said that what we've
seen, even in the successful North African revolutions such as those in
Tunisia and Egypt, is a difficulty to transform what has been garnered in
people power into potentially transformative political authority. What do
you think this bodes for the future of social protest on the continent—
including, for example, what's happening in Malawi right now, and who

knows where else in the near future—given what we know especially of the history of governance in Africa and postcolonial nations.

MAZRUI: If you witness a situation where there is an attempt at democratization from below, which is what has been attempted both in Tunisia and in Egypt this year, the trouble is that it is very much like the uprising from the collapse of the Bastille in the French Revolution. The proletariat taking over the system is eager to assert itself. And then it creates a period of adjustment. In the case of the French Revolution, that included a period of actual terror. The French terrorized each other. And then, unlike the Egyptians, that particular revolution from below was so anti-royalist that the entire royal family was executed. On the other hand, there is attempting democratization from above, of which in the Muslim World the best example is really Turkey. In that instance, Mustafa Kemal Atatürk engaged in major political, social, and cultural changes that were orchestrated by a political elite led by him. And, in general, they had a sense of where they wanted to take the country, which is much easier than if you are dealing with the equivalent of the Bastille being broken down by inmates. So we have to have our fingers crossed whenever there is this attempt at orchestrating big fundamental changes from below, by what begins as mob action. But it can work. And at the moment, in the case of Egypt and Tunisia, it does look hopeful. The problem with major uprisings in Sub-Saharan Africa is that they have not been primarily liberal except in terms of wanting liberation rather than liberty, ending colonialism, etc. When a major leader in Sub-Saharan Africa wants to change society from above, it hasn't been in the direction of liberal reform; it's been in the direction of *Ujamaa* in Tanzania—a form of socialism combined with African cultural nationalism, but without adequate guarantees for individual liberties and open society. I once described Kwame Nkrumah as a great African, but not a great Ghanaian because his policies domestically were not good for Ghana. But his policies for the African continent were ahead of his time. And then in the case of Gaddafi, I have had occasion to say that he is a good African but a bad Libyan. He is a paradox, like Nkrumah, being negligent of the immediate domestic constituency but being visionary with regard to continental ambitions, etc. Gaddafi was a bad Libyan because of considerable neglect of certain important liberties for the Libyan people. But I regard him as an important African leader who demonstrated that it is possible to be a leader of an Arab African country and still regard yourself as primarily African first, and Arab second.

TANOUKHI: Would you care to comment on developments in Malawi?

MAZRUI: It is less of a comfortable uprising, but it definitely shows eagerness to tame political power. The country started off very badly under Hastings Banda who monopolized power in Malawi for a long time. But the country gradually demonstrated that it was possible, even for such a major tyrant as Hastings Banda, to step down without major collapse. And you have an interesting experiment with a Muslim President in Malawi for a while. So the country has had fluctuations which make it different from what we've been talking about with regard to North Africa. And I think in general, Malawi is showing greater changeability than Zimbabwe. So I'm more optimistic about the future in central Africa of liberal democratic values, more optimistic about Malawi than about Zimbabwe right now. But I hope that both countries emerge triumphant after their present leaders.

TANOUKHI: So what are the prospects for stable democratic regimes in North Africa going forward, in your opinion, especially in light of Western intervention, not only by the US, in these civic conflicts?

MAZRUI: I'm not optimistic about liberal democratic order in Libya. But I think both Tunisia and Egypt do stand a chance of gradually consolidating. I think because Egypt is a very ancient civilization, it may have to overcome a lot of older traditions, if you like, the Pharaonic impediments to democratization. Egypt has had five thousand years of bureaucracy. I would regard Tunisia as standing a better chance of democratization. I'm even on record as trying to forecast that the first female President of an Arab country will be in either in Tunisia or Egypt. We have had female Presidents of Muslim countries in Turkey, in Bangladesh, in Pakistan, and in Indonesia. But there hasn't been a single female Arab rising to the top of political order. And my forecast, for what it is worth, is that the two Arab countries that stand the best chance of breaking down that particular gender barrier of democratization are Tunisia and Egypt. In the case of Tunisia, they have made more progress with regard to the empowerment of women than Egypt. The Egyptian women are better educated, but not necessarily better liberated than Tunisian women. But both countries are likely to lead the Arab World in this aspect of democratization.

TANOUKHI: What do you mean exactly by Pharaonic impediments to democratization?

MAZRUI: In societies which have a long history of dictatorship, there are major difficulties in breaking down those entrenched traditions because the population tends to accept Pharaonic power disproportionately, and sometimes to almost deify the leader at the time. In the case of modern Egypt, the nearest approximation to Pharaonic proportions of hero worship was Gamal Abdel Nasser rather than Hosni Mubarak. So Gamal Abdel Nasser became hugely popular. And when he died very suddenly in 1970, people were throwing themselves off roofs in suicidal mourning as they absorbed the death of this major figure. It is almost as if they were ready to build a pyramid in his honor. And he himself used to say he was the first real Egyptian leader after centuries of post-Pharaonic occupation by the Greeks, the Romans, Byzantium and the Arabs. I'm worried that these ancient tendencies of accepting power at the center which go back in Egypt thousands of years and not just centuries, may themselves prove an impediment to rapid democratization. Egypt's ancient political culture of deference to authority is dying, but not fast enough. I hope I am wrong. If Egyptians become democratic within the next fifty years, I hope my children will celebrate, because that will be faster than I was expecting it to happen because of that built-in lethargy of Pharaonic traditions.

TANOUKHI: In the international media at least, Libyan rebels are credited with the capacity to form a new state in the way that South Sudan is not, despite sympathy for the plight of southerners in news coverage. How would you compare the resources for state-making in a post-Gaddafi Libya versus South Sudan?

MAZRUI: This is definitely a legitimate concern that South Sudan is at risk of becoming a failed state and that Libya stands a better chance of becoming a viable modern, though perhaps not democratic, state with elements of tribal power. Endowed with great wealth, the Libyan situation is likely to be more positive than South Sudanese prospects at the moment. In South Sudan, part of the problem is gross neglect, not just by Arabs since the mid-1950s, but by the British before that. The British have been forgiven for their total neglect of South Sudan, incredibly! There they were, ruling Sudan under the banner of Anglo-Egyptian Sudan. Apart from trying to save southerners from Arabs and putting limits to Islamization, there is very little the British did for infrastructure, education, etc. And they have been forgiven by the international community. Northern Sudan bears the brunt of neglect in the south, when, in fact, most Arabs since 1956, and the British since they inherited Sudan from the Byzantine Empire, neglected basic infrastructural development of that country, which makes it much harder for both North and South right now to create viable states. Then, of course, they are quarreling about oil with the North. And that's another sad thing. The shared oil resources could be an opportunity for cooperation, not always an opportunity for competition and hostility. The Sudanese have not as yet, both North and South, found the right balance of sharing resources and being good neighbors.

TANOUKHI: On the topic of oil, and political Islam in particular, Fouad Ajami, in *The Arab Predicament* (2nd ed., p. 209) cites you saying that "the 'barrel of oil' and the 'crescent of Islam' were linked and October 1973 represented a resurrection of Islam." Please feel free to correct or clarify the statement, if the quote is inaccurate, or taken out of context. But if this quote is accurate, would you say that Islam declined when the price of oil did in the mid-1980s—and was resurrected in the last several years with the price of oil reaching its all-time high, at least in nominal dollars? If instead we understand Saudi economic power in relation to the United States' exploitation of Islam during the Cold War, primarily as a tool against secular Arab nationalism—as does Mahmood Mamdani in *Good Muslim, Bad Muslim?*—what role can we expect for oil-rich countries in Africa and the Middle East in the next years, especially in view of the selective interventionism displayed by the superpowers in recent months.

MAZRUI: There's no doubt that petroleum has been both a curse and a blessing for the Muslim World. And the particular piece of my writing to which you are referring had the title of "The Barrel of the Gun and the Barrel of Oil." It was a piece on how the oil sector created cultures of militarization in the Muslim World, partly because of the greed of industrialized countries' need for oil. So oil could be a source of power, which it has been for Saudi Arabia. Saudi Arabia is an important player in the world economy and indeed in world policy, mainly because of oil power. But I have always tried to distinguish between the real failures of Muslims and the alleged failures of Islam. And the failures of Muslims have included not being able to manage and use even Allah's bounties. The Muslim World is blessed by enormous resources of oil, led by the country which is the main custodian of Mecca and Medina, etc. And yet, although Islam must have contributed to this particular bounty, the Muslims themselves have abused those riches, and sometimes have allowed themselves to be bought by the West in ways which are anti-Islam. Unfortunately, these abuses have also impeded democratization of countries like Saudi Arabia, although there are elements in the Gulf area as a whole including Kuwait, which give us optimism that Arabs can begin to modernize their societies, and even have the beginnings of democratization, in spite of being rich in oil and in spite of being spoiled by extravagance. In the smaller Gulf areas, there are signs of hope. But in general, in Saudi Arabia, the signs of hope are not in the service of democratization, but in terms of being an important player in the global economy and in the world system.

TANOUKHI: Would you say that spring 2011—call it an Arab or African Spring—has already reshaped our understanding of political Islam?

MAZRUI: Yes, the year 2011 is definitely going to count as an important phase, comparable to the collapse of Communism in its potential towards reforming the societies which were previously ruled tyrannically. And then, in addition, some of the major convulsions during my lifetime in the Muslim World, have had 'plus' consequences. One was definitely the changes in Turkey, which are getting better now. For awhile, there was too much fundamentalist secularism in Turkey, to the extent of being intolerant of other people's more sacred beliefs. The Turks are beginning to find a better balance within secularism and Islam. And then there is the Iranian Revolution, also a major event in the Muslim World because it created repercussions in other areas of Islam, some of them under-observed because they're mainly cultural rather than political. The political side of the Iranian Revolution received disproportionate attention from the media, but there are major social changes which have occurred. And now this Arab Spring. The combination of the Turkish Atatürk Revolution, the Iranian Revolution, and the Arab Revolution, are likely to be counted in the period which covers my own lifetime as among the most important events affecting the Muslim World. The results of the partition of India, which created Pakistan, is still a work in progress with considerable anxiety as to whether it was a plus when the British, the Muslims, and the Hindus finally agreed to have the British India partitioned, or whether it was a minus in the repercussions which followed later on. So the Pakistani side of the Muslim story still hangs in the balance. The Turkish, Iranian, and Arab reforms have been hopeful and promising so far. And I have my fingers crossed, as they say.

TANOUKHI: I'd like to conclude with a question or two about the geography of the North African Revolution. Looking at the space of Tahrir Square since January, we find protestors carrying pamphlets displaying everything from personal grievances, civil demands, comic provocations, Qur'anic verses, and engaging in communal practices and displays ranging from revolutionary rock to group prayers, to silent protest. And as you might know, the very security of Tahrir Square has become the purview of revolutionaries after the elective withdrawal by the police force. What do we learn from the political and cultural negotiations and acts in loci of agitation such as the public square?

MAZRUI: The public square in Cairo symbolized by Tahrir—is definitely a platform which can accommodate large numbers of people and which is not too circumscribed by security forces. This has given the Egyptian protesters a bigger advantage than anything that the Syrians could remotely command in their more menacing political predicament. The Syrian security forces are less patriotic towards fellow citizens, than the Egyptians were. In general, we mustn't forget that these societies are still developing, have important areas of fragility, and revolutions take awhile to consolidate themselves. Some rapidly become civil wars, as in the case of both France and post-Czarist Russia with the coming of the civil war after the 1917 Revolution. Other societies that have seen revolution have sometimes deteriorated rapidly into major conflicts and terror. On the Arab side of the current Middle Eastern changes, there is a lot of hope that it won't deteriorate into massive civil war in spite of the Libyan Conflict. But we can't be too optimistic when we're confronted with what is happening in Syria and when we are confronted with the North Atlantic Treaty Organization's involvement in an African civil war. We are, as Africans and as Arabs and as human beings, both worried by what is happening in the Arab World and inspired by its potential. And I hope that potential is fulfilled politically before very long.

TANOUKHI: Finally, do you think it would be fruitful at this juncture to reevaluate 'North Africa' as a meaningful geographic designation—or as geographers would say, a "geographic scale"—of historical analysis as we think forward about social developments on the continent?

MAZRUI: Yes. If we just limit ourselves to talking about it as a sub-region, the way we talk about southern Africa or we talk about ECOWAS as a West African organization. It does make sense, when we are talking about sub-regions—western Africa, southern Africa, eastern Africa, and northern Africa. And also within North Africa, in the past, there's a tendency to distinguish the Maghreb section of North Africa from the rest of North Africa. So making North Africa into a more cohesive whole would help the Pan-African ideal, and may also reduce the tendency for North Africa to insist on emphasizing its Arabness and to be inadequately committed to the African continent. We need to cultivate a readiness on the part of North Africans to lead the rest of the Arab World. At different moments, Egypt has led the rest of the Arab World successfully. We need to widen the credentials of leadership from Egyptian (national credentials) to North African ones (sub-regional credentials), so that the relevance of a revolutionary movement in North Africa would be extended to the African continent as a whole. Africans, north and south of the Sahara, need to learn from each other—and distinguish between what to emulate and what to avoid.

Note

[1] This telephone interview was conducted in July 2011 for publication in the issue of the 50th anniversary of *Transition,* a magazine which was started in 1962 by the late Rajat Neogy in Kampala, Uganda, and is now based at Harvard University, Cambridge, MA.

INDEX

Bangladesh, 4, 6, 10, 81, 90, 113,
121, 123, 141, 144, 150, 160,
161, 163, 187
Barre, Siad, 28, 171
Battle of Dien Bien Phu, 124
Battle of the Camel, 157
Beijing, 83
Beirut, 98
Belgrade, 80, 131
Benghazi, 134, 136, 153, 157
Berber, 98, 99, 101
Berlin Conference, 123
Bevis Marks Synagogue, 97
Bhutto, Benazir, 4, 123
Bible, 2, 17, 26
Bilal, 112
bin Laden, Osama, 8
Bismarck, Otto von, 123
Blake, William, 168
Boers. See Afrikaners
Bosnia, 9, 37, 75, 77, 78, 79, 82
Bosnia-Herzegovina, 78
Botswana, 131
Bourguiba, Habib, 140
Boutros-Ghali, Boutros, 5, 72, 184
Brazil, 131, 132
Bretton Woods, 76
Britain, 7, 54, 55, 56, 57, 66, 67, 73,
76, 78, 81, 97, 118, 127, 130,
135, 166
British Broadcasting Corporation
(BBC), 94
British Parliament, 2
Brown, John, 18
Brunei, 89
Buddhist, 72
Buganda, 25
Bunche, Ralph, 128
Burundi, 99, 102
Bush Doctrine, 8
Bush, George W., 91, 103
Byzantine Empire, 189
Byzantines, 107

Caesar, 2

Cairo, 4, 34, 83, 113, 117, 145, 182,
191
Caliph, 2, 114
Caliphate, 2, 109, 114, 115, 116,
157
Cape of Good Hope, 48
Cape Town, 11, 172
Capitol Hill, 13
Caribbean, 133
Carr, E. H., 128
Catherine the Great, 142
Catholic, 32, 100
Central African Republic, 36, 77
Central Intelligence Agency (CIA),
8
Chaldean, 5
Chancellor, 4, 159
Chechnya, 9, 12, 18, 57, 77, 167
China, 67, 73, 83, 131
Chirac, Jacques, 70
Christianity, 17, 23, 24, 25, 26, 35,
36, 37, 48, 49, 50, 52, 96, 97,
109, 113, 128, 169
Church of England, 2
Churchill, Winston, 93
Çiller, Tansu, 4, 112, 123, 141
Cleopatra VII, 142
Clinton, Hillary, 90, 102
Cold War, 28, 51, 66, 68, 69, 74, 97,
130, 132, 133, 165, 166, 189
colonialism, 23, 26, 74, 82, 122,
123, 124, 132, 140, 166, 186
Communist World, 69, 70
Constantinople, 109
Copenhagen, 83
Coptic, 5, 184
Côte d'Ivoire, 9, 27, 183
Council of Cardinals, 114
Crow, Jim, 173
Cuba, 132
Cypriot, 102
Cyprus, 81, 98, 99, 102, 131
Czechoslovakia, 98, 99, 130, 133

D'Israeli, Isaac, 97
Dacca, 98